Understanding Motion Capture for Computer Animation and Video Games

Understanding Motion Capture for Computer Animation and Video Games

Alberto Menache

Morgan Kaufmann

AN IMPRINT OF ACADEMIC PRESS
A Harcourt Science and Technology Company

San Diego San Francisco New York Boston
London Sydney Tokyo

ACADEMIC PRESS
A Harcourt Science and Technology Company
525 B Street, Suite 1900, San Diego, CA 92101-4495 USA
http://www.academicpress.com

Academic Press
24-28 Oval Road, London NW1 7DX United Kingdom
http://www.hbuk.co.uk/ap/

Morgan Kaufmann Publishers
340 Pine Street, Sixth Floor, San Francisco, CA 94104-3205 USA
http://www.mkp.com

Library of Congress Catalog Number: 99-64633

ISBN: 0-12-490630-3

Printed in the United States of America
99 00 01 02 03 IP 6 5 4 3 2 1

*I dedicate this book to the memory
of my father, Mauricio Menache.*

Contents

꒐꒜

Acknowledgments

❦

Illustrations by David House.

Motion capture data files by:

Vicon
Biovision
TSi

Thanks to the following persons for their contributions:

Robert Abel

Graham Bruce

Benjamin Cheung

Peter Conn

Karen Goulekas

Tim Johnson

Fred Nilsson

Evan Ricks

Larry Bafia

Gordon Cameron

Richard Chuang

Eric Darnell

Rex Grignon

Jeff Kleiser

George Merkert

Carl Rosendahl

Thanks to the following persons for their support and assistance:

Ginger Barnwell	Darlene Bell
Julie Champagne	Sheigh Crabtree
Richard Chuang	Palmy Datt
Diane Grossman	Grue
Les Hunter	Kristine Kolton
Chris Mitchell	Brian Nilles
Thomas Park	Cordy Rierson
Carl Rosendahl	James Rowell
Tom Stone	David Spivak
Nick Tesi	Adam Valdez
Paige Whittaker	Regina Wright

Special thanks to PDI for their incredible support.

Infinite thanks, appreciation, and apologies to Ronit, Daniela, Mauricio, and Alexandra Menache. Your support and patience has been invaluable.

Introduction

In the late 1800s, Marey and Muybridge conducted independent studies of human and animal motion by shooting multiple photographs of moving subjects over a short period of time. These studies have had important ramifications in many disciplines, such as biology, medicine, photography, and even animation.

Thirty years later, cartoonist Max Fleischer used this idea to create the rotoscope, a device that allowed animators to trace cartoon characters over photographed frames of live performers. This was the first time that a real-life performance was used to help create an animated character.

The second incarnation of performance animation in entertainment officially started in the mid-1980s, when Robert Abel used it to create "Brilliance." This commercial marked the birth of motion capture for animation in three dimensions, or *performance 3D animation*. During the 1980s, mainstream character animation in 3D was born as well, and Wavefront became the first commercially available package for computer animation. Prior to these milestones, the computer animation market consisted mostly of flying logos and some image processing, and it was still dominated by technology rather than art, with very few exceptions. You had to be an engineer to use the tools because you had to write them.

The first and second stages of motion capture technology have many parallels. After their conception, both technologies went through a phase during which many believed they would replace animation created by traditional methods. The rotoscope obviously didn't, and it is clear to most people in the entertainment industry that today's motion capture will not either, but there are still some who think otherwise. During the period when rotoscoping threatened their craft, animators regarded it as an evil technology. To this day it is not widely accepted, although it is still used; however, the main goal is to achieve a certain look rather than automate the process of animation.

Although 3D motion capture is seen by many as a controversial technology, it is broadly used for video game characters and its use is growing fast in the film and television markets. It is still in the stage in which it is being tested as a mass production tool, and sometimes even as an animator replacement, but like the rotoscope, it will eventually become another style tool.

The main purpose of this book is to help accelerate this process by sharing experiences from different types of projects in order to provide a clear picture of what can and can't be done using motion capture. It should also serve as a guide for planning and carrying out projects with the help of performance animation, making sure that the reasons for using the technology are correct and that the goals are attainable.

Many of the cases and concepts outlined herein are based on the use of optical motion capture systems. However, the various different types of systems share basic ideas regarding data collection. After data collection, most concepts are the same, with perhaps the exception of real-time feedback, which is something for which all hardware types are aiming. Having said that, my feeling is that if you are interested in anything that pertains to performance animation, or even just character setup and the math associated with it, chances are you will find this book useful.

CHAPTER ONE

Motion Capture Primer

❦

MOTION CAPTURE AND PERFORMANCE ANIMATION

Motion capture is the process of recording a live motion event and translating it into usable mathematical terms by tracking a number of key points in space over time and combining them to obtain a single three-dimensional representation of the performance. In brief, it is the technology that enables the process of translating a live performance into a digital performance. The captured subject could be anything that exists in the real world and has motion; the key points are the areas that best represent the motion of the subject's different moving parts. These points should be pivot points or connections between rigid parts of the subject. For a human, for example, some of the key points are the joints that act as pivot points and connections for the bones. The location of each of these points is identified by one or more sensors, markers, or potentiometers that are placed on the subject and that serve, in one way or another, as conduits of information to the main collection device. From now on, when speaking generally about these, I will refer to them as *markers*.

Performance animation is not the same as motion capture, although many people use the two terms interchangeably. Whereas motion capture pertains to the technology used to collect the motion, *performance animation* refers to the actual performance that is used to bring a character to life, regardless of the technology used. To obtain it, one must go through the whole process of motion capture and then map the resulting data onto a three-dimensional character. In short, motion capture is the collection of data that represents motion, whereas performance animation is the final product of a character driven by a performer.

There are different ways of capturing motion. Some systems use cameras that digitize different views of the performance, which are then used to put together the position of key points, each represented by one or more reflective markers. Others use electromagnetic fields or ultrasound to track a group of sensors. Mechanical systems based on linked structures or armatures that use potentiometers to determine the rotation of each link are also available. Combinations of two or more of these technologies exist, and newer technologies are also being tested, all aiming for one result: real-time tracking of an unlimited number of key points with no space limitations at the highest frequency possible with the smallest margin of error. This is the Holy Grail of motion capture and probably the mission statement of every motion capture hardware manufacturer's research department. I later discuss how each of the current technologies falls short in this respect.

HISTORY OF PERFORMANCE ANIMATION IN THE ENTERTAINMENT FIELD

The Rotoscope

Motion capture in the entertainment field is the descendent of *rotoscoping*, a technique still used by some traditional animation studios to copy realistic motion from film footage onto cartoon characters.

The rotoscope device was invented and patented by cartoonist Max Fleischer in 1915, with the intent of automating the production of cartoon films. The device projected live-action film, a frame at a time, onto a light table, allowing cartoonists to trace the frame's image onto paper. The first cartoon character ever to be rotoscoped was Koko the Clown. Fleischer's brother, Dave, acted out Koko's movements in a clown suit. Fleischer wanted to use Koko to convince the big studios to use the new process for their cartoon projects. The sale was difficult because it had taken Fleischer about a year to produce the initial one-minute cartoon using the technique, so he couldn't market it as a mass production tool. Eventually, Fleischer realized that rotoscoping would be a viable technique only for certain shots that required realistic motion.

Walt Disney Studios used some rotoscoping in 1937 to create the motion of human characters in *Snow White*. Snow White herself and the Prince were partially rotoscoped. The decision to use rotoscoping wasn't a matter of cost, but of realistic human motion. In fact, *Snow White* went tremendously over budget due to the complexity of the animation.

Rotoscoping has been adopted over the years by many cartoon studios, but few actually admit using it because many people in the animation industry consider it cheating and a desecration of the art of animation.

A two-dimensional approach, rotoscoping was designed for traditional, hand-drawn cartoons. The advent of three-dimensional animation brought about the birth of a new, three-dimensional way of rotoscoping. Hence, motion capture.

"Brilliance"

Some of the current motion capture technologies have been around for decades, being used in different applications for medical and military purposes. Motion capture in computer graphics was first used in the late 1970s and early 1980s in the form of research projects at schools such as Simon Fraser University, Massachusetts Institute of Technology, and New York Institute of Technology, but it was used in actual production only in the mid-1980s.

In late 1984, Robert Abel appeared on a talk show and was asked if he would soon be able to counterfeit people digitally. "We are a long ways from that," he replied. "We haven't even figured out human motion, which is the basis, and that's a year away." A week and a half later, Abel received a visit on a Friday afternoon from a creative director from Ketchum, a prominent advertising agency. The visitor brought six drawings of a very sexy woman made out of chrome. She was to have Kathleen Turner's voice and would be the spokesperson for the National Canned Food Information Council, an association formed by Heinz, Del Monte, Campbell's, and a number of big players that sold canned food. They felt they had to make a powerful statement because the idea of buying food in cans was becoming obsolete, so they wanted to do something really different and outrageous, and they wanted it to air during the Super Bowl in January 1985. "Can you do it?" asked the client. "You're certainly here a lot earlier than I would have planned," replied Abel, and asked the client to wait until the end of the weekend for an answer.

At that time most computer graphics consisted of moving logos, landscapes, and other hard objects, and Robert Abel and Associates had already become a player in that market, along with MAGI, Triple-I (Information International, Inc.), John Whitney's Digital Productions, and PDI, all of which had their own proprietary software, because at that time there was almost no off-the-shelf animation software and whatever was available was still in its infancy. Abel's software was initially based on bits and pieces from Bell Labs, Evans and Sutherland, JPL, and other places, and was augmented over time by his group.

The next step would be to animate a digital character. "For storytelling, which was really our goal, we had to have human characters," recalls Abel, "because nobody better than a human character is able to convey emotion and story. We come from a long line of storytellers that go back maybe 35,000 years, and although the forms may change from cave paintings to digitally made motion pictures, it's still the same thing, it's the passing on of stories." Creating the first animated digital character would open a Pandora's box of many new challenges, such as creating realistic skin, hair, and expression. But first they had to deal with the motion.

Abel and his team decided to lock the doors and not leave the building until Monday morning. If by then they didn't have the solution figured out, they would have to pass on the project. Robert Abel and Associates' background in shooting miniatures with motion control cameras since the late 1960s and early 1970s was the key to the solution. They knew that the answer to their problem would have to do with motion and control, except this time it would be human motion. Keyframe character animation was not an option at the time, so they decided to find a way to track the motions of a woman acting the part of the character. It made sense to shoot the woman with several cameras from different points of view, and then use this footage to create a motion algorithm.

Seven people worked throughout the weekend. "Several of us got into our underwear," recalls Abel. "We got black adhesive dots and we put them on our bodies and we would photograph each other with Polaroid cameras and then we would lay out these Polaroids so we could see how they changed from angle to angle." They continued this slow deductive reasoning process until Sunday at 3 A.M., when they decided that it would take a few weeks to digitize all the motion. It would be close, but they felt that they could do the job in the eight-week schedule that the client had established.

Among the people involved in this project besides Bob Abel were Bill Kovacs and Roy Hall, who later became cofounders of Wavefront Technologies; Frank Vitz, now head of software at Kleiser-Walczak Construction Company; Con Pederson, cofounder of Metrolight Studios a few years later; Randy Roberts, who directed the project and is now a commercial director at Rhythm and Hues; Richard Hollander, recently president of Blue Sky/VIFX and now head of the feature film division at Rhythm and Hues; Neil Eskuri, currently visual effects director at Disney; Charlie Gibson, Oscar-winning special effects supervisor for *Babe*; and John Hughes, who later became cofounder and president of Rhythm and Hues.

They found a woman who was very pretty and graceful and had been a dancer and a model. They had decided that motion on 18 hinge points would be necessary to achieve the desired result, so with black magic markers they put black dots on each of her 18 joints. A stool with a 360° axis of rotation in the middle was assembled so that the model could sit and perform the moves without obstacles. The team photographed her from multiple points of view, and then managed to import the images to SGI Iris 1000 systems. These workstations appeared in early 1984 and were the first model produced by Silicon Graphics. They were then able to analyze the difference in measurement between pairs of joints (for example, the elbow and the wrist) for each point of view and to combine them to come up with a series of algorithms that would ultimately be used to animate the digital character. This process was done on a frame-by-frame basis and took four and one-half weeks.

At the same time, the wire-frame model was built in separate sections, all rigid parts. The motion algorithms were applied to all the combined moving parts, and the animation was output as a vector graphic. "We then had to deal with the basic issue of wrapping her body in chrome," says Abel. "Of course, there is no way in the world we could do ray-tracing to real reflective chrome the way those guys do it at SIGGRAPH, with those multimillion dollar supercomputers. We had VAX 750s, which were early DEC computers." This problem was solved by Charlie Gibson, who figured out a way of texture mapping the body so that when it moved, the map would animate following the topology of the body. Today we call this a reflection map.

The last challenge was to render the final spot, all 30 seconds of it, in the two weeks that they had left. "The good and the bad news is this," Abel announced. "We don't nearly have the horse power, but the VAX 750 is a staple of almost every university, laboratory, and engineering place in the country." They ended up using 60 additional VAX 750s around the country, from Florida to Alaska to Hawaii, and even a few places in Canada. The final spot, "Brilliance," was rendered and pieced together about two days before the delivery date. It is now known by most people in the industry as "Sexy Robot."

Pacific Data Images

Pacific Data Images (PDI) is the oldest operating computer animation studio, and it played a big part in the history of performance animation. Founded in 1980 in Sunnyvale, California, by Carl Rosendahl, and later joined by Richard Chuang and Glenn Entis, it wasn't until eight years later that the studio would produce its first project using some kind of human tracking technology.

Over the years, PDI used different types of tracking devices that fit particular project needs, ranging from custom-built electromechanical devices to electromagnetic and optical tracking systems, but it wasn't PDI's intention to specialize in motion capture. "We use technology where it is appropriate," says Richard Chuang. "We are not a one-technique company; our goal is not to be a master of any one thing, just be good at a lot of them."

The Jim Henson Hour

In 1988, PDI, now located in Palo Alto, California, began collaboration with Jim Henson and Associates to create a computer-generated character for *The Jim Henson Hour*. Henson had already done some tests with a digital character at Digital Productions and had been holding the idea until the technology was

Figure 1-1.   *Taping The Jim Henson Hour. (Photo courtesy of Rex Grignon.)*

mature enough to produce the result he wanted. Graham Walters, now a technical supervisor at Pixar, was the technical lead for PDI on the project.

The character was called Waldo C. Graphic. "One of the criteria on the project was that they wanted to be able to perform the character live when they were videotaping the TV show," recalls Carl Rosendahl. "It didn't mean that the final render needed to be live; they had to be able to record him live because of the spontaneity of the performance and such." Figure 1-1 is a photograph of the taping of *The Jim Henson Hour.*

Henson already had been doing some work with wireless telemetric robotics to animate characters for shots in which there was no way of controlling them directly, such as for a scene in *The Muppet Movie* in which Kermit is riding a bicycle and the audience sees the whole character in frame with his head moving around and singing a song. "It was a robot Kermit, and Jim had this foam Kermit head with some potentiometers on it that transmitted a radio signal to the robot on the bike," says Rosendahl. That device, shown in Figure 1-2, was used for the Waldo C. Graphic character, with some modifications. PDI built a mechanical arm to record the position of the character in space. Instead of the radio link, the robot

Figure 1-2.   *Steve Whitmire (L) and Rex Grignon operating the device used to control Waldo C. Graphic. (Photo courtesy of Rex Grignon.)*

had a direct hardware link to one of PDI's Silicon Graphics systems. A control box with buttons allowed them to do eye blinks.

"All the videotape recording was done in Toronto, so we moved all the equipment up there and basically got it to work live on the set," says Rosendahl, "so that we took a feed of the video camera and then comped in Waldo on top of it, and that's what the performance would look like, even though the video was recording the final image without Waldo in there, but the performers would look at the one with the rough-version Waldo."

Steve Whitmire, who is now in charge of bringing Kermit the Frog to life, was the puppeteer operating the device. "Essentially, it was a puppet, something that the puppeteer was familiar with at the end," recalls Rex Grignon, supervising animator at PDI. "He could put his hand in this and just fly it anywhere in the space within that region." During the show, the puppeteer's motion data was read in and interpreted to control Waldo on the screen as a low-resolution version. "We modeled a 50-polygon version of Waldo," says Grignon. "It was all within screen space. The puppeteers, when doing a normal puppet, would have their hand in the puppet, and they'd be looking down at a monitor, so they'd be able to gauge their performance, so they were absolutely used to this." The new technique had the added benefit that the puppeteer could bring the puppet down and not worry about hiding from the camera.

Grignon was in charge of recording the motion. "As we started a performance I'd essentially start the system recording, do the blinks, and when the director said cut, I'd cut and I'd save that take in a similar language to what they were using on the show," says Grignon. They kept track of the takes that Henson liked, because they needed to ensure that the data stayed in sync with the rest of the characters in the show. This was necessary so that after the editing of the show, PDI could use the data matching the chosen takes to produce the animation.

The device generated some interference, but although the character tended to jump and pop around, it looked pretty good for the live session. After the recording session, the data would be sent via phone line to the PDI studio, then located in Sunnyvale, California, and a PDI team would massage it to eliminate all the noise and add the necessary secondary animation, such as the belly wiggle. The team would also add several costume changes that required transitions, such as scenes in which the character turned into other objects (for example, a book or an electric saw), and would render the final high-resolution character.

They were doing one episode a week with about one minute of the Waldo character. "We'd go up on the weekend, we'd shoot the show on Monday, we'd send the tape back on Tuesday, and then Michelle Choi, who was here, would basically render the tape. We'd come back, we'd all work on this for about five days rendering a minute of stuff and adding any extra props and extra animation," recalls Grignon. "We lived here, we just lived here. We slept here every night."

"I still think this is one of the best uses of motion capture," notes Grignon, "You can take advantage of the puppeteer's skills, because these guys are masters. It's just amazing seeing them put their hand in a puppet and it just comes to life. I just remember Graham and I, both were just continually astounded with the subtleties that these guys could bring to these characters."

Waldo C. Graphic was brought back to life by PDI in 1991 for the *MuppetVision 3D* movie, still being shown at Disney–MGM Studios in Orlando, Florida.

Exoskeleton

In 1988, PDI commissioned Rick Lazzarini's The Creature Shop to build a Waldo device for the upper body and head. They called this mechanical device an "exoskeleton"; it was based on optical potentiometers on each joint (see Figure 1-3). "It took us two passes to get one that really worked well," recalls Carl Rosendahl. "Analog parts are too noisy," notes Richard Chuang. The second version had digital parts.

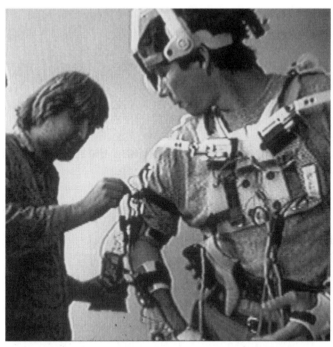

Figure 1-3. *Jamie Dixon wearing the PDI exoskeleton as Graham Walters makes adjustments during a shoot for Toys. (Photo courtesy of PDI.)*

The second exoskeleton was used for the Barry Levinson movie *Toys*, in a sequence for which PDI had to create an X-ray view of an ongoing meeting. "Jamie Dixon, who was our lead guy in the LA office, was the effects supervisor, and he actually was the one who did the performing," says Rosendahl. "And because there were multiple characters, he actually did it in multiple passes." Rosendahl also recalls that there were some glitches in the data that had to be cleaned up after the performance, but usable data was available in a reasonable amount of time. *Toys* was the first motion picture in which a digital character was successfully created using motion capture.

PDI later used a Flock of Birds, an electromagnetic device manufactured by Ascension Technology Corporation, on several projects in their Los Angeles office. One of them was a bit called "The Late Jackie Lenny" for a Comedy Central pilot in which a skeleton was a talk show host and would interview live comics or do a stand-up act.

For all the projects involving that device, PDI fabricated accessories to help hold the sensors in place and make the capture experience easier on the performer. Most of these were based on Velcro strips, but the head sensor was placed on top of a baseball cap so that when the performer took off the cap, the character would look like it had taken off its head. The device had some problems with interference. For example, the studio was located on the third floor of a three-story building, and the air conditioning equipment was located on the roof, right above the stage. When the air conditioning kicked on while the device was being used, the characters on screen would sway up and down.

deGraf/Wahrman

Brad deGraf experimented with performance animation while working at Digital Productions, using Jim Henson's Waldo device. After Digital Productions was purchased by Omnibus, Brad left and joined forces with Michael Wahrman, also from Digital Productions, and founded deGraf/Wahrman Production Company.

In 1988, Silicon Graphics contracted the services of deGraf/Wahrman to create a demonstration piece for their new 4D models. The piece was an interactive animation called *Mike the Talking Head,* which was showcased at SIGGRAPH '88. For the first time, an animated character was able to interact with the audience. The controls that animated the character in real time were operated by a puppeteer during the conference. deGraf/Wahrman's proprietary software was used to create an interface between the controls and the rendering engine and to produce interpolated instances of the character's geometry. The new Silicon Graphics 4D workstation had the horsepower to render the character in real time.

When deGraf and Wahrman dissolved their partnership, Brad joined Colossal Pictures and started rewriting the performance animation software. In 1993, he developed "Moxy," a character for the Cartoon Network that was operated in real time using an electromagnetic tracker. In 1994, he founded Protozoa, a spin-off from Colossal's performance animation studio. His focus has been on real-time performance animation solutions, including software and character development for different media, including television and the Web. ALIVE, Protozoa's proprietary performance animation software, supports multiple input devices, including motion capture systems, joysticks, and MIDI controllers. It also outputs to different formats, including live television and the World Wide Web via VRML (Virtual Reality Modeling Language).

Kleiser-Walczak Construction Company

In 1986, Jeff Kleiser began experimenting with motion capture while he was at Omnibus Computer Graphics. "We used the optical system from Motion Analysis in Santa Rosa, California, to encode martial arts movement for use in a test for Marvel Comics," recalls Kleiser. "Results were disappointing due to the alpha code we were working with."

In 1987, after Omnibus closed, Kleiser joined forces with Diana Walczak, who had been sculpting human bodies, and founded Kleiser-Walczak Construction Company. Their specialty would be to build and animate computer-generated actors, or *Synthespians*.

"After creating our first Synthespian, Nestor Sextone in 1988, we got together with Frank Vitz and went back to Motion Analysis to capture motion for our second digital actor, Dozo, in creating the film *Don't Touch Me,* in 1989," says Kleiser. "We were only able to get about 30 seconds of usable motion capture, and we had to recycle it to fill the 3.5 minutes of the song we had written." Vitz had been working with Robert Abel and Associates and had some motion capture experience, as he had been part of the team that created "Brilliance."

Over the years, Kleiser-Walczak has created digital actors for special venue, commercial, and feature film projects. They created dancing water people for the Doug Trumbull stereoscopic ride In Search of the Obelisk, located inside the Luxor Hotel in Las Vegas. Using a Flock of Birds electromagnetic system by Ascension Technology Corporation, they also created digital stunt doubles for Sylvester Stallone, Rob Schneider, and others for the film *Judge Dredd.* In their most recent use of motion capture, Kleiser-Walczak produced "Trophomotion," a commercial spot for Stardox athletic braces in which two basketball trophies come to life. They used a combination of keyframe animation and motion capture, which they achieved with an optical system manufactured by Adaptive Optics in Cambridge, Massachusetts.

Their latest project is computer imagery for The Amazing Adventures of Spiderman, a ride for Universal Studios' Islands of Adventure, in Orlando, Florida. "We tested mocap [motion capture] for this project, but it quickly became clear that superhero characters need to have super-human motion, and that keyframe animation gave us the look and flexibility we wanted," says Kleiser. "All the animation in the project was therefore done with keyframe animation."

Homer and Associates

In the early 1990s, projects utilizing motion capture in computer graphics were starting to become part of actual production work, so companies whose main business was based on this technology started to surface. Medialab, Mr. Film, Windlight Studios, SimGraphics, and Brad deGraf at Colossal Pictures concentrated their efforts on real-time applications that included character development and puppeteering, while Biovision, TSi, and Acclaim embraced the non-real-time technology for the up-and-coming video game market. At the same time, commercial production using the now traditional motion capture techniques was initiated by Homer and Associates.

"Party Hardy"

Although Homer and Associates had already created a shot for the film *Lawnmower Man* in 1991 using motion capture, they produced their initial entry in the advertising market in 1992: "Party Hardy," a spot promoting the Pennsylvania Lottery. It consisted of an animated crowd of lottery tickets at a costume party. The spot was especially challenging because it had to have humanoid motion and facial expressions, and each ticket had to be different. There also had to be a feeling of interaction among the characters.

Peter Conn, president and founder of Homer and Associates, decided to use a camera-based system to collect the motions for the spot. The system used was an Elite Motion Analyzer, a system manufactured by Bioengineering Technology Systems (BTS) in Italy primarily for medical and industrial applications, and provided by SuperFluo, a company dedicated to bringing these medical systems to the entertainment industry. SuperFluo added custom software geared to computer animation to the already existing configuration.

The spot was directed by Michael Kory, who also performed the motions for all the characters. For the body motions, markers were placed on human-size foam rectangles, shown in Figure 1-4, which Kory held while acting. The facial motions were also performed by Kory using the Elite system, but this time using smaller markers placed in specific areas of his face. The captured facial motion was used to help interpolate between facial shapes that were built by Kory.

"Party Hardy" is a good example of a project in which motion capture was used to collect data from an object or character puppeteered by a performer, as opposed to data collected from the actual performer's body.

"Steam"

Peter Gabriel's music video "Steam" was a coproduction between Colossal Pictures and Homer and Associates. The video was produced in 1992 and was directed by Stephen Johnson, director of other award-winning Peter Gabriel videos, including "Big Time."

"There was a period of several months when we were actively working with Brad deGraf and Stephen Johnson," recalls Peter Conn, president of Homer and Associates. "[Stephen Johnson] had a fertile imagination and an equally formidable lack of decisiveness and reality orientation. I remember that every meeting we had about what the video would include always involved going through dozens of storyboards of very elaborate effects. Although the beginning of the song was precisely worked out bar by bar, we never ever got through even half the song. There were dozens of elaborate concepts, which he seemed to want in the video. Since he was having inability to downsize the scope, he would fly to London or Senegal to get Peter's input. When he came back, there was never any consensus,

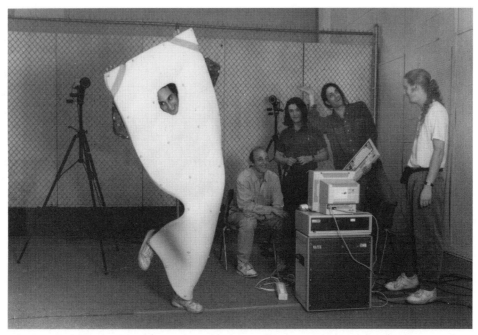

Figure 1-4. *The Homer & Associates team with the BTS motion capture system for the Pennsylvania Lottery commercial "Party Hardy": (left to right) Michael Kory, director (behind foam); Peter Conn, producer; Francesco Chiarini (Superfluo, motion capture specialist); Umberto Lazzari (Superfluo, motion capture specialist); John Adamczyk, technical director. (Photo courtesy of Homer & Associates.)*

just more and more concepts and ideas. A lot would have been almost achievable had the months of prep been actual production, but by the time the video was officially green-lighted there was no more than four weeks or so left to do everything. Motion capture was always specified as the great technique that would somehow make it all possible."

The motions would be collected using the same BTS optical system used on "Party Hardy." "By the time Peter Gabriel showed up for the motion capture sessions, the SuperFluo guys, Umberto Lazzari and Francesco Chiarini, had set up in our usual place, the large abandoned white storage room in the basement of the adjacent building," says Conn.

They spent two days capturing motion data from Peter Gabriel and a dancer. About 150 different movements were collected. "Peter had one rule for the room: no spectators," recalls Conn. "When the playback rolled, everyone had to dance and get into the music. He liked so much doing the motion samplings that he refused to quit. Knowing that we had only time left to animate a few scenes, it was way over the top, but hey, it was Peter Gabriel and we were getting data."

In the end, there were only a couple of shots in which captured motion data was used. The longest shot was one in which Peter was supposed to be made of ice, with dancing fire girls alongside. "He was to melt then reemerge as water," says Conn. Michael Kory animated the scene and Scott Kilburn wrote the particle software, which was based on Homer's proprietary code that had been written by John Adamczyk for *The Lawnmower Man.*

A crew of eight undertook the task of putting together the shots in a short period of time, while the director was in London. "Memorable moments included a conference call after they had seen a test over in the U.K.," says Conn. "Stephen was upset because he said that he had wanted the girls 'not on fire' but 'of fire.' We didn't really know what he meant, but we kept adding more particles. Then after the scene was delivered, he was still upset. It turned out that the girls weren't voluptuous enough, so we took the models and pulled the breasts out an ungodly much and then rendered just some breast fire and comped it on."

The other scene with captured motion data was the "Garden of Eden," in which both Gabriel and the dancer turn into digital characters after walking through an imaginary plane. "Actually, Brad [deGraf] did a great mocap piece with Peter Gabriel as a puppet but for some reason it never made the final cut," recalls Conn. "Despite the multitudinous mistakes and us knowing what it could have been given more time, the video went on to win some major awards, like the Grammy for Video of the Year in 1993," he notes.

Other notable motion capture works involving Homer and Associates include shots from the film *Lawnmower Man* and music videos such as Vince Neil's "Sister of Pain" and TLC's "Waterfalls," produced for Atomix with motion data from TSi.

TYPES OF MOTION CAPTURE

Human motion capture systems are classified as outside-in, inside-out, and inside-in systems. These names are indicative of where the capture sources and sensors are placed.

- An *outside-in system* uses external sensors to collect data from sources placed on the body. Examples of such systems are camera-based tracking devices, in which the cameras are the sensors and the reflective markers are the sources.
- *Inside-out systems* have sensors placed on the body that collect external sources. Electromagnetic systems, whose sensors move in an externally generated electromagnetic field, are examples of inside-out systems.
- *Inside-in systems* have their sources and sensors placed on the body. Examples of these devices are electromechanical suits, in which the sensors are potentiometers or powered goniometers and the sources are the actual joints inside the body.

The principal technologies used today that represent these categories are optical, electromagnetic, and electromechanical human tracking systems.

Optical Motion Capture Systems

Optical motion capture is a very accurate method of capturing certain motions when using a state-of-the-art system. It is not a real-time process—at least not yet; immediate feedback is not possible on the target character, but an almost real-time stick-figure visual aid is now possible. Data acquired optically requires extensive post-processing to become usable.

A typical optical motion capture system is based on a single computer that controls the input of several digital CCD (charge-coupled device) cameras. CCDs are light-sensitive devices that use an array of photoelectric cells (also called *pixels*) to capture light, and then measure the intensity of the light for each of the cells, creating a digital representation of the image. A CCD camera contains an array of pixels that can vary in resolution from as low as 128×128 to as high as 4096×4096 or even greater.

Obviously, the higher the resolution, the better, but there are other trade-offs. The samples-per-second rate, or frame rate, has to be fast enough for capturing the nuances of very fast motions. In most cases, 512 samples per second are more than enough. By today's standards, a CCD camera with a resolution of 4096×4096 would be able to produce less than one frame per second, but this is changing very quickly. Another important feature is shutter synchronization, by which the camera's shutter speed can be synchronized with external sources, such as the light-emitting diodes (LEDs) with which optical motion capture cameras are usually outfitted.

The number of cameras employed is usually no less than 4 and no more than 32, and they capture the position of reflective markers at speeds anywhere between 30 and 1000 samples per second. The cameras are normally fitted with their own light sources that create a directional reflection from the markers, which are generally spheres covered with a material such as Scotch-Brite tape. Infrared light sources are preferred because they create less visual distortion for the user. The marker spheres can vary from a few millimeters in diameter, for small-area captures, to a couple of inches. The Vicon 8 system, shown in Figure 1-5, is an example of a state-of-the-art optical system that can accommodate up to 24 cameras.

Most optical systems are manufactured for medical applications; as such, they lack many features that are important to computer graphics applications. The Vicon 8 system is the first system designed with computer graphics in mind. Until very recently, optical motion capture systems were unable to support SMPTE time code, a time stamp used by most film and television applications. Even if you videotaped your capture session, there was no easy way to

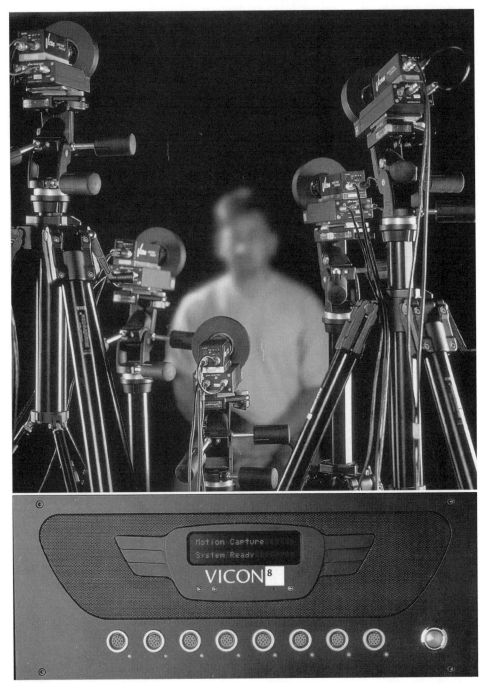

Figure 1-5.   *The Vicon 8 optical motion capture system. (Photo courtesy of Vicon Motion Systems.)*

match the video to the actual motion data. Having time code in the motion data allows you to edit the motion files, as you would do with live-action video, and properly plan the association of the characters with background plates. Another very useful new feature of the Vicon 8 is the fact that reference video of the session can be synchronized, or *genlocked,* with the actual data collection. In addition to video genlock, the Vicon 8 software can shoot AVI movie files at the same time as it captures. These movies are great references for data post-processing and application.

The optical system must be calibrated by having all the cameras track an object with known dimensions that the software can recognize, such as a cube or a wand with reflective markers. By combining the views from all cameras with the known dimensions of the object, the exact position of each camera in space can be calculated. If a camera is bumped even slightly, a new calibration must be performed. It is a good idea to recalibrate the system after every few minutes of capture, since any kind of motion or vibration can shift the position of a camera, especially if the studio is located on unstable ground.

At least two views are needed to track a single point's three-dimensional position, and extra cameras are necessary to maintain a direct line of sight from at least two cameras to every marker. That doesn't mean that more cameras are better, because each additional camera increases post-processing time. There are other methods for minimizing occlusions that are implemented in software and used during post-processing. The most time- and cost-effective solution is different for every case, depending on the type, speed, and length of the motion, as well as on the volume of capture and the available light. Figure 1-6 shows a performance being filmed on an optical motion capture stage.

Once the camera views are digitized into the computer, it is time for the post-processing to begin. The first step is for the software to try to produce a clean playback of only the markers. Different image processing methods are used to minimize the noise and isolate the markers, separating them from the rest of the environment. The most basic approach is to separate all the groups of pixels that exceed a predetermined luminosity threshold. If the software is intelligent enough, it will use adjacent frames to help solve any particular frame. The system operator has control over many variables that will help in this process, such as specifying the minimum and maximum lines expected per marker so the software can ignore anything smaller or bigger than these values.

The second step is to determine the two-dimensional coordinates of each marker for each camera view. This data will later be used in combination with the camera coordinates and the rest of the camera views to obtain the three-dimensional coordinates of each marker.

The third step is to actually identify each marker throughout a sequence. This stage requires the most operator assistance, since the initial assignment of each

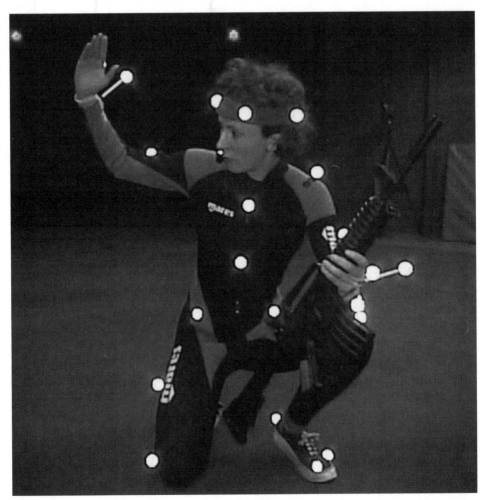

Figure 1-6.   *A performance in an optical motion capture stage. (Photo courtesy of Vicon Motion Systems.)*

marker has to be recorded manually. After this assignment, the software tries to resolve the rest of the sequence until it loses track of a marker due to occlusion or crossover, at which point the operator must reassign the markers in question and continue the computation. This process continues until the whole sequence is resolved and a file containing positional data for all markers is saved.

The file produced by this process contains a sequence of marker global positions over time, which means that only each marker's Cartesian (x, y, and z) coordinates are listed per frame and no hierarchy or limb rotations are included. It is

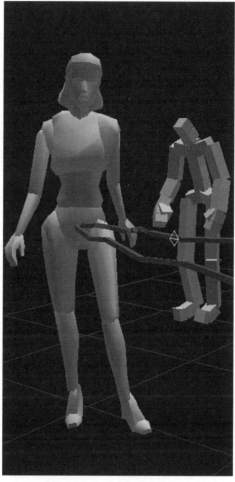

Figure 1-7. *The Vicon Mobius hierarchical motion editor. (Photo courtesy of Vicon Motion Systems.)*

possible to use this file for computer animation, but a more extensive setup is required inside the animation software in order to resolve the final deformation skeleton to be used. Experienced technical directors can benefit by using this file's data, because it allows more control over what can be done in a character setup. For the average user, however, the data should be processed further, at least to the point of including a skeletal hierarchy with limb rotations. Systems such as the Vicon 8 include data editing systems that allow the user to produce the rotational hierarchical data before importing it to animation software. Figure 1-7 shows a sample screen of the Vicon Mobius hierarchical motion editor that is shipped with the Vicon 8 optical motion capture system.

Advantages of Optical Systems

- Optical data is extremely accurate in most cases.
- A larger number of markers can be used.
- It is easy to change marker configurations.
- It is possible to obtain approximations to internal skeletons by using groups of markers.
- Performers are not constrained by cables.
- Optical systems allow for a larger performance area than most other systems.
- Optical systems have a higher frequency of capture, resulting in more samples per second.

Disadvantages of Optical Systems

- Optical data requires extensive post-processing.
- The hardware is expensive, costing between $100,000 and $250,000.
- Optical systems cannot capture motions when markers are occluded for a long period of time.
- Capture must be carried out in a controlled environment, away from yellow light and reflective noise.

Electromagnetic Trackers

Electromagnetic motion capture systems are part of the six degrees of freedom electromagnetic measurement systems' family and consist of an array of receivers that measure their spatial relationship to a nearby transmitter. These receivers or sensors are placed on the body and are connected to an electronic control unit, in most cases by individual cables.

Also called magnetic trackers, these systems emerged from the technology used in military aircraft for helmet-mounted displays (HMDs). With HMDs, a pilot can acquire a target by locating it visually through a reticle located on the visor. A sensor on the helmet is used to track the pilot's head position and orientation.

A typical magnetic tracker consists of a transmitter, 11 to 18 sensors, an electronic control unit, and software. A state-of-the-art magnetic tracker can have up to 90 sensors and is capable of capturing up to 144 samples per second. The cost ranges from $5000 to $150,000, considerably less than optical systems. To take advantage of the real-time capabilities of a magnetic tracker, it must be connected to a powerful computer system that is capable of rendering a great number of polygons in real time. Depending on the needs of a particular project, the cost of this computer system alone could exceed the cost of the magnetic tracker.

The transmitter generates a low-frequency electromagnetic field that is detected by the receivers and input into an electronic control unit, where it is filtered and amplified. Then it is sent to a central computer, where the software resolves each sensor's position in x, y, and z Cartesian coordinates and orientation (yaw, pitch, and roll). This data is piped into another algorithm that, in most cases, will convert each sensor's global orientation and position into one hierarchical chain with only one position and multiple rotations, which can then be streamed into animation software. Sometimes this conversion happens inside the animation software itself.

The whole process is not truly real-time, but it is close, depending on the amount of filtering, amplifying, and post-processing, and the speed of the connection between the control unit and the host computer. Slow and congested Ethernet connections can slow this process down considerably. Magnetic trackers have a specification called *latency*, which indicates the amount of time elapsed between the data collection and the display of the resulting performance. This specification can vary from a few milliseconds to a few seconds.

Magnetic trackers such as the Flock of Birds by Ascension Technology Corporation use direct current (DC) electromagnetic fields, whereas others, such as the Polhemus ULTRATRAK PRO (Figure 1-8), use alternating current (AC) fields. Both of these technologies have different problems associated with metallic conductivity. AC trackers are very sensitive to aluminum, copper, and carbon steel, but not as sensitive to stainless steel or iron, whereas DC trackers have problems with ferrous metals, such as iron and steel, but not with aluminum and copper.

Many of these conductivity problems are caused by the induction of a current in the metal that creates a new electromagnetic field that interferes with the original field emitted by the tracker. These new fields are called *eddy currents*. Some magnetic trackers use special algorithms to compensate for these distortions by mapping the capture area, but these calibrations only work with static, predefined problem areas such as metallic structures in buildings. In most cases, it is better to avoid any high-conductivity metals near the capture area. This limitation makes the magnetic tracker difficult to transport to different stages or sets.

The fact that a magnetic tracker can provide position as well as orientation data means that it requires less markers than its optical counterpart; however, it also means that internal skeleton data will not be calculated. This limitation is acceptable in many cases, since these kinds of trackers are normally used for real-time purposes and it is possible to calibrate the character setup to compensate for this deficiency by using joint offset measurements.

Magnetic trackers in the entertainment industry are used mostly for real-time applications such as live television, live performances, and location-based or Internet virtual reality implementations. Many times they are used in combination with other puppeteering devices. A performer can author the body motions of a character with the magnetic tracker while someone else is performing the facial

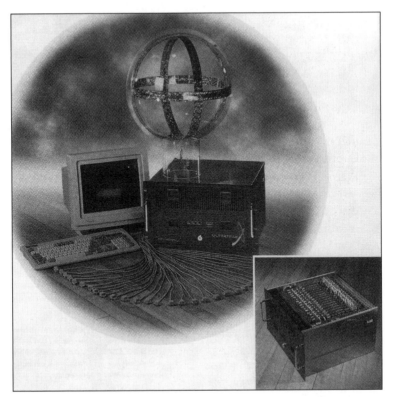

Figure 1-8.   *The Polhemus ULTRATRAK PRO system. (Photo courtesy of Polhemus.)*

expressions and lip-syncing using a face tracker or a data glove. At the same time, a puppeteer can be animating the character's eyes using a simple mouse.

Magnetic trackers are also used on non-real-time applications in which immediate feedback on a character is required. Non-entertainment-related applications include the already mentioned military applications plus simulations for various industries such as aerospace, medicine, and education. Figure 1-9 shows a performer wearing an electromagnetic tracker.

Advantages of Magnetic Trackers

- Real-time data output can provide immediate feedback.
- Position and orientation data are available without post-processing.
- Magnetic trackers are less expensive than optical systems, costing between $5000 and $150,000.
- The sensors are never occluded.
- It is possible to capture multiple performers interacting simultaneously with multiple setups.

Figure 1-9.   *Polhemus ActionTRAK electromagnetic tracker. (Photo courtesy of Polhemus.)*

Disadvantages of Magnetic Trackers

- The tracker's sensitivity to metal can result in irregular output.
- Performers are constrained by cables in most cases.
- Magnetic trackers have a lower sampling rate than some optical systems.
- The capture area is smaller than is possible with optical systems.
- It is difficult to change marker configurations.

Electromechanical Suits

The electromechanical motion capture suit is a group of structures linked by potentiometers or similar angular measurement devices located at the major human joint locations; it is driven by a human body's actions.

Potentiometers are components that have been used for many years in the electronics industry, in applications such as volume controls on old radios. A slider moving along a resistor element in the potentiometer produces a variable voltage-potential reading, depending on what percentage of the total resistance is applied to the input voltage. The potentiometers used for motion capture suits and armatures are much more complex versions of the old radio volume knob; they are sometimes called *analog* or *digital angular sensors.*

One big drawback of electromechanical systems based on potentiometers is their inability to measure global translations. In most cases, an electromagnetic sensor is added to the configuration to solve this problem, but that subjects the setup to the same disadvantages as the electromagnetic systems, such as sensitivity to nearby metals. In addition, the design of most of these devices is based on the assumption that most human bones are connected by simple hinge joints, so they don't account for nonstandard rotations that are common to human joints, such as in the shoulder complex or the lower arm. Of course, this can actually be a benefit if the mechanical setup of a particular digital character calls for such types of constraints.

A good example of an electromechanical suit is the Gypsy 2.5 Motion Capture System, by Analogus, shown in Figure 1-10.

Advantages of Electromechanical Body Suits

- The range of capture can be very large.
- Electromechanical suits are less expensive than optical and magnetic systems.
- The suit is portable.
- Real-time data collection is possible.
- Data is inexpensive to capture.
- The sensors are never occluded.
- It is possible to capture multiple performers simultaneously with multiple setups.

Disadvantages of Electromechanical Body Suits

- The systems have a low sampling rate.
- They are obtrusive due to the amount of hardware.
- The systems apply constraints on human joints.
- The configuration of sensors is fixed.
- Most systems do not calculate global translations without a magnetic sensor.

Digital Armatures

Digital armatures can be classified into two types: (1) keyframing or stop-motion armatures and (2) real-time or puppeteering armatures. Like the mechanical suit, both types consist of a series of rigid modules connected by joints whose rotations are measured by potentiometers or angular sensors. The sensors are usually analog devices, but they are called "digital" because the resulting readings are converted to digital signals to be processed by the com-

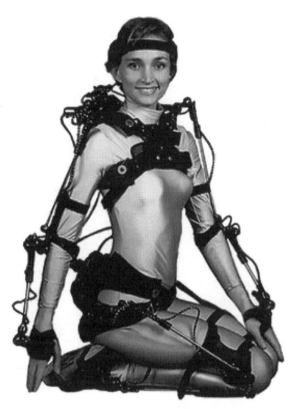

Figure 1-10. *The Analogus Gypsy 2.5 electromechanical suit. (Feb 1999, ID8 Media, San Francisco CA, 415-495-3930.)*

puter system. These armatures are typically modular in order to accommodate different character designs.

Keyframing armatures were initially used to help stop-motion animators animate digital characters; they are not really considered motion capture systems because they are not driven by a live performer. I mention them because most commercially available armatures can also be used as real-time armatures. Some proprietary armatures are dual-purpose, such as a device initially called the Dinosaur Input Device (DID), which was devised by Craig Hayes at Tippett Studio in Berkeley, California. The name was conceived because this unit was used to animate some of the digital dinosaurs in *Jurassic Park*. Later, the device was used to animate the bugs in *Starship Troopers*. It is now called the Digital Input Device (Figure 1-11).

The basic concept behind keyframing armatures is that the animator poses the device manually to generate each keyframe in the animation. The character in the animation software is set up with a mechanical structure equivalent to the armature's. By pressing a key, the animator uses the computer to record the armature's

Figure 1-11.   *Digital Input Device (D.I.D) designer Craig Hayes and the Raptor D.I.D. puppet. Jurassic Park 1992-93. (Photo courtesy of Tippett Studio.)*

pose into the digital character for a particular frame in time. This is done via a driver program that connects the device, typically plugged into a serial port, to the animation software. Once all the key poses are recorded, the software treats them as regular keyframes that might have been created with the software by itself.

Puppeteering armatures are very similar to keyframing armatures, except the motion is captured in real time as performed by one or more puppeteers. An example of such a setup is the proprietary armature developed by Boss Film Studios to capture the motion of Sil, the alien character that H.R. Giger designed for the film *Species*.

There are not many commercially available armatures, so most production companies have had to design their own. A commercially available example of a digital armature is the Monkey 2 by Digital Image Design in New York City (Figure 1-12). This unit can be used as both a keyframe and real-time armature. It is modular, so it can be assembled in different joint configurations. The first-generation Monkey had a fixed configuration, which made it unusable for any nonhumanoid applications. The typical cost for a 39-joint Monkey 2 setup is approximately $15,000, which includes all the necessary parts as well as driver software for most well-known animation packages. The device plugs into an RS-232 serial port.

Figure 1-12.   *The Monkey 2 armature. (Photo courtesy of Digital Image Design.)*

Advantages of Digital Armatures

- Digital armatures are easy to use for multiple characters animated using stop motion.
- Setup for different character types is easy.
- The cost is low.
- Armatures are good digital input devices for stop-motion animators.
- Data is available immediately.

Disadvantages of Digital Armatures

- Global translations are usually not captured.
- In most armatures, all the joints are hinge joints.
- Real-time armatures have low sampling rates compared with optical and magnetic systems.

Other Motion Capture Systems

The Waldo

The Waldo is a telemetric device that imitates the motions of whatever it is controlling. It was named after Waldo Farthingwaite Jones, a fictional disabled scientist in Robert A. Heinlein's 1942 short story "Waldo" who invents a device that allows him to act beyond his biomechanical possibilities. Telemetry is by definition the transmission of measurements; consequently, the Waldo transmits measurements of the motion of joints and other body parts to a mimicking device. There are many kinds of Waldos, controlled by different body parts, such as the head, arms, or legs, or even the body as a whole. Their main applications in entertainment are the control of digital or animatronic characters.

The name "Waldo" is rumored to have been first used at NASA to name an early telemetry device, and it was used for years as a generic name for such machines. It is now a trademark of The Character Shop, a company that specializes in animatronic characters. Figure 1-13 shows different kinds of Waldos manufactured by The Character Shop. The Jim Henson Creature Shop uses a device of this genre called the Henson Performance Control System to bring their animatronic or digital creatures to life.

Small Body Part Trackers

To capture the motion of small body parts, special trackers are needed, because full-body tracking devices lack the necessary resolution. However, there are some exceptions. For example, it is practically impossible to track facial movements and movement of fingers with an electromagnetic tracker because the sensors are bigger than the locations where they need to be placed. It is possible to handle such situations with optical trackers in some cases.

There are several mechanical and optical devices for capturing facial motion. The most popular are the real-time optical face trackers, consisting of a camera that is placed in a structure attached to the performer's head, so that it moves with the performer. The device captures the motion of small markers placed in different areas of the face. Unfortunately, these are 2D devices that cannot capture certain motions such as puckering of the lips, so the data is all in one plane and is not very realistic. Three-dimensional facial motion data can be captured

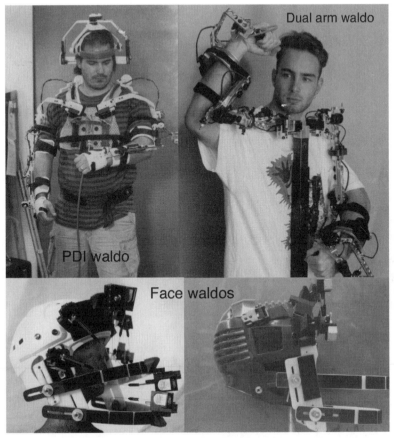

Figure 1-13. *Different types of Waldos manufactured by The Character Shop. (Photos courtesy of Rick Lazzarini/The Character Shop.)*

with an optical system using two or three cameras, yielding a much better result, but not in real time.

For hand motions there are several types of gloves that have small form-factor technologies, such as the Cyberglove, the DataGlove, and the PowerGlove. The Cyberglove (Figure 1-14) is manufactured by Virtual Technologies, Inc. (VTI). It has been available since 1991 and uses VTI's patented piezoresistive bend-sensing technology. It is available in 18- and 22-sensor models at prices ranging from approximately $9500 to $14,000 for a single glove. The 18-sensor model measures most finger rotations, abduction (the angle between adjacent fingers), thumb crossover, palm arch, and wrist rotations. The 22-sensor model adds a sensor for the distal joint of the index, middle, ring, and pinkie fingers. The sensors can capture a minimum rotation of 0.5° and can work at up to about 110 samples per sec-

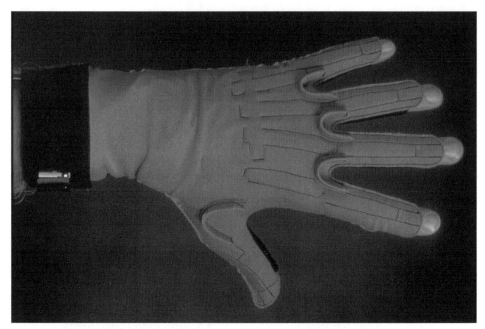

Figure 1-14.   *The VTI Cyberglove. (Photo courtesy of Virtual Technologies, Inc., www.virtex.com.)*

ond. Like many other similar devices, it requires a third-party device in order to measure global positioning and orientation.

The DataGlove, shown in Figure 1-15, has been around since 1987. It was manufactured by VPL Research, but the company's technical assets and patents were acquired by Sun Microsystems in February 1998, so the fate of DataGlove support and future availability is uncertain at this time. It is based on fiber-optic sensors placed along the back of the fingers. As fingers rotate, the fibers are bent and their transmitted light is attenuated. The strength of the light is turned into a signal that can be measured by the processor to calculate the rotation of the fingers. Most DataGlove models have ten sensors that measure the rotations of each of the two upper joints of the fingers. Some versions also have measurements for abduction. It can measure a minimum of $1°$ at up to 60 samples per second.

The Mattel PowerGlove was introduced in 1989 as an add-on controller for the Nintendo Entertainment System and has similar technology to that of the DataGlove. In fact, the PowerGlove was conceived as a low-cost alternative to the DataGlove. It was initially called Z-Glove by VPL Research, which later licensed it to Abrams Gentile Entertainment (AGE), the company that manufactured it for Mattel.

The difference that makes the PowerGlove's cost so much lower than the DataGlove's is in the components. The optic fibers were replaced with less expen-

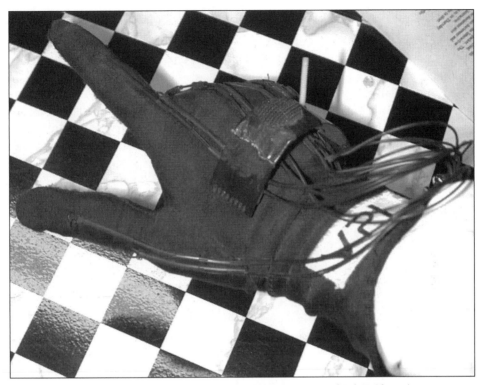

Figure 1-15.   *The VPL DataGlove. (Photo courtesy of Zak Zaidman.)*

sive conductive ink that is used as a resistor whose impedance variations indicate degrees of flexion. The global position and orientation are measured via ultrasonic pulses that are emitted from a few locations on the glove. The time taken for these pulses to reach the receivers is used to calculate in a very loose way the position and orientation of the glove. In fact, the glove emitters always have to be pointing at the receivers, which limits its range of motion. The PowerGlove only measures flexion of the thumb and three fingers, at a much lower resolution than the DataGlove.

The PowerGlove became very popular as an inexpensive virtual reality input device, mainly because its cost was around $100. It was sold as a peripheral device for the Nintendo game console and it had no standard interface. Thus, there was no easy way to connect it to anything else. When the popularity of the device became apparent, interfaces to use it with an IBM-compatible PC or an Apple Macintosh started to surface, released by AGE, third-party manufacturers, or people experimenting with the device. A very popular interface device among "garage virtual reality" enthusiasts is the Menelli Box, a public-domain interface design that helps transmit the PowerGlove's signals to an RS-232 port.

APPLICATIONS OF MOTION CAPTURE

Most motion capture equipment was developed with applications other than entertainment in mind. Such devices have been used for many years before becoming viable tools for 3D computer graphics.

The main markets that benefit from motion capture are medicine, sports, entertainment, and law, but there are smaller markets that are also taking advantage of the technology. For example, motion capture equipment is used to help design ergonomic environments. In addition, it is used for automobile safety tests: The motion of crash test dummies is captured and analyzed.

Medicine

In clinical circles, motion capture is called three-dimensional biological measuring or three-dimensional analysis. It is used to generate biomechanical data to be used for gait analysis and several orthopedic applications, such as joint mechanics, analysis of the spine, prosthetic design, and sports medicine.

There have been a great number of studies of gait performed with patients of all ages and conditions. The first ones were made by Etienne Jules Marey and Eadweard Muybridge in the late 1800s using photographic equipment.

Muybridge's studies started when he was hired by Leland Stanford, governor of California, to study the movement of his race horses in order to prove that all four hooves left the ground simultaneously at a given point during gallop. In 1876, Muybridge succeeded by photographing a galloping horse using 24 cameras (Figure 1-16). He then continued his studies of human and animal motion for many years. His paper on the subject, "Animal Locomotion," was published in 1884 and is still one of the most complete studies in the area.

A professor of natural history, Etienne Marey used only one camera to study movement, as opposed to the multiple-camera configuration used by Muybridge. Even though they met in 1881, Marey and Muybridge followed separate paths in their research. Studies continued in this fashion for a century, but until the introduction of optical motion capture systems in the 1970s, the research yielded almost no benefits.

Gait analysis is useful in medicine because it accurately separates all the different mechanisms that are used during the multiple phases of a walk cycle in a way that makes it easy to detect certain abnormalities and changes. For example, gait analysis helps to measure any degree of change in conditions such as arthritis or strokes. It is also used along with other tests to determine treatment for certain pathological conditions that affect the way we walk, such as cerebral palsy. Rehabilitation by gait training is used for patients with pelvis, knee, or ankle problems.

Figure 1-16. *Muybridge's galloping horse photographs. (Photo courtesy of Eadweard Muybridge Collection, Kingston Museum.)*

Sports

Sports analysis is a major application of motion capture. 3D data is being used extensively to improve the performance of athletes in sports such as golf, tennis, gymnastics, and even swimming by studying the performance of professionals and dissecting and classifying the different components of the movement. As motion capture technology improves to the point at which undisturbed data collection is possible, the potential uses will become even greater in this field.

There are a few motion capture studios across the country dedicated exclusively to the analysis of sports, especially golf. For a few hundred dollars, any golfer can have his or her swing analyzed or compared with the swing of a professional golfer. Visualization software allows the studios to study the athlete's motions to find any problem areas.

The market for sports analysis is mostly amateur sports enthusiasts, but professionals look for help as well. Biovision, a company that operates three sports analysis studios across the country, claims to have helped professional golfer John Daly to find a problem related to opposite movements of his hips and shoulders that happened for one-tenth of a second during his swing.

The benefit of using motion capture rather than videotape for this kind of sports application is that motion capture yields a three-dimensional representation of the motion that can be examined from any possible angle. A second important advantage is that at the normal speed a videotape records (30 frames per second), most fast-paced motions are not fully captured. Since motion capture is capable of recording at higher frequencies than regular video, much more of the motion is recorded.

The Entertainment Industry

The entertainment industry is the fastest growing segment of market for motion capture; although not yet the largest, it certainly is the segment with the highest profile. Of the different entertainment applications, the use of motion capture in video games is currently the most widespread and the most well accepted and understood. Television and feature film applications of motion capture are still an experimental market.

Video Games

Motion capture is used on almost every video game that involves human motion. The video game industry was the first segment of entertainment to embrace motion capture as a viable tool for character motion. It started doing so at a time when the motion capture hardware and software was still producing low-quality results at a high, but not extreme, cost. Even though the use of motion capture in entertainment started in television and film, those markets still remain resistant to widespread use of the tool, whereas the computer game segment has adopted it as the primary source of capturing human motion.

As recently as a few years ago, it was impossible to produce a game with character animation of sufficient quality to require the skill of a character animator. The hardware simply lacked the horsepower to render the images onto the screen at a desirable frame rate. When motion capture came into the picture, it was still in its infancy as a motion generation tool, but it was cost-effective and had more quality than any game that used real-time rendering could take advantage of. The data was usually good enough and didn't require any further tweaking for the kind of games that used it. As game engines become faster, motion capture is also maturing. It remains a cost-effective solution for these kinds of projects, but it now requires some massaging to make it look as good as possible. Eventually, the quality of the motion required for real-time video games will be equal to that of any other linear project.

Television

The use of performance animation in animated TV shows is a small market that is growing slowly and has met with several obstacles. The main problem is that motion capture has been used primarily as a cost-cutting tool, resulting in an unexpected quality trade-off. Shows that used performance animation in the past have usually not included a budget for modifying the animation beyond the performance. An example of a show with this problem is *The Real Adventures of Jonny Quest,* in which only a few minutes per show contain any kind of computer animation.

Other cartoon shows have been successful in using performance animation in their entirety. Most of these shows have been produced by the company that is actually collecting the motion, and the motion is captured in real time in most cases, so there are no surprises in what the quality of the final animation will be. Companies that have succeeded in producing these kinds of shows are Medialab, with *Donkey Kong Country,* and Modern Cartoons, with *Jay-Jay the Jet Plane.*

Commercials are still a very small part of the performance animation market. Because they are short projects, it is difficult to establish a pipeline for motion capture data that will only be used for a couple of shots. Specific shots that require a particular person's motion are what drives this market, such as the "Virtual Andre" spot that Digital Domain produced for Nike, which featured a digital version of Andre Agassi.

Music videos have benefited from motion capture since the early 1990s. Homer and Associates produced computer graphics based on performance animation for music videos by Peter Gabriel, Vince Neil, and TLC. More recently, two Bjork music videos have been produced using motion capture, one by Rhythm and Hues and another by Digital Domain.

Feature Films

The main applications of motion capture in live-action feature films are digital extras, digital stunts, and digital crowds. Digital extras are background human characters that for one reason or another have to be digitally generated. An example of such a case is a shot of the ship in the feature film *Titanic* as it leaves port. A live shot like this would be filmed with a helicopter and a lot of extras walking on deck, but since the actual ship did not exist, a miniature ship was shot, using a motion control camera. Because of the size of the shot, filming real people in green screen to composite over the ship would have been impossible, so the only solution was to create digital extras. The shot was produced at Digital Domain.

Digital stunts are actions that either are not humanly possible or that need to be seen on screen performed by a person other than the stuntperson. After a stunt is captured, it can only be enhanced to a certain level before the realistic motion is lost; thus, if a stunt is not humanly possible, it is best to hand it to a good character animator who specializes in realistic motion. Another kind of digital stunt involves applying motion data from a stuntperson to a digital version of a known actor. An example of such a stunt is the sky-surfing sequence in *Batman and Robin,* for which sky-surfers' stunts were captured by PDI and applied to digital versions of George Clooney's Batman and Chris O'Donnell's Robin.

Motion capture is a good tool to use for digital crowd scenes in which no inter-actions between characters occur. A perfect scenario would be a crowded stadium where some kind of sport is being played. A computer-generated crowd could be procedurally animated by first capturing different versions of each crowd reac-tion. As the game proceeds, the crowd may go into a cheering frenzy, or be bored, or angry. When one of the teams playing the sport scores, part of the crowd will be angry, others will be excited, and some will be ambivalent. A percentage of the crowd would be animated by using randomly selected angry cycles, another group would be animated by the cheering cycles, and the rest by the ambivalent cycles. An example of a sequence using multiple digital characters and motion capture is the group of crowd scenes at the end of *The Borrowers*, produced by The Moving Picture Company.

Law

Motion capture is applied in law to produce reconstructive videos of events. These videos are used as evidence in trials to aid the jury in understanding a witness's opinion about a particular order of events. According to a study conducted by the American Bar Association, this kind of evidence is much more effective with jurors than any other demonstrative evidence.

An example of an effective use of motion capture in the legal context is the video produced by Failure Analysis to recreate the events of the murder of Nicole Brown Simpson and Ronald Goldman during the O.J. Simpson trial. The video wasn't actually used as evidence in the trial, but it serves as an example of the kind of animation that could be used in a court of law.

To be admissible, the animation must be very plain, without any complex light-ing, texture mapping, or detailed models, and, like any other evidence, it must meet the local and federal rules of evidence. In most cases, it has to be accompa-nied by supporting testimony from the animation creators, during either trial or deposition. Many animation companies specialize in all aspects of evidence ani-mation, from its preparation to the presentation in court.

Chapter Two

The Motion Capture Controversy

☙❧

Motion capture, performance capture, Satan's rotoscope—call it what you may, it is a technology that has risen to the top of the hype machine among entertainment industry watchers, although for many insiders it has become a topic of major controversy.

The first of many problems was the initial perception of what could be done with motion capture. Years ago, when the technology was first used to generate animated characters in three dimensions, the results amazed most people because nobody had ever seen realistic human motion used for 3D character animation. Many people in the industry thought they had found the replacement for the traditional character animator. However, because the captured motion data available in those days was very noisy and expensive, it quickly became clear that it wasn't going to replace manual labor any time soon. In addition, off-the-shelf computer animation software with user-friendly interfaces, such as Wavefront, started to emerge, which helped more artistic and less technically oriented people enter the business. Character animators started to work in three dimensions.

In the last decade, the concept of the motion capture service bureau was born. Equipped with the latest in optical and electromagnetic technology, these studios detected the need for cheaper methods of character animation. The video game industry quickly became the first entertainment unit to sign up, finding the data fast and cost-effective. In fact, video game developers are still the number one consumers of optical motion capture, with about 85% of the total usage. Larger video game publishers, such as Acclaim, Electronic Arts, and Williams, have in-house studios that their game developers use, but most other developers still use the service bureaus.

The next logical market for service bureaus to pursue was film and television, but there was one problem: The applications were very different from video games. Video game characters were extremely low detail, and the motion data didn't need to be very clean. Most characters didn't even need to stay firmly on the ground. Also, most service bureaus didn't have anybody familiar with computer animation or even performance animation, and motion capture equipment manufacturers had even less knowledge of the subject, especially since their main market wasn't entertainment. This lack of knowledge combined with the desire to break into the entertainment industry drove manufacturers and service providers to make the same outrageous claims that had been made years ago: "Motion capture can replace character animators." This time around, the technology was more affordable and readily available for purchase, so the studios started listening.

Project-driven purchases of expensive motion capture equipment happened in many studios, such as Warner Brothers, DreamWorks, and smaller studios. The equipment in almost every case did not end up being used for the project for which it was intended, resulting in budget and creative problems and sometimes even the cancellation of projects. These studios were led to believe that any character-animated shot could be achieved with motion capture at a lower cost, even those with cartoon characters and requiring stylized motion and complex interactions with objects and other characters. In many cases, character animators were handed captured motion data and asked to modify it, a big mistake in my opinion, which only served to generate more heat against the technology.

Today this pattern is still happening because nobody wants to discuss their mistakes publicly in order to educate others. At the time of this writing there are at least three feature-length computer-animated films in production that claim to be using motion capture for almost every computer-generated character in every shot as a means of saving money. These projects will undoubtedly run into a brick wall eventually and will have to be rebudgeted or cancelled.

MOTION CAPTURE PERSPECTIVES

As a technical director in charge of character setup, I sometimes must make suggestions as to whether a certain shot should be carried out using performance animation. Even though I am very careful in suggesting the use of motion capture and do so only when I feel that it is vital for the shot, I still meet with tremendous resistance from the character animation group. The problem isn't only that choosing motion capture is like telling a character animator that his or her job can be done faster and better with the use of a machine; it goes deeper than that. Motion capture has a reputation of being unreliable and unpredictable, and animators are afraid of being stuck with having to fix problems associated with it. Many of today's experienced character animators who work with computer-generated (CG) images have had such encounters. Many of them have stories about having to clean up and modify captured motion data, only to end up replacing the whole thing with keyframe animation. Also, many animators dislike the look of performance animation. Some say it is so close to reality that it looks gruesome on CG characters; others say it is far from real. People who have no experience with the technology also have many misinformed opinions, mostly based on horror stories from others.

I don't believe motion capture is unpredictable. It is very easy to predict when it will or will not work if you've had experience with it. Its bad reputation is based on poor choices made by misinformed people, including executives, animators, and even manufacturers. By presenting informed commentary from experienced people in the CG industry, I expect to help form a better comprehension of the reality behind motion capture. If used in the right way and for the right reason, it can be a very useful tool; if not used properly, it will lead to chaos. You don't have to stake your career on the next project you decide to use motion capture on, as long as you are familiar with the pros and cons and you don't overestimate its capabilities.

Richard Chuang, vice president at PDI, has a deep understanding of the benefits and shortcomings of the technology. He says that many of the problems of performance animation have to do with the state of the technology. "Sampling the external skin of the person, you don't have the true anatomical motion," points out Chuang.

Chuang believes that keyframe animation is better for depicting very fast motions, like jumping or flipping, but that motion capture can capture subtleties associated with slower motions. In Chuang's opinion, motion capture's best applications in visual effects are background crowds or complex stunts, but not foreground characters.

According to Carl Rosendahl, the best uses of performance animation in PDI's experience were the projects produced in collaboration with Jim Henson. "It was a great use, because of its puppetry, and you were trying to perform with people where, yes, there's a script, but they don't stick to it. And the magic of the Hensons, whether it is with the Muppets or any other characters they do, is really that spontaneity, that improv that they do on the set that is guided by the script. And in order for them to be able to do that, they really have to be able to interact live, and that's a perfect application for it," he says. "It worked for all the skeleton stuff we did because there you're trying to get a human character to move in a really human way, so it was really effective for that. For the *Batman* stuff I think a lot of the times we'd gone back and reanimated so much of it. It's kind of questionable as to whether there really was enough value in it."

Rosendahl points out that a big part of the reason why motion capture has such a bad reputation is that many of the proponents of motion capture have set up a false expectation in Hollywood that motion capture is a real-time technology. "Production, whether it is television or film, they want it fast and they want it cheap. And you can just look at a keyframe technique and say it's certainly not fast, because you have people sitting there doing that stuff, and it costs money—it's not cheap," he says. "Then in comes this promise that it's real-time fast, and because of that, it's cheap." He also talks about the fact that nobody ever says that performance animation won't look like finely tuned keyframe animation. "People who were doing keyframe animation suddenly had to unfairly justify what they were doing because somebody was out there saying 'We can do the same kind of stuff faster and cheaper,'" he adds.

Benjamin Cheung is a CG artist at Square USA's Honolulu Studio, where he is working on animation and character setup for *Final Fantasy: The Movie*. He used to work at TSi as a technical director (TD), where he had to deal with captured motion data on an almost daily basis. "Motion capture is described as 'Satan's Rotoscope' because people are afraid to use it, and have used it in the past in an inappropriate way. The real problems of motion capture lie not in the capture itself, but in the planning and the capture support that animators need," Cheung asserts. "The planning of the whole process is the most important part. A well-planned capture session will save animators and character TDs a lot of time and effort."

Eric Darnell, codirector of *Antz,* believes that the main problem with motion capture associated with characters has to do with mass distribution, weight, and exaggeration. He says it is impossible for a performer to produce the kind of motion exaggeration that a cartoon character needs, and the mass and weight of the performer almost never look good when applied to a character of different proportions. Richard Chuang concurs: "The mapping of human motion to a character with nonhuman proportions doesn't work, because the most important things you get out of motion capture are the weight shifts and the subtleties and that balancing act of the human body. If the proportions change, you throw all that out the door, so you might as well animate it." He concedes that there may be performers that could portray these differences, but he points out that animation is just as powerful.

Nobody has a better-spoken opinion than Tim Johnson, codirector of *Antz.* He says his biggest problem is that performance animation is used as though it were a substitute for animation. In his view, the principles of the craft of animation, whether it is done with clay, cutouts, drawings, or the computer, are the same: characterizing and exaggerating acting with nonhumans. On the other hand, performance animation uses humans to capture gestures in real time that are translated onto another body. He uses this comparison: "There's Kermit, and there's Mickey Mouse. Both of them have their own audience, but you would not necessarily want Kermit to appear in a Mickey Mouse cartoon."

"Animation is an art form that is unbelievable and unprecedented in its leap," notes Johnson. "Animators have to use still frames to create motion and acting. There's no other art form that is that removed from its destination. In dance, painting, and music you are one on one with your art form—you are making the music, doing the gesture. But animators are a step removed from the finished product. It's a very unique and precious twentieth-century art form. What is upsetting is to take that and say you're going to get anywhere near the joy and the quality of the aesthetic by using motion capture."

On the other hand, Johnson does concede that performance animation has its place: "Performance animation deserves a champion. It deserves a Jim Henson, a visionary to come along and understand that this does not look like character animation. Understand that it does not look like Mickey Mouse, and make a Kermit—a character that is best designed for the medium, that moves in a way suitable to the narrative and to the characters at hand, and really celebrates whatever story or venue they're doing. Not because it's cheaper, and they're trying to imitate Mickey Mouse, but because they want Kermit."

"It takes years and years to do good animation. I don't think motion capture is ever going to get you anything for free. You need a skilled artistic person somewhere in that process to know what it takes to make a performance good," says Rex Grignon. "Trying to figure out what the aesthetic could be for this new medium is what should drive it, not the technology."

In Johnson's opinion, performance animation is consistently defining itself by imitating other things. He feels that what is lacking is an application where motion capture is not used to imitate something else, like a live-action superhero or a hand-drawn animated character, but rather is used in an original way that would take advantage of the feel and gestalt of performance animation. In his view, modern dance could possibly be that medium. "They use props and other things that allow modern dance to give you a reshaping of the human form," says Johnson, "so those are people that are already dabbling in what I think performance animation's future might be."

Animators use videotaped reference material regularly when animating, but using captured motion data as a reference is, like rotoscoping, a controversial topic. Tim Johnson says that using motion capture as a reference is a "fool's error." Speaking about using videotape as a reference, Johnson points out that "what [animators] are doing is selectively pulling those things that to a human eye are most representative of that character, that moment, that motion, and that gets right at the heart and soul of what makes character animation an art form. It can't be duplicated or caught on a camera." He adds, "To use performance animation as a reference just doesn't work. You can give me all the data in the world and it doesn't help me, as an artist, have a vision which leaps beyond the technical to seeing what's in the heart of a particular motion."

Benjamin Cheung disagrees. He believes that it is better to use captured motion data as reference material. He recalls that while interviewing at Digital Domain, he mentioned the idea to Rob Legato, visual effects supervisor, and others. Digital Domain was in production on *Titanic* at the time; shortly thereafter, they started using the process, which they named *rotocap.*

MOTION CAPTURE AND THE MEDIA

Motion capture generates a lot of press, much more than keyframe animation. The media love to show people geared up with cables or markers, especially if it is a celebrity performing for a digital character. On almost every motion capture job that I worked on at TSi, the client had a "behind the scenes" crew videotaping the session. Motion capture and the performer would take all the credit, although we had animators that sometimes had to throw away some of the motion-captured shots and keyframe-animate them. Many media reports on the subject also claim that the technology will eventually replace traditional animators.

Some studio executives who got wind of the "new" technology through the media decided to study the possibility of integrating it into their special effects and CG animation projects. Most of these studies consisted of having some data captured by a motion capture studio and then testing it on a particular character. The results were misleading, because the studies didn't really include what the motion capture people went through to clean up the data and apply it to the character. They only considered cost, but didn't take into account that motion capture studios were often discounting the price of the data in order to get in the door. In addition, the motions studied were usually walk cycles and other simple moves that are less complicated to process than the average movements for a typical film or game project.

This motion capture frenzy was further fueled by the success of *Toy Story* as the first CG animated feature-length film. Performance animation was seen as a way to achieve the same success at a fraction of the cost. It was also heralded as the key to cost-effective CG television cartoons. At TSi there was a period when studios would show up and ask us to bid on capturing data for full-length feature film projects or television shows without even having a specific project yet. It really didn't matter what the content was, as long as it was motion captured. In the studios' views, such a project would cost less and guarantee great press exposure, especially if an actual movie star performed the character.

The media also have made no distinction between the look of real-time digital puppeteering and that of keyframe animation and have covered them as if they belong to the same medium, which is upsetting to most animators. Following are some examples of statements that have been released by the media in the past few years:

> *"Motion capture is a highly efficient way to produce animation. Depending on what it is, you can produce 10 minutes in a single day."*
> —Animation Magazine, *February 1998, quoting Dan Smith, CEO of SimGraphics*

> *When computers gather together all the digital data from the shoot, the product is a three-dimensional, animated figure yielding a stunning image for the audience at a fraction of the cost of traditional animation techniques.*
> —CNN *report by Dennis Michael, 10 June 1998, talking about* Sinbad: Beyond the Veil of Mists

> *By using the motion capture technique, Rajan says he'll be able to make the film for a third of what a traditionally animated feature costs. That makes Sinbad's fictional adventure one that movie studios may be watching closely.*
> —CNN Tomorrow-Today *report by Dennis Michael, 19 June 1998, talking about Sri Ram Rajan, producer of* Sinbad: Beyond the Veil of Mists

> *"When Pixar animates* Toy Story's *Woody or Buzz, it might take them a whole day to complete a 15-second scene, but we can animate Woody or Buzz in real time."*
> —Red Herring Magazine, *January 1997, quoting Brad deGraf, founder of Protozoa*

MOTION CAPTURE STORIES

In the recent past, the use of performance animation in a project was largely driven by cost. Many projects have failed or fallen into trouble due to lack of understanding, because the decision to use motion capture was taken very lightly and made by the wrong people. Some of these projects have entered into production with the client's informed knowledge that motion capture may or may not work, and a budget that supported this notion. Other clients have blindly adopted performance animation as the primary production tool, based on a nonrepresentative test or no test at all, and have invariably run into trouble. In some cases, the problems occurred early in production, resulting in manageable costs; in other cases, the problems weren't identified until expenses were so excessive that the projects had to be rebudgeted or cancelled.

Projects such as *Marvin the Martian in the 3rd Dimension,* the first incarnation of *Shrek, Casper,* and *Total Recall* were unsuccessful in using performance animation for different reasons. Others, such as *Titanic* and *Batman and Robin,* were successful to a certain degree: They were able to use some of the performance animation, but the keyframe animation workload was larger than expected. A few projects managed to successfully determine early in production whether it was feasible to use motion capture or not. Disney's *Mighty Joe Young, Dinosaur,* and *The Amazing Adventures of Spiderman* are good examples of projects in which motion capture was tested well in advance and ended up being discarded.

The projects that will benefit the most from motion capture are yet to come. In live-action films, large crowd scenes and background human stunt action will be the best applications, such as in *The Borrowers,* for which London-based effects studio The Moving Picture Company created, among other effects, a crowd of over 1000 digital humans for a sequence at the end of the film. Character animation pieces, such as *Marvin the Martian in the 3rd Dimension, Antz,* or *A Bug's Life,* will probably never have a use for performance animation.

Total Recall

In 1989, Metrolight Studios attempted what was supposed to be the first use of optical motion capture in a feature film. The project was perfect for this technology and was planned and budgeted around it, but it somehow became the first failure of motion capture in a feature film.

The project was the futuristic epic *Total Recall,* starring Arnold Schwarzenegger. The planned performance animation was for a skeleton sequence in which Arnold's character, the pursuing guards, and some extras, including a dog, would cross through an X-ray machine. It was similar to the shots that PDI did on *Toys* using their exoskeleton, where characters had to have an X-ray look.

Metrolight hired an optical motion capture equipment manufacturer to capture and post-process the data. The motion capture session had to be on location in Mexico City, and the manufacturer agreed to take its system there for the shoot. The manufacturer also sent an operator to install and operate the system.

"We attached retro-reflective markers to Arnold Schwarzenegger, about fifteen extras, and a dog," recalls George Merkert, who was the visual effects producer for the sequence, "then we photographed the action of all of these characters as they went through their performances." Regarding the placement of the markers, Merkert recalls that the operator "advised Tim McGovern, the visual effects supervisor, and me about where the markers should be on the different characters. We placed the markers according to his directions."

They captured Arnold's performances separately. The guards were captured two at a time, and the extras were captured in groups of up to ten at a time. Even by today's standards, capturing more than one performer in an optical stage is a difficult proposition; and more than three or four is almost impossible, depending on how they are moving. "It seemed a little strange to me; I didn't see how we could capture that much data, but the operator guaranteed us that everything was going to be okay," recalls Merkert. The motion capture shoot went smoothly as far as anybody could tell, but nobody knew much about motion capture except for the operator sent by the manufacturer. Therefore, nobody would have been able to tell if anything went wrong.

After the shoot, the operator packed up the system and went back to the company's headquarters in the United States to process the captured data, but no usable data was ever delivered to Metrolight. "He [the operator] needed to do a step of computing prior to providing the data to us so that we could use it in our animation, and we never got beyond that step. He was never able to successfully process the information on even one shot. We got absolutely no usable data for any of our shots," says Merkert. "They had excuses that it was shot incorrectly, which it may well have been. My response to that was, 'Your guy was there, telling us how to shoot it. We would have been happy to shoot the motion capture any way that you specified. The real problem is that you never told us what that right way was even though we asked you every few minutes what we could do to make sure this data gets captured correctly.'" The production even sent people to the motion capture manufacturer to see if anything could be done to salvage any data, but all of it was unusable.

"I think what happened is that their process just entirely melted down, didn't work. They couldn't process the data and they were unwilling to say so because they thought they would get sued. It wound up costing my company maybe three hundred thousand dollars extra," notes Merkert. "Regardless that the motion capture simply didn't work, we were still responsible to deliver to our client. The only way we could do that was by using the videotapes, which were extremely difficult to use for motion tracking. Unfortunately, because the motion capture company advised that we do it in this way, we had lit the motion capture photography in such a way that you could hardly see the characters to track them. You could see the retro-reflective balls attached to the characters very well, but you couldn't see the body forms of the characters very well." Optical systems in those days worked only in very dark environments. Almost no lighting could be used other than the lighting emitted from the direction of the cameras. "Our efforts were very successful, however. Tim McGovern won the 1990 Academy Award for Best Visual Effects for the skeleton sequence in *Total Recall*," he adds.

A few lessons can be learned from this experience. First, a motion capture equipment manufacturer is not an animation studio, and thus has no idea of the requirements of animation. In this case, the operator didn't even know the system well enough to decide whether it should be used to capture more than one person at a time, which brings us to the second lesson: Motion capture always seems to be much easier than it really is, so it must be approached carefully, using operators with a track record. Extra personnel are also needed to make sure nobody is creating any noise or touching the cameras. Third, if possible, never capture more than one performer at a time. In this example, it was clear that each performer could have been captured separately because they didn't interact, but it was decided not to do so. Fourth, both the captured data and calibration must be checked before the performers take off the markers and leave the stage, and extra takes of everything must be captured for safety. Fifth, marker setups have to be designed by experienced technical directors and not by operators who know little about animation setup requirements. Sixth, when working on an unknown remote location, the motion capture system has to be tested before and during the session. Extra care must be taken because lighting conditions and camera placements are always different than in the controlled environment of a regular motion capture studio.

Shell Oil

After 1992, many companies were involved in commercial work using motion capture. A campaign that was especially prominent was one for Shell Oil that featured dancing cars and gasoline pumps. It was produced by R. Greenberg and Associates in New York using a Flock of Birds electromagnetic device manufactured by Ascension Technology Corporation.

Fred Nilsson, now a senior animator at PDI, worked at R. Greenberg in 1994 when the Shell campaign was produced. "We got the main skeleton guys from Softimage to come down and they taught us how to build a skeleton for motion capture," recalls Nilsson. "We set up a skeleton that had goals where all the motion capture points were, and then there was another skeleton on top that was a parent of all the joints of the other skeleton, so that we could capture the motion and then animate on top of the other skeleton." The main complaint that Nilsson had about the motion capture data was that the characters were never firm on the floor, but the second skeleton was used by the animators to ground the characters, with the help of inverse kinematics.

The skeleton that contained the final motion was used to deform a grid, which was used to deform the final character—a car or gas pump. Because of the strange proportions of the characters, a lot of cleanup work was necessary. They also had to deal with interference. "We were on a sound stage and there was some big green screen wall that was all metal and it was really interfering," says Nilsson.

"A year later we did three more Shell spots and all of us said no, we don't want to use motion capture," recalls Nilsson. They animated the last three spots by hand and it took about the same time to produce them. "They turned out a lot better," says Nilsson.

In this particular case, the biggest benefit gained by the use of performance animation was the extensive press coverage that Shell obtained because of the "new" technology that was used to animate the cars and pumps. The free publicity didn't dissipate with the creation of the last three spots by keyframe animation, since most people thought that performance animation was used on those as well.

Marvin the Martian in the 3rd Dimension

Marvin the Martian in the 3rd Dimension is a 12-minute stereoscopic film that has been shown at Warner Brothers Movie World theme park in Australia since 1996. It is meant to look like a traditional cartoon, but because it is stereoscopic, it had to be created using two different angles that represent the views from both the right and left eye. The best way to achieve this was to create all the character animation using CG. To obtain the necessary stereoscopic effect required placing two cameras in the right locations. The challenge was to make sure the rendering and motion looked true to the traditionally animated cartoon.

In 1994, Warner Brothers acquired a Motion Analysis optical motion capture system, thinking that they could have actors perform the parts of the Warner Brothers' cartoon characters. Among the companies involved in the project were Will Vinton Studios, PDI, Metrolight Studios, Atomix, and Warner Brothers Imaging Technology (WBIT). "They asked if we could do Daffy Duck with motion capture," recalls Eric Darnell, codirector of *Antz*. After several months of testing, Warner Brothers decided to scratch the motion capture idea and use traditional animation after all. They ended up providing keyframes on pencil to all the 3D animation studios to use as reference for motion. The Warner Brothers motion capture equipment was auctioned in 1997, after WBIT closed its doors.

The Pillsbury Doughboy

In 1996, TSi was approached by Leo Burnett, the advertising agency that handles the Pillsbury account, to create two spots with the Pillsbury Doughboy using performance animation. The agency had already explored the technology once by doing a spot using an electromagnetic tracker at Windlight Studios, and now they wanted to try optical motion capture.

The first step was for us to produce a test with the Doughboy performing some extreme motions. We decided to bring in a dancer/choreographer we had often employed, because she had a petite figure and was a good actress who could probably come as close to performing the Doughboy as any human could. Since the client didn't specify what kind of motions they were looking for, we decided to have the Doughboy dance to the tune of M.C. Hammer's "Can't Touch This." We captured the main dance and a couple of background dances we would use for background characters and, after post-processing, converted them to the Alias format.

The main dance was applied to the Doughboy, and the background dances were mapped to models of Pillsbury products. The resulting piece was quite disturbing: the Pillsbury Doughboy performing a sexy dance surrounded by three or four cylindrical chocolate-chip cookie-dough dancers doing a pelvic-motion-intensive step. It wasn't exactly what you'd imagine the Doughboy would do, but they did say "extreme motions." I was a little worried about what the client's reaction would be, but I figured that if they really wanted to use motion capture for the Doughboy, they had a right to see the kind of motion they would get. We sent the test to Chicago.

The day after we sent the test we got a call from producers at Leo Burnett. Their first comment was that the dark lighting that we used would never be used on a Doughboy commercial. We explained that the point of the test was for them to see the motion, not the lighting, and that the lighting had been approached that way to match with the sexy nature of the motion. As for the motion, Leo Burnett said that it was offensive to their client (Pillsbury), but that it had proven the point. They gave us two Doughboy spots to do simultaneously.

Part of the deal was that we would set up a motion capture session that the Leo Burnett and Pillsbury people could attend. We used the same woman who performed the sexy Doughboy for the test. One of the shots involved the Doughboy vaulting over a dough package using a spoon as a pole. We knew we could never use captured motion data for the interactions of the spoon and the Doughboy, but we captured it anyway, because our client wanted this method used on all their shots. We figured we could use it for timing, and that's exactly what we did. All the other shots were standard Doughboy fare: the Doughboy pulling a dish, smelling the steam from baked products, just standing and talking, and, of course, being poked in the belly. The session went very smoothly. Our clients and their clients were very interested in the technology that we were using and had a lot of fun watching the performance.

The data was processed and converted to the Alias format, where we already had set up the Doughboy model for the test. A big problem we had on the test was that the legs of the Doughboy would never stay on the ground. We knew we would run into this problem again while working on the shots for the commercials. Benjamin Cheung was the technical director in charge of applying the data and lighting the Doughboy. He used only portions of the data, throwing away most of the legs' and some of the arms' motions, particularly when they interacted with the spoon. We probably used only 15% of the captured data on the character, and the rest just as reference for poses and timing. We were already expecting that, so it wasn't a surprise and we didn't miss our deadline.

The client, as we had agreed, stayed faithful to the captured performance and didn't make any major animation changes. It was a very smooth pair of projects, and although we were charging very low rates, we managed to make a decent profit. The project would have cost a little more if it had been keyframed, but it wouldn't have made a huge difference.

The main risk on a project such as this concerns the art direction, such as when a client that is not familiar with performance animation suddenly discovers that the motion looks different than expected and starts making changes. In this case it didn't happen because we did our homework to educate the client on what our system could do; however, they did not return for more motion-captured Doughboys, preferring to go back to keyframe animation. I was not surprised.

Batman and Robin

PDI had provided a computer-generated Batman stuntman for *Batman Forever*, using optical motion capture as a means to collect the performance of a gymnast performing on a stage doing flips and other movements on rings. *Batman and Robin* required much more elaborate digital stunts, many of them happening in the air. PDI was again contracted to create these stunts using motion capture.

The motion capture services were provided by Acclaim Entertainment, the computer game company that had the video game rights for the Batman property and that had earlier provided the motion capture services for *Batman Forever*. They used their proprietary four-camera optical system to capture all the necessary motions for the stunt sequences.

Acclaim's team captured several of the shots at Acclaim's motion capture stage in New York, except for the shots that belonged to the sequence in which Batman and Robin skyboard away from an exploding rocket while in pursuit of Mr. Freeze (played by Arnold Schwarzenegger), trying to recover a diamond he had stolen. Because all the action in this sequence happened in the air, John Dykstra, visual effects supervisor, decided to bring Acclaim's optical motion capture equipment to a vertical wind tunnel used for military training. The tunnel was located at the Fort Bragg military base in North Carolina, and the performers were not actors, but members of the U.S. Army's Golden Knights parachuting team. Dykstra directed the performances in the tunnel, and Acclaim processed the data and delivered it to PDI.

"We took the skeleton files from Acclaim and converted them to a setup," explains Richard Chuang, who was the digital effects supervisor for PDI. "We also converted all the motion data into our own animation space." Dick Walsh, character technical director at PDI, had set up a system that allowed them to adjust the differences in physical attributes between the digital model and the performer (Figure 2-1). "We actually had a certain flexibility with the use of motion capture data from

Figure 2-1.   *Dick Walsh working on the Batman character setup. (Photo courtesy of PDI.)*

different performers on the same character," recalls Chuang. The data was then used to move a skeleton that would drive PDI's muscle system, also written by Walsh. In addition, animators had the ability to blend the captured data with keyframe animation, with or without inverse kinematics. The system didn't require animators to modify the motion data. They worked on clean curves and were able to blend the animation and the captured data using animatable ratios. The system was especially useful when blending between captured motion cycles.

"In both cases we ended up using probably around 20% motion capture and 80% animation," notes Chuang, referring to both *Batman* films. "What we found is that because the motion is always captured in a stage, it really has nothing to do with the final performance you need for the film. For the director to have control of the final creative, we ended up taking motion capture as a starting point, and then animating on top of it. Then we'd be able to dial between motion capture and animation whenever we needed to."

Part of the problem with motion capture in this case was that the motions were for the main action of the sequence and the director wasn't present to direct the performance. When you capture motion for background characters, it is okay for the director to delegate the task, but in a case such as this, the director would expect to have first-hand creative control over the final performance. That meant the performance would have to be modified by the PDI team to his specification.

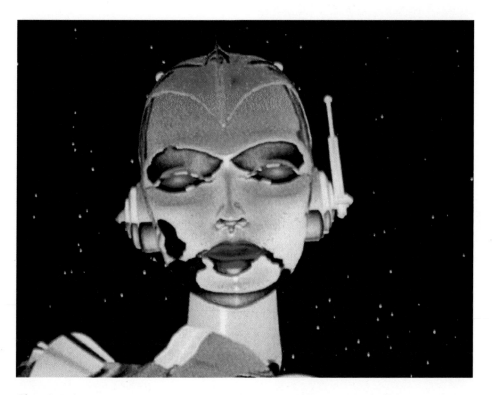

Plate 1. *"Brilliance," a commercial for the National Canned Food Information Council that was created by Abel and Associates and ran during the Super Bowl in 1985. It is best known as "Sexy Robot."* (Image courtesy of Robert Abel.)

Plate 2. *Waldo C. Graphic was produced as a collaborative effort between Jim Henson and PDI for "The Jim Henson Hour."* (Image © 1988 The Jim Henson Company. All rights reserved.)

Plate 3. *PDI used a mechanical device called the "Exoskeleton" to create this shot for the movie* Toys. (Still from *Toys* © 1992 Twentieth Century Fox Film Corporation. All rights reserved.)

Plate 4. *Dozo, a Synthespian[SM] performer created by Kleiser-Walczak Construction Company, sings and dances in the music video "Don't Touch Me."* (Dozo is the first female Synthespian[SM] performer created by Diana Walczak and Jeff Kleiser. She stars in their computer-generated film "Don't Touch Me," which premiered at SIGGRAPH in 1989. © 1989, Kleiser-Walczak Construction Co.)

Plate 5. *"Party Hardy," a commercial for the Pennsylvania Lottery created by Homer and Associates.* (Image courtesy of Homer and Associates.)

Plate 6. *Homer and Associates and Colossal Pictures collaborated to produce this music video for Peter Gabriel's "Steam." The video won the 1993 Video of the Year Grammy.* (Image courtesy of Homer and Associates.)

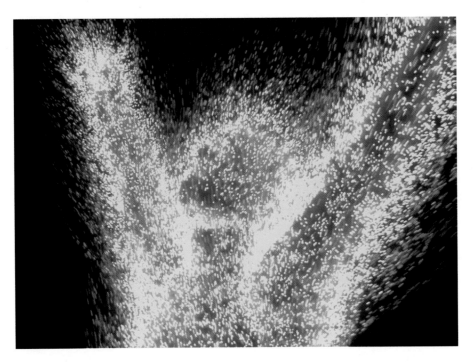

Plate 7. *This shot in the film* Lawnmower Man *was produced by Homer and Associates.* (Image courtesy of Homer and Associates.)

Plate 8. *This shot in Vince Neil's "Sister of Pain" music video was captured using an optical system by Homer and Associates.* (Image courtesy of Homer and Associates.)

Plate 9. *This dancing robot is part of a demonstration piece created at TSi.* (Copyright 1996 ThreeSpace Imagery, Inc.)

Plate 10. *Several shots were created using motion capture in "Waterfalls," the award-winning TLC music video created by Atomix and Homer and Associates in collaboration with TSi.* (Image courtesy of Homer and Associates.)

Plates 11a–d. *Various skeletons created from captured motion:*

11a. *Dalmatian*

11b. *Chimpanzee*

11c. *Alien*

11d. *Simultaneous capture of two performers*

Plate 12. *Image of a 30-second in-house commercial showcasing Virtual Celebrity Productions' most glamorous celebrity, Marlene Dietrich.* (Image courtesy of Dr. Barnabas Takacs / Virtual Celebrity Productions.)

Larry Bafia, animation director at PDI's commercial and film effects division, worked on the air sequence. "It was the first time that I ever had to deal with motion capture data at all, so I had no idea what I was getting into at the time," recalls Bafia. "This is a character that comes from a comic book and it really has to look like a superhero," he adds. "Some of the poses had to be exaggerated and it wasn't something that a human could do in a wind tunnel." The team kept most of the captured data for the motions of the character's torso, especially the actions of weight shifting on the skyboard. They used keyframe animation on many shots to enhance the pose of the arms and to animate the fingers, which were not included in the motion data. Inverse kinematics was used mostly on the legs.

The motion capture session was directed by the special effects supervisor, John Dykstra, who tried to capture as many different shots as possible for the director to choose from. This was done even before background plates were available, so no final camera angles and framing was available. "What you do is you capture all the possibilities, and then based on that you try to edit something that will fit your film," says Chuang. "But by the time you get your background plates you can end up with something completely different."

PDI technical directors prepared desktop movies of all the captured motions so that after the plates became available, the team could decide which actions would apply for each particular shot. "One of the problems was the fact that a lot of the shots were long enough where the particular motion capture cycle didn't have quite enough activity," recalls Bafia. Because of this, the team had to blend several captured motions into single shots. An example of this is the shot in which Robin catches the diamond after Mr. Freeze loses it. "I had to start the front end of the shot with one piece of motion capture where [Robin] is basically staying alive and balancing himself on the board and getting ready for spotting this diamond and catching it," recalls Bafia. After catching the diamond, Robin had to do a spin-around, not unlike that of a surfer. "Because of the restrictions inside the wind tunnel, the guy could do the spin but he had to pull up early so that he wouldn't fall too far and drop down toward the fan that was actually suspending him," says Bafia. PDI had to use inverse kinematics to maintain the character's feet on the board, and keyframe animation to blend between two motion files that had a reversed feet stance—all this while keeping the elements in the captured data that John Dykstra was interested in maintaining.

The fact that the performers weren't aware of where the final camera would be located was a problem that translated into the performance. "I would like to see a situation where you actually try motion capture after you shoot the film versus before, so you know where the background plate is going to be, and the director directs the action accordingly," notes Chuang.

Regardless of the expected problems with captured performances, the resulting shots were extremely successful. PDI had the experience to use whatever they could out of the motion data and discard the rest. Therefore, the project was completed in a timely manner, the clients were happy, and PDI made a good profit. The difference between this and other projects using motion capture was that for *Batman and Robin*, motion capture was used to achieve a certain look, not to save money.

The Real Adventures of Jonny Quest

The Real Adventures of Jonny Quest, produced by Hanna-Barbera, was a reproduction of an old cartoon series. Each episode consisted of at least 18 minutes of cel-animated cartoons and a computer-generated virtual reality segment of up to 3 minutes. The CG segment for the first season was produced by Buzz FX. They decided to capture the body and facial motion of all the human-shaped characters because the budget was too low for keyframe animation. The motion data was provided by House of Moves, located in Venice, California.

Data for several episodes was captured at the House of Moves studio, and post-processing started as the rest of the production was being orchestrated. As the motion data started to arrive, it became obvious that more work would be required to enhance the quality of the characters' motion; unfortunately, time and money constraints did not allow this to happen. The actual motion data wasn't the main problem—it was the size difference between the performers and the actual characters. The characters were unsteady on the ground and seemed to be floating or skating. In addition, many shots that included interactions between characters or characters interacting with props did not match when applied to the digital models. The characters sometimes needed to be shown walking on uneven terrain or climbing rocks or other objects, which was impossible to match using motion data.

The Real Adventures of Jonny Quest is an example of a show for which motion capture data could have been a good idea, but that ended up as a failure because of the many mistakes that were made, starting with the budgeting. It is always a mistake to assume that all the characters' body motions in every shot can be captured. The data that can be captured has to be planned on a shot-by-shot basis. Furthermore, the captured body motion data is never plug-and-play. Always expect some kind of human involvement. You also cannot assume that the same character setup will work for all shots. In some cases, such as when there are interactions between characters or props, some areas of the character need to be animated by hand or by using the data combined with inverse kinematics. When a pipeline is set up for mass production, these cases have to be considered in advance. Some testing should be done before making a commitment to such a large undertaking. Finally, when using a motion capture studio to collect data, one must remember that it is a motion capture studio and not a computer animation studio. It is up to the people who will use the data to decide if and how a certain shot will work.

Facial capture is a different story. As long as the performance is acceptable to the director at the time of capture and the character setup is well designed, facial motion capture can be a plug-and-play solution. In the case of *Jonny Quest*, such data was integrated into the pipeline much better than the body data. It produced a medium-quality result, but still acceptable for the kind of television budget this project had.

Shrek

Before it came to PDI, *Shrek* was a project that DreamWorks Feature Animation had been developing. It was, and still is, meant to be a full-length animated motion picture, based on the children's book by William Steig. During its first incarnation, the animation production depended a great deal on performance animation. At PDI, the project will be totally animated by keyframe animation.

The decision to use performance animation on *Shrek* was based not only on cost (which indeed played a big part in the decision), but also on the desire to achieve a certain look. Before *Shrek* was even in preproduction, PropellerHead Design (Rob Letterman, Jeffrey Abrams, Andy Waisler, and Loren Soman) produced a test of a similarly shaped character called "Harry" for a potential television show for HBO. The motion capture for the test was done at TSi.

For the Harry test, the propellerheads (as they were known in the *Shrek* production) prepared an appliance that was worn by their performer. The appliance would add the volume that the performer needed to approach the proportions of Harry. This was a new idea that we had never seen done before, and it seemed like a good one. During our first of two sessions, we placed the markers on the appliance and captured the body motions with our optical system. The tracking of the data was a challenging feat because it was an uncommon setup, but we managed to get it done.

In the second session, we were supposed to capture Harry's finger motion. We had never tried to capture the motion of fingers with an optical system, and we didn't guarantee that it would work. It was strictly a developmental session. We placed the small markers that we usually used on face capture on the finger joints. The performer sat down in a chair, and we immobilized his hands as much as possible because the wrist movement had already been captured in the previous session and we knew we couldn't capture the fingers if the wrists were moving. We captured several passes of the actor moving his fingers with the timing of the dialogue, but in the end it was impossible to track those motions, and we had to scratch the idea of optical finger capture. Facial capture wasn't even tested for this project.

The propellerheads finished the Harry test, filling in the additional animation, plus texture and lighting. The end result was stunning. The Harry test laid the foundation for the production of *Shrek* at DreamWorks. The propellerheads would coproduce the film, which would be animated using techniques similar to those in the Harry test: optical motion capture with body extensions or appliances.

The DreamWorks studio in Glendale was geared up with Silicon Graphics computers running different animation platforms and a brand new ten-camera Motion Analysis optical motion capture system. A production staff was assembled and production of a 30-second test began. Character animators started to work with the optical motion data. Several months later, the test was shown to Jeffrey Katzenberg, DreamWorks's cofounder and the partner responsible for animation films. Shortly thereafter, the production was halted and the project went back into development. The propellerheads were no longer involved. Exactly what happened is still a mystery, but motion capture was ruled out for this project. Among other things, the production made a mistake by using character animators to work with the captured motion data. It is not certain if that actually affected the test, but it would have eventually become a big problem.

"I was kind of excited to see what *Shrek* could have done with performance animation," notes Tim Johnson, "just because it seemed like everybody was trying to say something with that aesthetic. Certainly as it will be done here [at PDI], *Shrek* could be really well animated. But it seemed to me that if they approached it with the same principles as Jim Henson approaches one of his films like *Labyrinth*, they could have generated something that would acknowledge, rather than try to hide, its performance animation qualities."

Godzilla

Another character that was supposed to be animated by performance was Godzilla, in the 1998 film with the same name. Future Light had developed a real-time motion capture system based on optical hardware by Northern Digital. The system was connected to a Silicon Graphics Onyx with a Reality Engine, and it could render an animated creature in real time. Future Light is a division of Santa Monica Studios and sister company of Vision Art, one of the CG studios involved in the visual effects production for *Godzilla*. Director Roland Emmerich liked the system because he could see the creature motion in real time, so the production proceeded with the idea of using the system as much as possible for the animation of the creature.

The character design was proportionally close to the human body, so it was possible to map human motion into the character's skeleton without much recomputing. According to Karen Goulekas, associate visual effects supervisor, the motion capture worked technically, but it didn't yield the results they were looking for aesthetically, so they decided to abort that strategy and use keyframe animation instead. In the end, the animation for all the creatures, including Godzilla and its offspring, was done with keyframe animation.

"The reason we pulled the plug on using the motion capture was, very simply, because the motion we captured from the human actor could not give us the lizard-like motion we were seeking. The mocap could also not reflect the huge mass of Godzilla either," adds Goulekas. "During our keyframe tests, we found that the Godzilla motion we wanted was one that maintained the sense of huge mass and weight, while still moving in a graceful and agile manner. No human actor could give us this result." In addition, they had Godzilla running at speeds as high as 200 mph, with huge strides; this proved to be impossible to capture.

"Once we had nailed the 'look' and 'feel' of the keyframe animation we were looking for, the animation was going faster than the mocap sessions. Roland was able to see multiple iterations of Godzilla in previsualization animation daily and changes became very fast," says Goulekas.

In general, using human motion to portray a creature like Godzilla, even if it is proportionally close to a human, is a mistake. In previous Godzilla films, it was always a guy in a suit performing the creature. In this version as initially conceived, it would also be a guy in a suit, except it would be a digital suit.

Godzilla wasn't the only project for which performance animation was contemplated to portray an animal digitally. DreamQuest Images conducted early tests in preparation for production of *Mighty Joe Young,* and Disney tested optical motion capture for *Dinosaur.*

In the next chapter, I talk about a test done with a chimpanzee and a human performing the same motion. Both motions were applied to a three-dimensional chimpanzee model. It is a similar example to the cases just discussed, in that human motion was used to portray an animal's movements, and, as with all these cases, the end result was less than encouraging.

Sinbad: Beyond the Veil of Mists

Sinbad: Beyond the Veil of Mists is a computer-generated feature-length film that is now in post-production. The film is being produced by Improvision, a Los Angeles production company, and Pentafour Software and Exports, one of India's largest and most successful software companies, headquartered in Chennai, India. Pentafour specializes in Y2K problem-solving solutions.

The story concerns an evil magician named Baracca, who switches places with a king by giving him a potion. The king's daughter, who is the only one that knows that the switch took place, escapes, eventually running into Sinbad. The Veil of Mists refers to a mythical place where Sinbad and the princess have to go to find the answer to defeating Baracca and saving the king. The main character, Sinbad, is voiced by Brendan Fraser. Additional cast includes Leonard Nimoy, John Rhys-Davies, Jennifer Hale, and Mark Hamill.

Sinbad will be the first all-motion-captured computer-generated feature-length film. With an initial budget of seven million dollars, it is no secret that motion capture was adopted by the producers primarily as a cost-effective alternative to character animation. They had originally planned to finish the whole film in six months, thinking that using motion capture would be a huge timesaver. Evan Ricks, codirector of the picture, was approached by the producers with a rough script. "They already knew that they wanted to do motion capture," recalls Ricks, who is a cofounder of Rezn8, a well-known CG production and design studio in Los Angeles. He told the producers that a film of this magnitude would probably take at least two years of production, but they insisted on trying to finish it on schedule.

Given the constraint that the production would have to utilize motion capture, Ricks initially explored the possibility of using digital puppeteering to animate the characters in real time, using that as a basis for animators to work on. After conducting a few tests, they found that there weren't enough off-the-shelf software tools available to produce this kind of project in real time, so they decided to use an optical motion capture setup.

Motion capture would be used for human characters' body motions only. They couldn't find a good solution at that time to capture facial gestures optically, so they tried to use digital puppeteering instead. Finally, they decided that all facial animation would be achieved by shape interpolation. Pentafour had acquired a Motion Analysis optical motion capture system that was sitting for some time unused in India, but the production decided to use the services of the California-based House of Moves and their Vicon 370E optical system. The reason was that in Hollywood there were more resources and expertise readily available for the shoot, such as stages, actors, set builders, and motion capture specialists.

The production rented a large sound stage at Raleigh Studios and started building all the props and sets that the actors would interact with during the capture session. They even built a ship that sat on a gimbal that could be rocked to simulate the motion of the ocean. "That introduced all kinds of problems in itself," notes Ricks, "because all of a sudden you don't know exactly where the ground is and you have to subtract that all out."

In addition to the people from House of Moves, the production had the services of Demian Gordon, who was brought in as motion capture manager. Gordon had worked extensively with motion capture before, when he was at EA Sports. His job was to help break down the script, work closely with House of Moves, help design marker setups for all characters, and find solutions to problems that arose during production.

The House of Moves' Vicon system was brought into the sound stage and installed using a special rig that rose about 30 feet off the floor, which kept all seven cameras away from the action on the stage. In addition, special outfits were made for the performers to wear during the sessions.

Ricks wanted to shoot the motion capture sessions on tape from many angles as if it were a live television show. He was planning to edit a story reel after the motion capture was done and to use it while producing the computer-generated images. A camera crew was hired initially, but was eventually dismissed by the production company because of its high cost. "We paid the price later," says Ricks. "The camera can really help the director to visualize what's going to be on the screen. I guess you can stand by and use a finder, but with live action, the very next morning you can see dailies. You can see what you actually shot and if the angle works. With motion capture you get a single reference and end up with mechanics more than cinema."

Even if they had been able to tape all the captured shots, they had to deal with the motion capture system's inability to synchronize video and capture scan rates. They couldn't use SMPTE time code, because at that time no optical system was able to generate it, although it is a very important aspect of production work. The newer Vicon 8 system is capable of supporting SMPTE and genlock, but that system wasn't available at the time of the shoot. According to Ricks, the lack of a good way to synchronize all the elements played a big part in the extension of the production schedule.

Because of the compressed schedule, the crew had to capture thousands of shots in about two months. According to Ricks, four months would have been ideal. "We weren't able to finish all the storyboarding before we started the capture, so sometimes we would be literally looking over the editor's shoulder, telling him what we wanted, or looking at new storyboards that had just been drawn, and then go over to the stage around the corner and capture it. Not the ideal way to work."

Typical problems during the motion capture sessions included performers losing or relocating markers. On projects of this magnitude, it becomes very difficult to keep track of exact marker placements, which creates inconsistencies in the motion data. They also had to deal with obstruction problems, where cameras didn't have a direct line of sight for all markers.

Many of the shots had more than one performer interacting at the same time. They were able to capture up to four characters simultaneously, although it became somewhat problematic to clean up the data. "A lot of it took place aboard ship, and there's six people on the crew, so there's a lot of interactions," says Ricks. Fighting sequences were especially difficult to capture, particularly when somebody would fall on the floor and lose markers.

The production was set up so that all design work, preproduction, initial modeling of characters, and motion capture work were done in the United States. The animation side, including the application of captured data, modeling of sets and secondary characters, shading, and rendering, would be handled by the Pentafour CG studio in India, which was a relatively new studio whose experience was mainly in the production of art for CD-ROM titles. Ricks wanted to use very experienced people to handle the most challenging parts of the project, creatively and technically, leaving the supporting tasks to the inexperienced crew.

Overall, the first six months of production had been extremely productive. Evan Ricks and Alan Jacobs had managed to rewrite the script practically from scratch, while Ricks and the production designer developed the look. They hired the staff and cast, recorded the voice track, storyboarded, built sets to be used for motion capture, tested motion capture alternatives, and designed and built all the digital characters and sets. They even stopped regular production for over a month to create a teaser for the Cannes Film Festival. All the motion capture was also finished within those first six months. Everything was looking great and the staff was energized. "I was continually told by visitors and investors how beautiful our designs were, and how new and different as opposed to a 'Disney' look," says Ricks.

Unfortunately, after the completion of the motion capture, the producers had a mistaken perception of the work left and didn't understand what had been achieved in those six months. In their view, most of the technical hurdles in the production had been surpassed. Not only did they not see the need to fulfill repeated requests to hire additional experienced personnel, but they also started laying off their most experienced staff members. Finally, the remainder of the production was moved to the Pentafour studio in India.

The difficult part started after House of Moves finished post-processing and delivered the data. "There was a serious underestimation in how long it takes to weight the characters properly," notes Ricks, who describes some bizarre problems with the deformations of the characters. The deformation setup was much more time-consuming than they had originally estimated. The problem was augmented by the fact that they relied exclusively on off-the-shelf software, and there's a lack of commercial tools for handling captured motion data. A project of this scale would normally have some sort of in-house R&D support, but the budget didn't provide for it.

The mechanical setups for the characters were created using the rotational data provided by House of Moves, as opposed to translational data. For a large project like this, with so many characters and interactions, it would have been beneficial to create customized setups using the translational data, using markers as goals for inverse kinematics or as blended constraints. When using rotational data, the mechanical setup has already been done by the motion capture studio, and not necessarily in the best possible way for the project at hand. "[House of Moves] hadn't done tons of this stuff at that point either, and they had to staff up. It was a learning experience for everybody," notes Ricks, "but they did a very good job under the circumstances."

A typical problem with captured motion data is in the unmatched interactions between characters and props or other characters. The crew in India has been responsible for cleaning up all these problems, including the inability to lock the characters' feet on the floor. This particular problem can be fixed by using inverse kinematics, but it can also be hidden by framing the shots in such a way that the characters' contact with the floor is not visible. Ricks was trying not to let this problem rule the framing of shots.

As Ricks predicted, the length of the production of the film will be close to two years. "If you deconstructed just about any recent film, you'd find out what the director originally wanted and what actually took place are very often two different things, and that was no different here," says Ricks. He is hoping that the producers will give the crew enough time to correct most of the technical issues before the film is finally released.

"I believe our story is interesting and the look unique enough for this to be a very good film. The key is to use this experience to identify the strengths of mocap, to realize that its value is currently not as broad as many think. It is a new camera, not an end in itself," concludes Ricks.

CHAPTER THREE

The Motion Capture Session

☙❧

This chapter covers everything that pertains to the motion capture session, starting with the decision whether to use motion capture or not. It is important to learn how to make that choice in an intelligent manner so that it doesn't backfire later during production.

DECIDING TO USE MOTION CAPTURE

A client has sent storyboards and character designs for your review. You are supposed to come up with a budget for a digital character performing certain actions. The project does not need to be rendered in real time. The client has a very small budget and there is no way you'll be able to compete with other studios if you use keyframe animation. You don't have a lot of experience using captured motion data. Do you suggest performance animation immediately?

If you said no, you're right. This scenario has been proven to result in chaos time after time. It is safe to assume that in most cases performance animation will not save time, except when used to create a product with expected quality trade-offs, such as a motion library for an interactive video game, a virtual reality experience, or a live television show. Similarly, it is safer to believe that it won't save you money. I'm not saying that it is impossible to save time and money using motion capture, but that you should never assume it will unless you have demonstrated this by testing. Testing, of course, will cost time and money. What you should do in a case such as the one outlined in the previous paragraph is propose exploring the possibility of using performance animation, and then proceed cautiously.

I believe that a decision to use motion capture has to be initially based on look alone. If the realistic look of human motion is not what you want, do not even consider motion capture. This is the first bridge that you should cross. Once you have determined that this is the look you are aiming for, you need to start worrying about the second consideration: How can you capture reliable motion data for your project?

Stage 1: Do You Want Realistic Motion?

It is sometimes difficult to visualize what your character will look like after realistic motion has been applied to it. If the character is not shaped like a human, the motion might look strange and even disturbing. It is impossible to predict if this will happen because it depends on the character and the performance. Even if the character is human shaped and the data is clean, the animation might look weird if the context is not right. For example, my first tests using optical motion capture were done with sample data of a dancer's performance captured with an optical system, which I imported into Side Effects' Prisms. I applied the data to a human skeleton that I had from a previous job. I didn't want to acknowledge it then, but the skeleton motion looked strange. I wasn't used to seeing that kind of motion associated with a make-believe character. Nevertheless, I was still awed by the result and decided to look further into the technology.

Recently I have seen two productions that involve optical motion capture and a human skeleton. One is a Michael Jackson short film called *Ghosts*, produced by Digital Domain, and the other is a short video called *Exo-Skeleton* by Pyros Pictures. The two are alike in that both use optical motion capture data and both present a human skeleton dancing. In addition, both have extremely clean motion, without any artifacts. The difference is that *Ghosts* portrays a skeleton integrated in a real live-action environment, whereas *Exo-Skeleton* has computer-generated surroundings and stylized lighting. *Ghosts* works very well because it is meant to look real. The main character is supposed to move like Michael Jackson and was actually performed by him; in addition, it is surrounded by actual dancers. *Exo-Skeleton*, on the other hand, looks strange to my eye because I feel the context is wrong. I wasn't expecting to see the skeleton moving as a real human with such fluidity after coming out of the grave. It helps to have realistic surroundings when using realistic motion, and the performance has to be in context with what the character is trying to portray. The dancer creating the motion for *Exo-Skeleton* wasn't acting the part of a skeleton, but the part of a human. Keep in mind that I'm not trying to criticize anyone's work, but to use it as commentary to illustrate my point.

On one occasion we did a test for the now-defunct Boss Film Studios in which a chimpanzee had to move along a branch of a tree, holding on to it with its hands and swinging its legs. The purpose was to create a demo for a feature film client.

During that process, we would find out if a human could perform the animal's motion in a convincing way, and also if we could collect motion from a chimpanzee.

In preparation for the test, we found an animal trainer who had two well-behaved chimpanzees with acting experience, and a very flexible human gymnast. Our motion capture stage supervisor spent time with the monkeys at the suggestion of the trainer, helping them familiarize themselves with the markers that they would have to wear during the session. At some point, he had problems with the monkeys putting the markers in their mouth. This could have been dangerous because the markers are covered with tiny crystals that, if swallowed, could cause internal bleeding, but after a couple of days the trainer was able to control this behavior and we thought we were ready for our session.

The day of the session, Boss brought to our studio a structure that would represent the branch. Before starting the capture, we had the chimpanzees rehearse the motion without the markers; this rehearsal was without major problems. The chimps were very friendly and even allowed all of us to take photos with them. Then the gymnast performed the motion and we collected her data. It looked very convincing as we saw it at the studio.

After a few takes with the gymnast, it was time to put markers on the first chimpanzee. We wanted to use the bigger chimp because the markers could be placed farther away from each other. We had made Velcro belts that would strap around his arms, legs, neck, and chest, plus a little cap with markers for the head. Our stage supervisor tried time after time to put the markers on the monkey with the help of the trainer, but the chimpanzee wouldn't allow it and broke several markers in the process. We decided to try using the small chimpanzee. He was more docile and accepted the markers without problems. He came to the stage and performed the motions several times, following exact directions from the trainer. He was better than many of the humans that we had captured over the years.

The data post-processing was no walk in the park. We had minimum problems with the human data, but the animal data wasn't totally clean. The markers were very close to each other in some areas and the software couldn't follow them very well, so a lot of operator-assisted tracking was required. When all the data was clean, we noticed that the Velcro strap in the chimpanzee's belly had been sliding around. Fortunately, it had two markers, and it didn't really matter in what part of the perimeter of his belly the two markers were because we could always calculate the center based on their diameter. We managed to stabilize this data as well, and it worked.

We converted all the data to every available format and delivered it to Boss. They in turn gave us a chimpanzee mesh they had created. From this point on, we would do our own tests and they would do theirs. I used Prisms and Softimage software to do our tests, and I found that although the human motion looked convincing when I saw it performed, it didn't when it was applied to the monkey mesh. However, the monkey data looked perfect. The monkey with the human data looked like a chimpanzee in a human suit.

The problem with animal performance is the same as with human performance: The talent has to be able to perform in a convincing way. If a particular motion is not feasible for an animal to do, then you cannot capture it. You can do small enhancements after the fact, like increasing the distance of a jump, but not much more. Animals cannot perform a part other than their own, and humans cannot perform convincing animal motion in most cases. Recall the use of motion capture in *Godzilla*, discussed in Chapter 2. The production of the digital character was initially based almost totally on performance animation, but later in production it was reworked to mostly keyframe animation because the final character looked "like a guy in a Godzilla suit." The special effects producers of *Mighty Joe Young* also considered performance animation, but did the right thing by testing before production actually started. They had a better excuse for considering it, because their character actually *was* a guy in an ape suit for most of the film. They decided to drop the motion capture idea because there was no easy way of modifying the captured data. Because this decision was made before production started, they managed to avoid a costly mistake.

As a rule of thumb, you should not use motion capture to animate characters that should have cartoon-style motion. To be more specific, take Disney's twelve basic principles of animation as outlined by Frank Thomas and Ollie Johnston. These principles are standard learning material for character animators and should be taken into consideration when deciding whether to use motion capture. Some of them cannot be achieved by a performer no matter how talented, and others can be easily accomplished realistically with motion capture. The principles are as follows.

1. *Squash and stretch.* The character goes through extreme shape changes but maintains its volume. This is the first principle that cannot be achieved by a performer. Some people have attempted to add this property to captured motion data either by hand or procedurally, but the results have not been promising.

2. *Timing.* The performance, whether animated or acted, has to have the right timing to convey the necessary perception.

3. *Anticipation.* Anticipation is an indication of an action to come. This is typical of cartoon characters and not necessarily of human performance, but in some cases it is consistent with realistic actions, such as bending your knees before jumping. A good performer can show anticipation to a certain degree, but is limited by the laws of physics.

4. *Staging.* A principle of filmmaking in general, the layout of the scene and positioning of the camera and characters are equally important in animation and live-action performance.

5. *Follow-through and overlapping action.* Follow-through is the opposite of anticipation. The reaction happens after the action, such as bending the knees as one reaches the floor after a high jump. Again, a live performer can accomplish physically feasible follow-through. Overlapping action is inherent to live performance, but in animation, it is easier to start an action after another one is finished, resulting in either paused or rigid motion.

6. *Straight-ahead action and pose-to-pose action.* These are two animation methods. Straight-ahead action calls for the animation of a scene on a frame-by-frame basis, whereas pose-to-pose action entails the creation of key poses scattered over time periods. The frames in between these key poses are drawn later. In computer animation, most of the character work is done using a variation of the pose-to-pose action method, creating key poses for different parts instead of posing the whole character at a particular frame. This is done by creating keyframes and letting the software produce the in-between frames by some kind of interpolation defined by the animator. This method is easier to manage because there is less data to deal with. Motion capture is completely straight-ahead action; as such, it generates keyframes at every frame. This makes it very difficult to modify. Pose-to-pose action can be achieved through motion capture by selecting significant keyframes, deleting the rest, and allowing the computer to do the in-betweening as before.

7. *Ease-in and ease-out.* It is very rare for an object to become active without a period of acceleration, or to become static without a stage of deceleration. Ease-in and ease-out are principles based on real-world physics, so they can easily be achieved by capturing the motion of a live performance.

8. *Arcs.* Most actions are not linear. When animating, you almost never want to use linear interpolation between keyframes. This is another principle aimed at emulating realistic movement, which can be represented as a set of different types of arcs. When using keyframe animation, these curves are usually smooth between keyframes. With motion data, however, they are coarse and noisy, representing the natural nuances of realistic motion.

9. *Secondary motion.* When animating, you first create the primary motion of the character, which is usually the motion of limbs and face. You then create the motion of other parts or objects that react to the primary motion, such as hair and clothing. Secondary motion represents a lot of extra work with hand animation, whereas with motion capture it is a part of the performance. One has

to be able to collect it, however, which may not be possible with some systems. For example, clothing motion can be captured by an optical system if markers are added to the clothes, but an electromagnetic tracker or electromechanical suit would not be able to collect that kind of data easily.

10. *Exaggeration.* The principle of exaggeration implies approaching or crossing the boundaries of physical reality in order to enhance or dramatize the character's performance. You must decide if capturing a live performance would be acceptable, or even feasible, for the level of exaggeration needed.

11. *Appeal.* The audience must find the characters interesting and appealing. This principle applies for both live action and animation.

12. *Personality.* Two identical characters can appear totally different by conveying different personalities. This is a principle of acting in general that should be applied to animation. When using motion capture, this is the number one reason to use a talented performer, as opposed to just anybody that can move.

The following principles of animation cannot be accomplished with motion capture:

Squash and stretch
Anticipation beyond physical boundaries
Follow-through action beyond physical boundaries
Exaggeration beyond physical boundaries

The following principles of animation are natural to live performances:

Overlapping action
Straight-ahead action
Ease-in and ease-out
Arcs
Secondary motion

Finally, the following principles of animation require work whether a character is animated or performed:

Timing
Appeal
Personality
Staging

Procedural and manual methods exist for adding some of the principles to motion data after the fact, such as squash and stretch, anticipation, follow-through, and exaggeration. The question is, Why would you want to capture realistic data if you want a cartoony look? Modifying captured motion data by hand can be more expensive than keyframe animation, and a procedural solution usually doesn't yield an interesting performance. Of course, there are exceptions, but you shouldn't rely on them.

I'm not saying that you should never capture human motion and apply it to a cartoony character, but it is safer to go through this process as a test to find out if it will yield the result you want before you commit to a high expense. In fact, many cartoon characters are animated through performance, mostly with real-time feedback systems in combination with other controls. An example of such a show is *Donkey Kong Country*. These kinds of projects are usually created by studios that specialize in that kind of medium and have experience with real-time character puppeteering. Companies such as Medialab, Protozoa, and Modern Cartoons have created a business from the real-time rendering of characters and have established it as a medium separate from the rest of character animation; it is not accurate to call this medium motion capture or even performance animation, because it involves many kinds of manipulations other than performance. This type of animation is called *digital puppetry*, and it involves a different decision-making process from what I describe here.

A good example of a project in which human motion data was applied to a cartoony character was the 1996 set of spots that TSi did for the Pillsbury Doughboy, which are explained in more detail in Chapter 2. We decided to use captured motion data on the Doughboy because (1) we determined that his motion didn't require any squash and stretch or extreme exaggeration or anticipation, and (2) we supplied our client with a test of the Doughboy performing extreme motions mapped from a human, so they knew what to expect. Some of the shots were not well suited to the subject, but we knew we could collect the data anyway and use it as timing reference. As long as the client did not change the timing of the motion we would be fine, and they agreed not to do that.

Stage Two: Can You Successfully Capture the Data?

I will start by separating the two kinds of projects that you are likely to deal with. Film or video productions and game cinematic sequences follow a predetermined continuity, so I refer to them as *linear* projects. On the other hand, user-controlled video games are *nonlinear* projects, since the player's actions determine the sequence of events that, in real time, shape the character's motions in different patterns. These two types of projects are handled differently in some aspects when it comes to performance animation. There is a third type of project that I do not cover specifically: real-time digital performance applications, such as live television and trade-show performances. These kinds of projects have to be based totally on performance animation. I do feel, however, that the concepts I outline here can be used at the planning stage of such a project.

If a character design is already available, and it has been determined that realistic motion is the way to go, it is time to evaluate if it is possible to capture the data you are looking for. For this purpose, I like to use a divide-and-conquer approach, breaking the project into small, similar groups of shots and using these categories to evaluate strategy and plan the sessions. A *shot* is an uninterrupted camera take that is later combined with other shots to form a scene. It will fit our purpose to define a shot as an uninterrupted piece of character motion, because this definition applies to all media, including linear and nonlinear projects. A step-by-step explanation of how to perform the evaluation follows.

Create a Candidate Table

I'm assuming that if you are planning a motion capture session, you already have either a script, production boards, or a game design from which you are supposed to determine which characters to animate via performance. For the characters you are considering, you have already concluded that realistic data is the way to go.

The candidate table is a preliminary step that is designed to save you time, helping you avoid creating storyboards for shots that are not even in consideration. As you create the table, define if a digital character is supposed to be visible and decide how it is supposed to be animated, if at all. For example, if a character is talking, it is possible that it isn't facing the camera. Similarly, a character may be so tiny in the camera viewpoint that you may not have to animate it at all, or maybe you only see the character's foot in the shot, so animating the rest would be irrelevant.

If all you have is a shooting script, you should be able to extract and list those shots that appear to be candidates for performance animation. You will be lacking valuable information, as no visual reference is yet available, but you must assume that if the digital character is present in the shot, it is visible. If possible, talk to the director to find out what he has in mind for each shot. Later in the production, shot breakdowns and production boards are created; as you get hold of them, you will have to revise the candidate table based on this new information. If the project is a nonlinear video game, the design must already include a list or a flow chart of motions for each character. Such a list is required before starting to create the table, because no script is available for a nonlinear project.

The table should include at a minimum a shot name (which will be used to designate the data file as well), a list of the character or characters involved, and a description of each shot. You can also include a client reference name, which could be the board number or a page number in the script. You don't need to include other information such as timing just yet, since it is not the purpose of this list to calculate costs and schedules. A Categories column is also necessary, but it should be left blank for now. I will get to that later.

Table 3-1. *Sample Candidate Table*

No.	Name	Client reference	Characters	Categories	Description
1	SO-02	Pg. 1-3	Stan, Ollie		Ollie is sitting in the dune buggy, driving recklessly. Stan is being pulled and is skiing behind it. Camera is in front of car.
2	SO-04	Pg. 2-1	Stan		Stan hits a dune and flies in the air, losing control. Camera follows from the side.
3	SO-08	Pg. 4-2	Stan, Ollie		Stan and Ollie sit comfortably in car, enjoying their drink. Camera is in front of car.

Table 3-1 is a fictitious example of what an actual candidate table would look like. The candidate table is not supposed to be a final table, so don't be afraid to include shots that are questionable. Be careful not to exclude any shots that have any possibility of qualifying.

I didn't have the luxury of knowing about this method when I was starting, and I often ended up capturing a lot of data that was discarded for a variety of reasons, from not being able to track the desired motion to not being able to use the data in the shots. As you become more experienced, more of the shots cataloged in the candidate table will actually make it to the motion capture session, because you will be able to tell which ones are not feasible without going through the whole evaluation process.

Prepare Motion Capture Blueprints

Storyboards are commonly used for representing and understanding live-action and animation shots, but performance animation requires more information than storyboards alone provide. You need a certain kind of blueprint that includes storyboards and much more. You need to know what your subject is interacting with, starting from the ground itself to other characters and props. You also need to know the placement of each of these interactors. If the floor is uneven or sloped, you need to know. If the character leans on the wall or touches anything, that is also important information. So are measurements of all props and the volume that will envelop all the action. All these variables may seem unimportant at the stage of planning a shot, but at the time of capturing and importing data into a character they become big issues that one ends up wishing had been dealt with at the beginning.

For nonlinear applications, you most likely don't need some of the information I describe in this section, especially the camera orientation, because the camera will be controlled by the user. You do need other items, however, such as a list of shots that will be tied with the shot in question, because you will want to make sure that the attachment point is similar for all of them.

The subsections that follow list items to include in motion capture blueprints.

Shot Description

A small description of what happens in the shot.

Client Reference Name

A name by which your client refers to this shot (if it applies).

Character Names

This is a listing of all the characters that will be captured simultaneously or separately in this particular shot.

Storyboards

It is imperative to know exactly what has to happen for each shot that you are evaluating. The best way of doing this is actually videotaping the shot using live actors, but this is quite expensive and in some cases impossible; thus, the most common way is to use storyboards. Whether you create them or your client supplies them, they should be detailed enough that you should be able to visualize the shot perfectly.

Some of the things that depend on good understanding of the performance are the sample rate at which it is best to collect, the placement of the markers or sensors on the performer's body, the character setup, and the topology of the 3D model. In addition, if you will be using an optical system, this information will affect the number of cameras to use and the placement of cameras according to the area of capture.

A typical storyboard is a drawn representation of a scene, which is a combination of shots that take place in a particular setting. A shot is represented in a storyboard by one or more drawings that are commonly used to block character movements and camera work in relationship with dialogue and timing. The storyboards needed for motion capture pertain only to a particular shot and not to a whole scene, and they need to be more specific for complicated motions, sometimes showing various views of the action.

Shot Timing, Including Handles

Motion data is expensive, so you don't want to capture more data than you need. Make sure that your timings include *handles,* that is, a few frames at the beginning and a few at the end. The number is up to you, but it should be anywhere from a third of a second to a couple of seconds. I measure it in seconds because the number of samples per second will vary according to the type of project or motion capture system used. To obtain the frame count, you can always multiply the timing by the sampling rate. If you use a motion capture service provider, this number can be key to avoiding cost surprises.

It is very common when designing video games to create a list of motions and just capture them without going through this step. In many cases, I would receive a motion list without timings or handles and be asked to quote the cost of capturing the data. I would calculate the cost, making sure to try to time the shots with reasonable handles, but the difficulty of envisioning what the client had in mind occasionally resulted in very different final costs than what was estimated.

It is also common to slap timing on a shot without even thinking about it. For example, I once had a client who wanted to collect data for an ice hockey game. I asked him to provide in advance a list of motions with timings, but all the timings he provided were inaccurate because most actions on skates require a certain degree of build-up, which translates into long handles. You cannot start a skating cycle like a walk cycle: You have to slowly pick up the right speed until you have the speed and rhythm you need. This was one of my earliest motion capture jobs, my first video game job, and perhaps the first motion capture session ever done on a skating arena, so I couldn't detect the problem immediately. I figured we could cut the files to the right length after the session, but this became impossible because we couldn't decide what segment of each shot to delete without consulting with the client, who happened to be based out of the country, and we were afraid of deleting the point where motions would tie into each other. Also, we had close to 500 files, so it would have been impossible for the client to help remotely. We decided to track most of the data, removing only parts in which the skater left the capture volume. The resulting cost was about triple what I had originally estimated, and although we had only provided an estimate, the client refused to pay the extra amount.

The Measured Boundaries of the Performance

Make sure you know the volume and area limitations of the motion capture stage. Most systems have a maximum volume that cannot be breached, so you need to ensure that each shot will comply with it. With some systems you can sometimes play with the volume to add area in a certain plane while decreasing the area in another plane, maintaining the volume constraint. For example, the capture of a slam dunk will require much more height than the capture of a baseball batter, so you may want to trade some stage area for more altitude.

When using an optical system, the closer the cameras are to the area of capture the better they can see the performance. This translates into better and less expensive motion data. In addition, as the motion moves away from the center of the stage, the cameras become less accurate due to lens distortion. This problem is partially solved by the lens distortion correction software that some optical motion capture systems include, but it is never completely repaired. Similarly, with a magnetic tracker you need to make sure the action will happen within the electromagnetic field, so the placement of the transmitter needs to be planned in advance.

Including all the performance's measurements in the storyboard will ensure that you can divide your shots into groups based on stage volume and configuration. This makes the tracking post-process more efficient. If you don't include the measurements, the stage will usually be set up for the maximum possible capture volume. It could be very time consuming to reconfigure a setup, especially if it is optically based. Nevertheless, if you are well prepared, a long session can be divided into two or three different configurations.

The ice hockey game discussed earlier is a good example of how one can benefit from good planning. The scenes had very low and tight motions and very wide and high motions. Most of the goalkeeper actions could be collected with a very tight camera setup, which made the post-processing stage easier. Other motions (such as skate cycles) required a huge volume because the cycle itself used up a long distance. The height had to cover a tall skater, his skates, and sometimes even his arm raised with the hockey stick in it. Of course, we didn't have to collect the whole stick since it was a rigid object, so we used three markers close to the handle that would represent the whole thing. However, it still was very challenging to collect all the necessary data. We certainly had a hard time cleaning up those motions. Had the client provided us with the critical timing information, we could have optimized our volume. A corridor-like configuration (a narrow, but long and tall, volume) would have been appropriate for this situation. It would have saved a lot of time and money in the post-processing of the data.

Character Setup

Character setup and marker setup are two different things. Marker setup pertains to the locations of markers, sensors, or potentiometers that are used to collect data. Character setup deals with the locations of joints or bones in the body of a character that will provide the final motion and deformations. This is usually done using the 3D animation software, such as Maya or Softimage. The character setup depends on the marker setup, because the data collected must be enough to calculate all the information needed by the joints. For example, if you have a knee joint in your character setup, you will have to add the necessary markers at collection time to calculate the rotations of the knee.

You don't need to determine a marker setup at this time, but you must prepare a character setup design that will later allow you to come up with a marker configuration for your character. Only a design is necessary since in a perfect world you will not actually model your character until after the motion capture session. Even if you already have a character, it shouldn't be set up for motion until the captured base position is available.

If your system can only handle one marker configuration, then your character setup will have to be designed based on this setup constraint. However, if you can design different marker setups, then you can work the opposite way, which is much better. With an optical system, you can define where you put the markers and you can use combinations that will allow you to determine the motion of any location on the subject that you may want.

World Axis

It is important to maintain a common world axis throughout the project, especially if you are capturing data from several characters that must interact in some way. Always use the same orientation and position of the world axis as in your target animation software or game engine. Looking at the front viewport in most off-the-shelf animation programs, the positive Y-axis is oriented toward the top of the screen, and the positive X-axis is directed toward the right side of the screen. The positive Z-axis is sometimes facing the outside of the screen; other times, it points toward the inside of the screen. These two variations represent right-handed and left-handed space, respectively.

If your software uses right-handed space, you would want your talent looking toward the positive Z-axis as you collect the base position (a file in which the talent is standing in a pose similar to the 3D character's neutral pose). For left-handed space, the performer should be oriented toward the negative Z-axis.

Some off-the-shelf animation programs use left-handed or right-handed space with variations in world axis orientation. A good example is Alias, in which you can specify either Y or Z as the up axis.

Try to assume you will place the axis at the origin and use it as the root of your character's setup. If necessary, you can add a translation offset in case you need to place the character elsewhere in a set.

Measurement Units

You can add a scale offset to the world axis in order to size the character proportionally with other elements in your project, but proper planning calls for uniform units across the project. It is best to base digital models on real-world units, especially when using captured motion data. Make sure to specify the measurement units you'd like your data to conform to and use those units when modeling characters, sets, props, and any other elements in your shots, especially if they will interact with the digital character. For example, if the character has to avoid certain digital obstacles, you could conceivably mark the position of the obstacles in the capture area. This is not guaranteed to work exactly as planned because you still have to deal with character versus data proportions, but it will definitely be close.

Obviously, having the right units doesn't mean that your captured data will match perfectly for a specific character. You may have to manipulate it before and after applying it to the character, but at least you will have a common starting point for your whole project.

Main Camera Angle and Framing

Unless your data is to be used for a nonlinear application, chances are you will have a camera angle that will be used for the final rendering of the shot. This is important for two reasons. First, when you capture the performance, you always want to have a taped reference. This applies to both linear and nonlinear projects. If the project is linear, it is always best to have at least one camera placed with the angle and framing of the final camera to be used. Of course, this rule probably won't apply if the camera of the final shot is moving, but the camera should be at least placed in the general direction. The taped reference will be used in some cases to decide between takes, or as a placeholder for editing purposes, and definitely as reference when applying the data to the final character.

Second, the performer needs to know where the camera is. When acting, you perform to the camera, which is where the audience is. If you don't know where the audience is, you cannot establish contact with it through body language, and the performance becomes flat. If it isn't possible to place the video camera in the general direction of the final camera, you need to let the performer know where that final position is.

The camera position should not be confused with the world axis of the motion. Camera placement can change from shot to shot, but all shots have to maintain a

Figure 3-1. *World axis versus camera placement.*

common world axis. Thus, when you capture a base position that will be used for character setup, it must always face your preferred front axis (see Figure 3-1).

All Interactions Explained with a High Level of Detail

Anything that the character touches or reacts to has to be accounted for in advance in order to decide if it is possible or feasible to use motion capture on that particular shot. Some shots will require more human involvement than others at the time of applying data to a character; that time is usually based on the number of interactions.

Let's imagine we are capturing a baseball batter waiting for a pitch. The first capture is the batter walking with the bat in one hand. In this case, the only interaction is the bat in one hand and the floor, but the floor is flat, so we don't worry about it. We put markers on the batter, including his hand, and two markers on the bat (except for the base, because we know it is in his hand). This type of object is called a *constant interactor,* because it remains for the length of the shot. These kinds of interactions are solved mostly by character setup only and can be occasionally simplified by using fewer markers during the capture session. Applying this data to a character is not plug-and-play, but it is fairly uninvolved, assuming the size of the character is proportional to the size of the performer.

The second capture is the batter putting the bat under his arm as he rubs powder in his hands. This situation is more difficult because there are two interactions to worry about: the bat under the arm and the two hands. In addition, none of them is constant, since the bat is first in the hand, then under the arm, and the hands are first apart and then together. These are called *variable interactors,* and we cannot use shared markers with them. For example, we cannot use the hand marker to capture the position of the bat anymore because the bat is not in the hand for the length of the shot. Therefore, we end up using three markers on the bat. At the time of applying the data, the bat most likely will not end up under the arm of the batter, so we'll need to either animate the motion by hand or add a parent joint to the bat that we can use to add variation to the original motion. We never want to modify the captured motion data directly. We'd also use markers on each hand. At the time of application, if the hands don't end up together due to size problems, we'll have to discard the elbow data and use the wrist positional data as a constraint for inverse kinematics goals.

The third capture is the following scenario: As the batter waits, he hits his shoe twice with the bat, holding it with both hands. Then he holds it with the left hand and passes it to the right one, starting to swing it into the ready position. He finally swings, hitting the ball. He drops the bat as he starts running. If we don't care about the bat after it leaves his hand, the interactors are as follows:

1. The bat in both hands
2. The bat in both hands and the shoe
3. The bat in both hands
4. The bat in both hands and the shoe
5. The bat in both hands
6. The bat in the left hand
7. The bat in both hands
8. The bat in the right hand
9. The bat in both hands
10. The bat in both hands and the back of his neck
11. The bat in both hands
12. The bat in both hands and the ball
13. The bat in both hands
14. The bat in one hand

You may think I'm being repetitive, but there really are 14 variable interactors in this shot, without counting the floor (which is flat). Initially the batter has the bat in both hands, then he hits his shoe, then the bat is again in both hands, and then it hits his shoe again. It is back in both hands before it goes to the left hand, and as it goes to the right hand, it passes in between both hands again. Then it goes to both hands. Later it touches the back of the neck. As he swings, the bat is in both hands, then it hits the ball, and then is in both hands again. As the bat is tossed, it leaves one hand first and then the other one.

Interactions need to be listed in this manner: cataloged as either constant or variable, and, if variable, in order of occurrence. You need to be very thorough in determining that all the interactions are listed, including the ones that are in-betweens. If you do this it will be easy to estimate the operator time that will be used, and no money will be lost by miscalculating the actual cost of a difficult shot. It is even possible to come up with a cost and time formula based on the number of constant and variable interactors combined with the shot length.

All Props, with Size and Location

If your character must interact with any props, you have to specify the prop's exact size and position, based on the units and world axis provided. This is an area in which common sense needs to be used because there are many factors at play. Assuming you have a well-organized project in which all units are the same and in which the character's proportions match closely the ones of the performer, the correct placement of these items should result in a very close resemblance of reality once you translate the action into the digital realm.

When using a real-time capture device such as an electromagnetic tracker, you can usually place the digital prop along with the digital character for real-time feedback. The performer can interact with it by watching a screen. This technique avoids the need for creating a live version of the object for the performer to interact with.

In the case of non-real-time capture devices, such as optical systems, there is no way of looking at the digital prop at the time of the performance. Therefore, a live stand-in object must be placed in the stage area that will represent the digital prop. This object could be anything from a replica of the digital prop to a painted area that represents where the object is located.

Depending on the complexity of the interaction, you must decide what level of detail is needed for representing the object. If the prop is a column that the performer needs to avoid without touching, perhaps a painted profile on the floor will be enough. Maybe a few ropes or thin pipes from the floor to the ceiling indicating the corners of the column are needed, depending on how close the interaction will be. Keep in mind that these objects could hinder the actual collection process by occluding markers or introducing interference.

Rigs

Some motions cannot be achieved by the performer alone, so special contraptions need to be created to help. These are not really props, because they will not form part of the digital scene. For example, a wire rig for flying requires the performer to wear a type of harness, which will affect the marker configuration. Some rigs can even interfere with the data collection, so it is very important to be aware of this as you evaluate the project. If any of the shots to be evaluated require a special rig, you must figure out what that will be as you create the motion capture blueprint.

File Naming Convention

When you're dealing with lots of motion files, you can't afford to be disorganized. Each shot that you capture requires a predetermined name and number that will give you exact information as to what character the file belongs to, what setup was used, the calibration file to be used when tracking, what base position the file is compatible with, and other specific items defined by the grouping that you will come up with afterward.

Since this is a preliminary evaluation stage and you probably still don't know most of the information, you can start designing the file names using the character or characters' names, a sequence number, and a description of the motion. The name will grow as you find out more information, and at the time of collecting the data, the full name will be listed here and used for saving the file.

If the data is for a client, you must find out their naming convention, because you will have to establish a cross-reference table in order to be synchronized with them. Also, one shot in a production could represent more than one shot in the motion capture list, and vice-versa; that relationship will have to be kept organized as well. Finally, if file name length is limited, a detailed index must be kept to correlate file names to their contents.

Dialogue

When capturing a facial performance, it is obvious that the entire dialogue is needed beforehand, but the dialogue also has importance when collecting full body data. In real life, body language enhances communication when one speaks. Thus, if a shot has dialogue, it is important to consider it when collecting full body data because it effects timing and performance.

The nuances that you are able to capture with motion capture are so realistic that if you omit a simple item like this, the final performance will not look believable. In my opinion, it is because of the lack of importance placed on the actual situation of the performance that so many people dislike watching performance animation. The eye is so well trained for the real thing that a little deviation will nullify the whole effect.

Shots to Be Blended

When capturing data for a nonlinear project, each shot will most likely have to blend with many others. For example, in a video game, a player controls what the characters do, and the game engine plays back the motion corresponding to the player's action in almost real time, blending it with the preceding motion. It these two motions don't fuse well, the game loses fluidity.

A list of shots to be blended and a flow chart should already be included in a good game design, and this material should be transferred to the blueprint, making sure to specify if it should match from the head or tail. Whether a shot is a cycle or loop must also be specified, because the shot's head must blend with the tail. The start and end positions must be specified in these kinds of shots, preferably by drawings or photos.

A shot in a linear project doesn't usually have to blend with any other motion, but there are special cases. If the motion has to occur in a volume greater than the one available for collection, it is possible to break the motion in two and blend it together later. On the other hand, if a production storyboard lists two or more shots that represent the same motion from different camera angles, they should be performed and captured in one step, splitting it later into different shots.

Number of Files

To be used later, this is the number of files in which this shot will be divided. It could be more than one file if there are multiple characters to be captured separately or if a particular motion needs to be collected in two or more passes.

Sampling Rate

Sampling rate is also referred to as frames per second. There are two kinds of sampling rates that you need to worry about: the capture sampling rate and the delivery sampling rate. Capture sampling rate is the frequency at which you collect the data, and delivery sampling rate is the frequency at which you apply the data to a character. At least the delivery sampling rate should be included in the blueprint. The capture sampling rate is possibly not known yet, but it will become important later.

If the project will be rendered at NTSC video resolution, the delivery sampling rate will probably be 30 frames per second. For film, it is 24 frames per second. The sampling rate for video games is defined by the engine capabilities and should be included in the game design. You may need the final data delivered at a higher sampling rate than the final medium requires in order to do certain operations, such as motion blur, field rendering, or time distortion effects. This data should be delivered at a rate divisible by the final medium rate. That is, if film is the final medium, the delivery sampling rate could be 24, 48, or any similar number divisible by 24, because it is easy to down-sample data when the divisor is an integer number. Converting film to NTSC video or vice-versa always presents a problem because every 24 frames of film correspond to 30 frames of video.

Configuration Name

This field is for future use and will list the name of the marker configuration to be used. In large projects, it is common to have several different configurations, each of which will include a marker setup map and a base position file. You must keep track of what configuration matches each shot because you will need the information later in the process, especially during character setup and data application.

Calibration Name

When you collect data that will be tracked as a post-process, such as with an optical system, you must take note of what calibration name pertains to each shot. At the time of data analysis, the operator will have to associate the calibration with the actual shot raw data file in order for the software to start tracking.

The calibration of an optical system is kept in a file and is used by the software to calculate the exact position of each camera in space. Without this information, it is impossible to calculate anything else's position in space. Several times during a daily session, a calibration file must be recorded by capturing data from a known object, such as a large cube with markers.

For systems in which the data is tracked in real time, it isn't necessary to save the calibration information, because once the motion data is tracked, the calibration parameters are no longer needed for a particular shot.

This field will be left blank at this stage, as it will only be used at the time of data collection.

Talent Used

It is important to always use the same performer when you capture data for a character within a particular project. Otherwise, it would be like switching actors in the middle of a film. Later in the process, you will have a casting session, where you will determine the name or names to put in this field.

Special Instructions

Based on the number of interactors, camera framing, props, and other special considerations, here you will write notes that pertain to the collection, character setup, and data application. You don't need to—and cannot—write all your notes at this point, but you will use this field throughout the project.

Among other things, this field's objective is to pass on pertinent information to the next levels of the project. For example, if you have a motion file in which, for session economy, you collected data for markers that are not supposed to be used

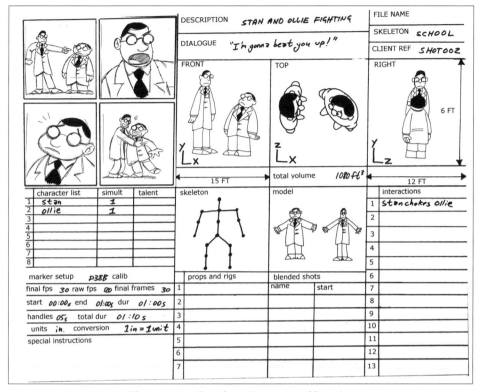

Figure 3-2. *Sample motion capture blueprint.*

in that particular shot, the technical director in charge of applying the data must be informed. Another scenario would be to pass specific instructions to the data collection and analysis team to follow at collection or tracking time.

Figure 3-2 shows an example of a motion capture blueprint.

Catalog Your Shots

Once your motion capture blueprints are complete and you are sure that you have all the pertinent information about each shot, it is time to organize them in different categories. You can forget about the chronology of the shots, because you have already assigned shot and file names to each of them, so everything should come together nicely when you are done.

The object in this step is to group the shots into categories based on motion capture parameters that will allow you to organize your session, post-processing, and data application, and to reject shots that don't meet your requirements. This is the final bridge to cross; any shot that survives will be captured.

First, you have to come up with categories based on the differences of the particular shots in your project. I cannot tell you exactly what categories these will be, but I can show you the general areas that are significant in order to help you come up with them. Second, you need to be able to sort your data based on these new categories. A database program may help in this regard.

The listing of significant areas that follows is not in any particular order, as each project has different variables and priorities.

Volume

When you have a large number of shots, you should use special software to help you get organized. By using such software, it should be easy to produce charts that will visually help you identify the shots that either fall outside of the maximum volume or have deviations that would cause them to become special cases of stage configuration. Let's look at the group of shots shown in Table 3-2. For simplicity's sake, Table 3-2 has only 17 shots, but the example can be applied to any project size. In addition, we will assume that the system in question can handle a maximum volume of 2000 cubic feet. You can reject shots that fall outside the range of capture of your particular system by charting the total volume per shot. The bar chart in Figure 3-3 shows that shot 8 surpasses the maximum volume; therefore, it must be discarded from the list.

Table 3-2.   *List of Possible Shots*

Shot	Width	Length	Height
1	12.0	8.0	8.0
2	4.0	5.0	7.0
3	7.0	11.0	9.0
4	7.0	7.0	7.0
5	9.0	11.0	9.0
6	12.0	21.0	7.0
7	15.0	4.0	8.0
8	20.0	17.0	7.0
9	18.0	12.0	7.0
10	12.0	12.0	8.0
11	5.0	3.0	9.0
12	3.0	4.0	12.0
13	13.0	12.0	9.0
14	8.0	12.0	7.0
15	6.0	12.0	7.0
16	4.0	6.0	7.0
17	9.0	6.0	7.0

For optical systems, with which the capture volume can be reconfigured, you can divide the remaining shots into volume groups. If all shots fall into a narrow volume range, this may not be necessary. Depending on the spread between the minimum and maximum area, you may have to divide your shots into two or thee

Total Volume

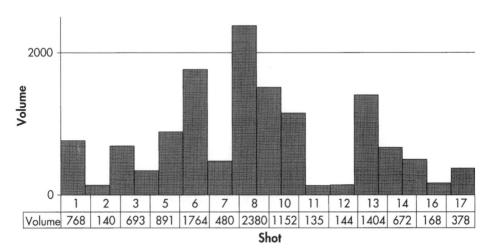

Volume	768	140	693	891	1764	480	2380	1152	135	144	1404	672	168	378
Shot	1	2	3	5	6	7	8	10	11	12	13	14	16	17

Figure 3-3. *Volume chart.*

basic groups, adding special groups to encompass special cases such as corridors or tall setups.

A project with 500-plus shots could easily end up with three rectangular volume groups, plus several special groups. An easy way to see if you have any special cases that require additional configurations is to plot the width/length ratio and the height per shot. The chart in Figure 3-4 shows the proportions of the floor area of the stage. The perimeter values represent the shots, and the aligned numbers represent the ratio between width and length. The higher the value, the less square the stage needs to be. This value is given by the following code:

```
if (width/length < 1) {
ratio = length / width;
else
ratio = width / length;
}
```

Out of 17 shots, notice how 16 fall within the 1:2 ratio value. Shot 7, however, is noticeably different from the rest and will have to be cataloged as a special case, requiring its own stage configuration.

Figure 3-5 shows a similar scenario based on the height requirements of each shot. In this case, 16 shots fall within the 6 to 8 feet range, whereas shot 12 requires 12 feet. It is possible that this shot will require another special configuration.

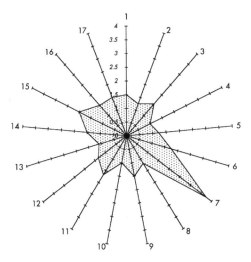

Figure 3-4.   *Width/length ratio chart.*

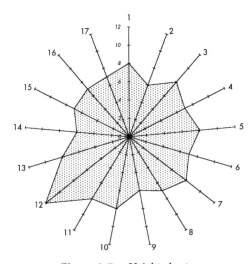

Figure 3-5.   *Height chart.*

Characters

A listing of all shots by character is always a good idea, especially for talent scheduling and rehearsing purposes. When scheduling your capture session, it may also help to calculate a certain performer's cost, or to calculate the character's total screen time.

Three very important categories that pertain to characters are multiple, split shot, and split-multiple. A *split shot* is the type of shot in which more than one character is present, but which can be split into two different subshots in order to collect the data of each character individually. When this is done, a postfix needs to be added to the shot name to represent the fact that it is divided. A shot with multiple characters can only be split in this manner if there are minimal or no interactions between characters. If there are minimal interactions, the timing between the performances might need to match perfectly, a match that will only be achieved by extensive rehearsing and maybe multiple data captures. Never assume that you can modify the timing of a performance after the fact.

Multiple refers to a shot in which more than one character's motion has to be collected simultaneously. There are shots in which characters interact with each other in ways that would make it impossible to split the shot into several parts. Think about it in terms of video. If you could shoot each character separately performing this action and then merge them, being able to reconstruct the action perfectly, then you should split the shot; otherwise, it falls into the multiple category. If you have an electromagnetic or electromechanical system that can only handle one performer at a time and you don't have access to a second setup, you must now reject all the shots that fall into this category. With an optical system you have a little more leeway, since you can add markers to a second subject; however, depending on the interaction, you will have to design creative ways of positioning markers so that they don't get occluded for lengthy periods of time. I don't know any optical system that can handle more than four or five performers as of yet, but this will change as systems evolve and accept more markers at a time.

Split-multiple shots are performed by multiple performers, not all of whom have markers. This is a good idea when timing is a consideration, and it helps the talent achieve a certain movement. I saw this done in my studio a few times, especially during sports games projects. A good example is capturing the motions of a soccer goalkeeper, because there has to be somebody shooting the ball. For a martial arts game, a martial artist performed certain moves, such as air kicks and flying turns, with the help of another artist without markers, who also served as the target of punches and kicks. We later captured the action of receiving these punches and kicks, again with both martial artists on the stage but with only the receiver wearing the markers.

Interactions, Props, and Rigs

You must have a category for each type of shot based on interactions. For example, all shots in which there are variable interactions involving one arm should be grouped together, as should all the shots that have constant interactions with a certain prop. You need to define what is the maximum number of interactions that you will have to handle manually and decide if it is worthwhile or even possible to capture that performance.

For example, suppose you have a shot in which a character has variable interactions with both his arms and legs. It is likely that you will have to eliminate the captured data on all those limbs and animate them manually. You still have the body left. It may be worthwhile for you to capture the data just to have the body motions, but if the arm and leg interactions will affect the body in any way, such as in timing, it is best to reject that particular shot. In most cases, the legs' motion affects the body motions, unless the character is swimming or sitting without his feet touching the ground.

Another example would be the baseball player that I mentioned previously, who moves the bat back and forth between his hands several times. This kind of shot should be captured, as the bat interactions do not affect the body data in any way. It will require human involvement to finalize this shot, but you can still retain a good amount of the data without modification.

Constant interaction with a prop can also be tricky. Suppose a character is climbing a rock of ambiguous shape. Unless you have a replica of the actual rock on stage and your character is proportionally equal to your talent, you are most likely looking at problems. You will have to turn off the legs' data and perhaps change the body's timing, and that makes that shot a reject.

Props and rigs can also be problematic without interactions if they prevent the collection device from capturing the data. This includes anything that would introduce noise or occlude cameras in a way that would make it impossible to collect the data. In any case, all props and rigs that interact, occlude, or even exist in a shot must be in a separate category.

Blending

Two categories need to be created based on blending, namely, head and tail blending. A particular shot could belong to either of these categories or both. This list will be used to make sure during the capture session that the shots have similar starting and/or ending points, keeping in mind that as the sampling resolution of a shot increases, blending will be more difficult and will require extra work after character application.

Character Setup

This category is particularly important, as it will be key to designing the marker setup. You may have one particular setup for each character or even a few different ones per character. If you will do facial and body captures for a particular character, you need two separate setups. You must define one category per character setup. This will most likely yield a similar number of marker setups, but it may also result in more or less, so it has to be independent.

Imagine you have already designed one particular character setup in Softimage that is used in all of your character's shots, but one shot calls for the character to sit on a couch. If an optical system is used, the couch will obviously occlude all the markers placed on the back of the performer, so they need to be moved to the front.

The marker setup for this shot will be different, but in the end, the same character setup can be used in Softimage if the motion capture data analysis and conversion was done correctly. This book includes a practical example of this particular case.

If you have any kind of control over the placement of the markers, I advise continuing only if the character setup design is ready, because then the marker setup will be dependent on the character setup and not vice versa. Try to use this benefit to your advantage.

Priority

Some shots have a priority for reasons not related to the motion capture technical process. Most of the time these priorities concern delivery restrictions. In the past, my clients have divided shots into different delivery categories with different due dates. This would dictate the order of post-processing that we'd follow.

Depending on the size of the project, you may have many categories to consider. If the information becomes unmanageable, use a database or spreadsheet program to help. It will help you get organized and you will save money in the process. Make sure you have printouts of candidate tables sorted by every one of these categories. Doing so will help you come up with your final motion capture schedule. Also, make a single list with all the categories you defined, and put all your motion capture blueprints in a binder for easy access. You will reorder them later when you have a list with the final shooting schedule. Table 3-3 shows the same candidate table as in Table 3-1, but with categories added.

Table 3-3.   *Sample Candidate Table with Categories*

No.	Name	Client reference	Characters	Categories	Description
1	SO-02	Pg. 1-3	Stan, Ollie	Split shot Sitting setup Skiing rig	Ollie is sitting in the dune buggy, driving recklessly. Stan is being pulled and is skiing behind it. Camera is in front of car.
2	SO -04	Pg. 2-1	Stan	Rejected	Stan hits a dune and flies in the air, losing control. Camera follows from the side.
3	SO-08	Pg. 4-2	Stan, Ollie	Multiple Sitting setup	Stan and Ollie sit comfortably in car, enjoying their drink. Camera is in front of car.

You are now finished with the evaluation process, and much of the work you've done will prove very valuable at the collection and character-mapping stages. I'm sure you've also managed to reject some shots that you didn't consider as problematic to begin with. You should have rejected all shots that didn't meet the system's maximum capture volume, shots that had more characters than is possible to collect per shot and that were not feasible for splitting, shots with many interactions that affect limbs and body, and other shots that would have required too much human manipulation later. Now you can start planning your motion capture session.

PREPARING FOR THE SESSION

You have successfully prepared a list of shots that will be performed at the motion capture stage and are getting ready to schedule your session. Whether you have an in-house system or are hiring a service provider, some preparations are still needed. You need to find a good performer, organize all your props and rigs, order all your shots as efficiently as possible and, if necessary, come up with marker configurations that will fit your character's setup.

Using an External Motion Capture Service Provider

There are several service companies in the field of data collection. Some specialize in the entertainment business, and others in areas such as sports analysis, forensic science, or biomechanics. Obviously, you would prefer to deal with a studio that has some animation experience, especially in the field that will correspond to your project, whether it is a video game or a film effect shot. Also, you want them to have the kind of system that you think is best suited for your application, plus a capture volume greater or equal than your maximum required volume. You would like them to be as close as possible to these criteria. In Appendix B, I have listed the primary service providers, the type of equipment they use, their specialty, the value-added services offered, and their supported animation and motion capture data formats. Most studios will provide you with sample data in the format you need. Some will even capture a free test if your project is large enough.

Find out if the studio can provide the data already mapped to your character model using your preferred software package, and if so, figure out to what level. Simply applying data to a character is very different from applying data plus solving all interactions and size problems. Applying data takes just a second once the character setup is in place, but all the extra tweaking that will be needed can take a long time. Make sure they have the qualified technical directors required to do this job. If you decide to have the service bureau do this work for you, you will need to provide them with all your models, including props.

A state-of-the-art motion capture studio should have the ability to deliver SMPTE time code in motion data and synchronized video and movie files. This is a new feature in the most advanced motion capture systems, such as the Vicon 8 optical system.

Some studios can provide other value-added services. At TSi, we used to deal with most of our clients' casting, rigging, prop building, custom programming, and even directing needs, but this was only possible because we also had CG animation and game development departments. This may be too much to ask for a motion capture service bureau that is not part of a bigger operation, as they may not have the volume required to justify all the personnel needed by these services. Nevertheless, if you decide to let the studio provide any of these services, make sure to stay involved so you can get exactly what you want.

When you negotiate a price with the service bureau, make sure you show them as much information as possible to avoid misunderstandings. Have them sign a nondisclosure agreement if necessary, but make sure they know what they're talking about when giving you a quote, especially if it is only an estimate. It is very common for a client to call a motion capture studio and say, "Give me a ballpark figure for 200 moves for a polygonal shooter." Based on their experience with these kind of game projects, the studio may give you an estimate that could be close but could also be totally off. After doing dozens of these types of games, I've learned that there's nothing standard about doing game character's motions. They no longer involve just walk and shoot cycles, but very complex movements that designers introduce to make their games different from the rest. Sports games are no exception, and some get extremely complicated.

If your capture project is for a linear animation, you will probably require more services from the studio because these types of projects tend to have more time, and revisions are very usual. In addition to your main studio session, try to allow your budget to cover an extra maintenance date, because you will probably have to modify your animation. It is always better to collect the performance again than to modify captured motion data.

When the data collected is to be used on a nonlinear project with a long development schedule, it is wise to break the capture schedule into two separate sessions. That way, you can correct errors from the first session that will become known only after data was applied to the character models.

Different service bureaus have different billing practices. Some studios charge for the day, and the price includes studio and data. Others charge a bulk rate per project; still others charge a fee for stage time plus post-process operator hours, but give you an estimate before the session. I prefer the method of charging an hourly fee for the stage, plus a fixed rate by the finished second of data. As a client, you thus know exactly what you will pay, and it is fair to the studio because they will set the fee per second based on the type and complexity of the project.

Paying a bulk rate is also fine, but because it can be risky for the studio, it usually is higher than other billing plans. The daily charge is usually reserved for real-time systems, where you can walk out with your data when the session is over.

The worst type of billing, in my opinion, is by operator post-process hour. Even if you get an estimate at the beginning, it doesn't mean the studio is obligated to charge that amount, and, believe me, it will almost never be less than the estimate. Try to avoid this system at all cost if you don't want to be horrified at invoice time. This type of billing puts you at the mercy of the studio, and, even assuming that everybody is honest in this world, you want to know in advance what you will be paying for a service. In addition, the studio may give you a low estimate to ensure you will come there for business. When TSi opened its motion capture studio, there was maybe one other optical motion capture service bureau around, and the norm was to charge by the operator hour. We had so many problems explaining to the clients why the final charges were different from the estimate that we finally decided to start charging by the finished second, and very soon other companies followed suit. Leave hourly billing to the attorneys.

Prices for optical data per second today range anywhere from $20 to $200, but the average is about $45. Stage hourly rates can be as low as $150 per hour and as high as $1,500 per hour, depending of the level of service needed. Prices are more expensive when using a real-time tracking system, but the cost includes the data as well. Value-added service rates don't follow any particular norm. Each studio has its own way of billing for data mapping, casting, rigs, props, and other services.

You don't want to do business with a motion capture service bureau that doesn't deliver the quality of data you expect. A demo session is always recommended, but if you couldn't arrange for one, you should, at a minimum, arrange for the studio to provide you with sample data files in the format or formats that you will be using for your project. Unless your final animation solution is proprietary, the service bureau should be responsible for delivering data compatible with your off-the-shelf animation software. When you inspect the data, make sure it has no imperfections, such as sudden pops and snaps, and that it isn't noisy, but fluid and realistic. Remember, if this is a sample file that the service bureau is distributing to clients, it probably represents the best quality that the studio has ever achieved, not necessarily its average quality, which is why a custom test is always better.

The inspection of the data should first be carried out visually, using a simple object like a stick figure or just a skeleton within your animation program, making sure when you set it up that the data is not being scaled or modified in any way. You should also look at the data itself with the aid of a curve visualization tool, such as the one included with any off-the-shelf animation program. In rotational data files, look for sudden multiple of 90° jumps in rotation angles for any axis. You may think a 360° jump from one frame to the next will not cause any problems because the axis's orientation remains the same, but when you start tweaking the data—especially if you want to blend between motions or reduce the number of keyframes—you will find that it does cause major problems. It also causes problems when assigning vertices to joints for deformations. Some of these jumps are due to a problem called *parametric singularity*, commonly known as *gimbal lock*, in which a rotational degree of freedom is lost due to the alignment of the axes. Other jumps are caused simply by the tracking software as it converts transformation matrices to Euler angles (x, y, z). Any motion capture service bureau should be able to deliver data without these kinds of defects.

Another important item to consider when capturing data that requires post-processing is capacity. Whether or not the studio is able to deliver the data you need in a reasonable time frame has to do with the number of data analysts it employs and the number of other jobs that will be processed during the same period. If this becomes a problem, try to work out a schedule whereby you will receive partial deliveries. Also, arrange to receive your data in all its stages: from the global translation file to the hierarchical rotations file to the file compatible with your animation software. You never know when you will need these files, and it probably doesn't cost the studio any extra money to provide them to you.

Before closing a deal with the service bureau, make sure to reserve the dates needed, and put the agreement on paper. Also, find out about liability insurance. If the studio is not covered for any accidents that may occur at the stage, you will have to arrange coverage for your session.

In summary, these are some of the items you should require from a motion capture service bureau:

- Experience in your particular field
- Desired motion capture equipment
- A capture volume as large as your needs require
- Motion data without noise and other defects such as gimbal locks
- Support for your animation format
- Ability to deliver synchronized video in both tape and digital movie files
- Ability to apply data to characters, including interactions and other improvements
- Other value-added services
- Enough capacity to fit your deadline
- Insurance

Props and Rigs

If your session requires any special prop, now is the time to put it together. When a certain item has a digital counterpart, it can be critical that both match perfectly. In other cases, only a small representation of the actual prop is needed. You should follow the guidelines concerning units of measurement that I discussed previously.

It is a good idea to capture data from props if possible. In an optical stage, this should always be done. If an item is to remain stationary during the capture session, there is no need to collect its data at the same time as the actual performance; the more markers there are, the more post-processing is needed for a shot. A single capture of only the stationary props can be layered with the performance after the fact. You can do this before the actual session in order to make sure everything will match afterward. Having this data will help the digital artists in charge of the scene layout to know exactly where everything is on the stage. All moving props, such as guns, swords, and footballs, should be captured during the performance, but prepared in advance.

Some rigs are simple, such as a rope and a harness, but others are very complex mechanical contraptions that can interfere with a motion capture session either by introducing unwanted interference or by occluding reflecting markers. Make sure this won't happen by testing the rig at the stage. Familiarize yourself with it before designing the marker setup, as you may have to place markers on the rig as opposed to the performer.

Talent

Performance animation is so named because the animation emanates from a performance, but the importance of the actual performance is often underestimated. If one has to produce a filmed project, you usually search for good acting talent. Likewise, if one puts together an animated cartoon, you'd want to have trained animators working on the characters. For some reason, when the two are combined, people just don't believe such experience is needed. This may be true if you are dealing with a video game that will play back at four frames per second, but for any other kind of performance animation project, talent is as important as any other artistic source, whether it is acting, animating, painting, singing, or sculpting.

This train of thought started because a few years ago, the final animation of a character created by performance animation was very different from the actual performance. Today this still happens in some cases, but we already have the tools to create exact replicas of the realistic motion, which makes the performer all the more important.

Take your time finding the right talent for your project. Do not simply decide to use your lead programmer just because you want to get some bang for your payroll buck, or your level designer because he had some martial arts training when he was a child. Performance is the source of the art in performance animation, and as such, it should not be the place to cut corners.

Match the right project with the right type of performer. If your project is a football video game, use football players; for a fighting game, use martial artists. If you have to collect the performance of a particular celebrity, try to use that celebrity. Stunt people are very good if you are doing rough motions, but you shouldn't use them as they do in film, only for dangerous shots. For each character you must use the same performer throughout the project in order to avoid multiple character setups.

It is always best to modify the character model to approximate the proportions of the performer, but many times this is not possible, so you must try to find talent that matches as close as possible. Take all measurements from the people you are considering and compare their proportions to the model's. It will save time later in the process.

The best way to find talent is to prepare a test audition, where you will have a few applicants perform certain motions that will best represent the content of the project, perhaps involving the required props and rigging. Make a short list of the best ones and, if possible, schedule a second session in which you will capture their performance. The data by itself reveals more subtleties that are not obvious when looking at the live performance, like small idiosyncrasies particular to specific people that would not be acceptable for your digital character. Try looking at the data without knowing who the performer is, and you will probably make the best choice. If you are using a motion capture service bureau, this step may seem like overkill, but you could combine it with the test session and kill two birds with one stone. You may also think that it is a big waste of your time to put markers on each of the applicants, but the fact is that the performance will suffer if the talent doesn't feel comfortable dressed in black leotards or carrying a heavy tethered contraption, so a dress rehearsal is in order. When hiring a performer, make sure he or she will be available for follow-up sessions. Also keep in mind that one performer can play many parts if necessary.

Other issues that are important relate to insurance, union requirements, rights over the performance, and other contractual questions. I never had to deal with some of these, especially unions, because the medium was pretty new at the time, but today at least the Screen Actors Guild (SAG) has established guidelines for its members' participation in digital performances. The ownership of the captured data remains a gray area. The norm still in force today is that the owner of the data is whoever pays for the session; however, this assumption is bound to be questioned sooner rather than later, as performers acquire more practical understanding of the medium. In the near future, the use of a performance will probably be equated with the use of a person's likeness. Granted that a performance may not be as descriptive of a person as a photograph or a painting would, but when the performer's movements are widely known it could be, as is the case with world-known celebrities such as Marcel Marceau or Michael Jackson.

A performer with motion capture experience is also very desirable. There are special issues that a performer must understand when at the motion capture stage. In any situation, the talent must look at the stage in terms of the animation space, knowing where the origin is and being able to move within the boundaries of the capture area. These restrictions are not common to other media and sometimes present difficulty to the inexperienced performer. Previous experience also helps in the capture of motions that are intended to be blended together. The performer must be good at starting and ending his or her performance in a predetermined pose.

If your talent happens to be a celebrity, spend some time explaining to him or her how things work at a motion capture shoot. The performer has to be willing to abide by the guidelines or no good data will be collected. Sometimes bringing in a director that the celebrity can trust is a lifesaving move. If the director is well educated in the motion capture procedures, everything should go smoothly, so invest some of your time to make sure of that. When working with a celebrity, you almost never get rehearsal time, but try to push for it.

Designing the Marker Positions

If you are using an optical system, chances are you can define the marker locations. You should take advantage of that, especially if you have a preliminary character setup design.

At TSi, we had a default human marker setup that basically covered all the main bone groups. Most of our clients' projects were covered by this configuration, especially the real-time video game projects. For those projects we almost always captured more data than needed, because the client usually did not have a preliminary character setup design; however, this situation also sometimes caused us to capture less data than needed. Clients always thought that we were responsible for obtaining all the information that their particular project would require. As soon as we realized that, we started querying them about their projects. The point is that you need the marker configuration to be as efficient as possible for the capture session, but by the same token, it should enable you to collect all the data that your character setup will require. That is why I recommend a character setup design in advance.

A default marker setup is a great starting point because it will cover major joints, and you can add and remove from it as needed. Figure 3-6 shows a default marker setup for an optical system. As opposed to an external device that collects rotational values, such as an electromechanical suit, an optical system captures translational data for individual points. The advantage is that you can calculate internal joint rotations by grouping specific markers. The default optical marker setup should be able to capture all internal rotations of the major joints, including at least four sections of the spine (see Figure 3-7).

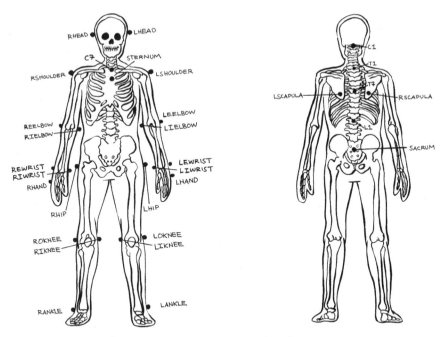

Figure 3-6. *Default optical marker setup.*

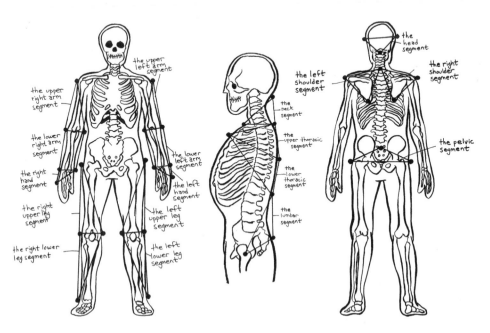

Figure 3-7. *Major bone groups covered by the default marker configuration.*

To collect all the needed information for each of these moving segments, you need to add enough markers to form a triangle. The markers need to be placed in locations where the skin is close to the bone, because the more tissue and fat between the marker and the bone, the more distortion of the initial triangle is induced. The size of the triangle can be unified for all frames as a post-process, but the less modification is applied to the data, the better the result will look.

The default marker setup allows for the collection of all possible motions of the rigid segments composed of the pelvis, vertebral column (in four separate segments, including the neck), head, left and right shoulder, upper arm, lower arm, hand, upper and lower leg, and foot (in two segments). Although they share markers, I will cover each of these segments separately after describing the terminology of motion.

Terminology of Motion

There are six degrees of freedom, or possible movements, available in whole or in part to any given joint. In biomechanical terms, these movements are called flexion, extension, abduction, adduction, medial or internal rotation, and lateral or external rotation.

Flexion is the motion of bending between two adjacent segments that decreases the angle between them, whereas *extension* is the opposite or reverse bend, whereby the segments return to their initial position. Examples of flexion and extension are shown in Figure 3-8. In all the character setups that I describe, flexions and extensions are represented by the X-axis.

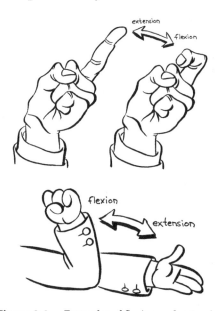

Figure 3-8.   *Examples of flexion and extension.*

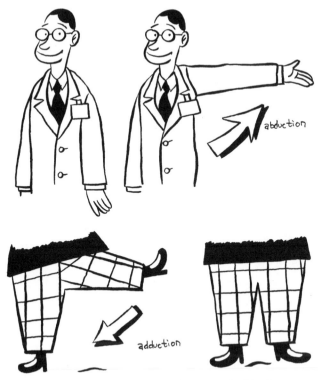

Figure 3-9.   *Examples of abduction and adduction.*

The next pair of movements, abduction and adduction, pertain to the Z-axis of character setups. *Abduction* is the movement away from the center of the segment, such as a leg rotating toward the outside of the body; *adduction* is the returning motion. Figure 3-9 illustrates typical abductions and adductions.

The last group of motions are the rotations along the axis that travels through the segment (see Figure 3-10). These are normally called *medial* (or *internal*) and *lateral* (or *external*), depending on whether the rotation is taking the segment and its children closer or further away from the body, respectively. They are also known as *twists*. The body and head rotations are called *left* and *right rotations.* The Y-axis represents these rotations in character setups.

Pelvis

If you trace a straight line from the center of the skull, passing through the center of the atlas down to the ankle joint, and you traverse it with a line going through the center of the sacrum, the intersection point will be close to the human body's center of gravity (Figure 3-11). This point is very important for any character setup, especially when using a hierarchical chain of nodes, because it will be the

Figure 3-10.   *Examples of rotations.*

parent of the body-based node chain. As such, it will hold the global translational data for the body.

Figure 3-12 shows the triangle that depicts the motion of the pelvis, which is formed by the markers LHIP, RHIP, and SACRUM. Both LHIP and RHIP are placed along the sides at the same height as the head of the femur. The SACRUM marker is located in the back around the middle of the sacrum.

Vertebral Column

The human vertebral column is formed by 24 vertebrae that make up its three divisions: lumbar spine, thoracic spine, and cervical spine. The lumbar spine is the lowest segment, consisting of vertebrae L1 through L5, which are similar in shape and motion characteristics (Figure 3-13). Left or right rotation is not easy for the lumbar spine vertebrae, but all other movements are common. The whole lumbar segment can be labeled as one rigid motion segment defined by markers LHIP, SACRUM, and L1. The L1 marker, as its name indicates, should be placed in the back of the L1 vertebra. Other combinations of markers can be used, but the one I describe here will work fine.

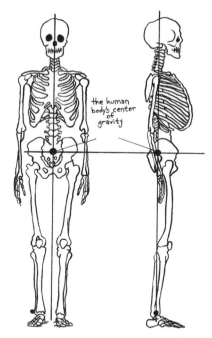

Figure 3-11. *Human body's center of gravity.*

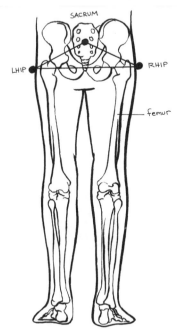

Figure 3-12. *The triangle that depicts the motion of the pelvis.*

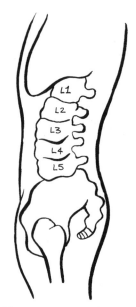

Figure 3-13. *Lumbar spine.*

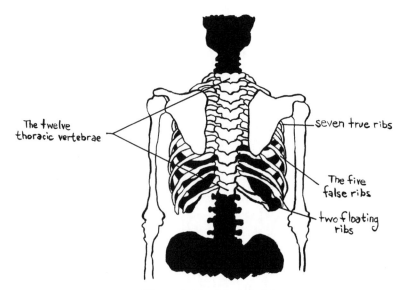

Figure 3-14. *Thoracic spine.*

The thoracic spine contains 12 vertebrae, T1 through T12. I divide this part of the column into two motion segments called the lower and upper thorax, based on their motion characteristics (see Figure 3-14). The vertebrae in the lower thorax (T8–T12) have much more mobility than the ones in the upper thorax (T1–T7),

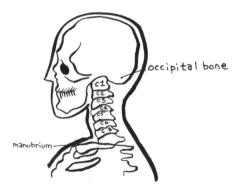

Figure 3-15. *The neck.*

because the latter have the first seven ribs attached to them. These ribs are called *true ribs* and are connected directly to the sternum, which constrains their motion. The next three ribs are called *false ribs* and are attached to the front part of rib 7 instead of to the sternum. The last two ribs are called *floating ribs* and are not attached to the anterior or front side at all. Even though the thoracic spine could be divided into three motion groups based on its motion characteristics, I will only divide it into two segments. This division is based on the fact that only two vertebrae compose the smallest segment, so the lower thoracic segment will be formed by the vertebrae that hold the false and floating ribs.

The lower thoracic segment is calculated by the combination of markers L1, STERNUM, and T7; the upper thorax is determined by T7, STERNUM, and T1. The STERNUM marker should be placed at the bottom of the sternum, whereas T7 and L1 should be located behind their respective vertebrae.

The final segment pertaining to the vertebral column is the neck (Figure 3-15). It is formed by vertebrae C1 through C7, which have increased mobility over the lumbar and thoracic vertebrae, and will be represented by markers T1, C1, and C7. Marker C7 should be placed on the anterior side, at the height of the manubrium. C1 should be located at the bottom of the occipital. Figure 3-16 shows the entire vertebral column and its four motion segments.

Head

The motion of the skull is easy to collect because it is rigid and has almost no tissue. I use markers C1, RHEAD, and LHEAD. The two latter markers can be placed on a cap and, if preferred, can be located in front and back instead of side by side. Figure 3-17 shows the triangle that represents head motion.

Shoulder

The shoulder is one of the most difficult segments to capture accurately. It is formed by a combination of three joints: the *glenohumeral joint* between the

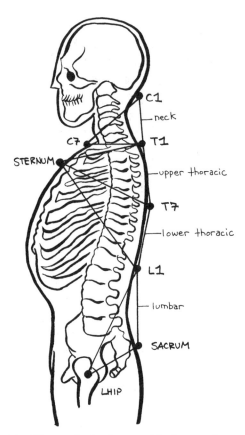

Figure 3-16.   *The vertebral column and its four motion segments.*

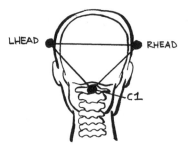

Figure 3-17.   *The head motion triangle.*

humerus and the scapula, the *acromioclavicular joint* between the distal clavicle and the acromion, and the *sternoclavicular joint* between the medial clavicle and the manubrium (see Figure 3-18).

The sternoclavicular and acromioclavicular joints are driven by the motion of the scapula, which adds range to the movements that the shoulder can do, along

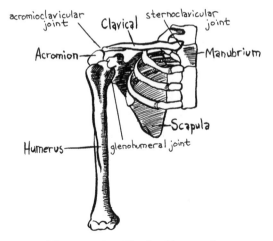

Figure 3-18. *The shoulder complex.*

with the glenohumeral joint. The shoulder motions can be captured using the C7 marker along with the LSHOULDER and LSCAPULA or RSHOULDER and RSCAPULA markers, depending on the side. Each SHOULDER marker should be placed just above its respective acromion, trying to keep it unaffected by the glenohumeral joint's motion. Each SCAPULA marker should be positioned on the posterior side at the bottom of its respective scapula. Unfortunately, scapular motion is very difficult to collect because the scapula slides under the skin, so post-processing is always required. Most software included with optical motion capture equipment does not deal with this type of problem, so I recommend correcting it before converting the data into hierarchical rotational format. Of course, the most widely used solution is to ignore the problem; that may work in some cases, but in others it results in nonrealistic shoulder motions.

Figure 3-19 depicts the triangles that represent the shoulder segments.

Upper Arm

The humerus is the bone that supports the upper arm. It starts at the glenohumeral joint and has the capability of flexion, extension, abduction, adduction, and lateral and medial rotations. You need a triangle to define the motion of this important segment (see Figure 3-20). The first vertex is represented by the already known SHOULDER marker, while the other two are represented by IELBOW and EELBOW. These two markers should be placed at the elbow, over the medial epicondyle and lateral epicondyle, respectively. The IELBOW marker in some cases may be occluded from the cameras. In such a case, it would be acceptable to place an additional marker somewhere else on the upper arm—perhaps along the lateral humerus, where muscle action is not too apparent, unlike over the biceps or triceps.

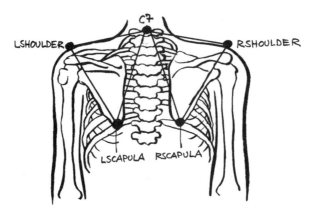

Figure 3-19.   *The triangles representing the shoulder segments.*

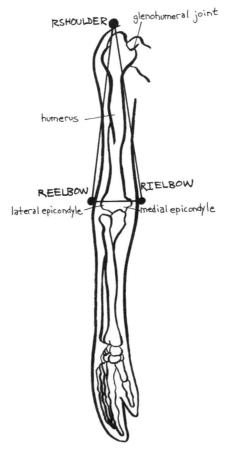

Figure 3-20.   *The upper arm segment.*

Lower Arm

The forearm is formed by the radius and ulna, and is linked to the humerus by the elbow joint, which is restricted to flexion and extension. It is easy to confuse the motion characteristics of this joint because as we see the rotation of the hand, we think we are rotating the elbow, or even the shoulder, but in reality we are crossing the radius over the ulna. This motion is called *pronation*, whereas the reverse motion in which the radius and ulna return to their parallel location is called *supination* (Figure 3-21)

Understanding the arm mechanics is key to the realistic setup of a humanoid character. Most marker setups that I've seen in the past do not take into account all of the arm's underlying structure, and they create data that assumes the whole arm to be formed by two segments that share lateral and medial rotations, while the wrist has its own. When the final character is set up for deformation, therefore, one usually sees horrible abnormalities along the shoulder and wrist areas that need to be dealt with.

The forearm's motion will not be represented by a triangle, because at least four points are needed to catalog its complexity. The lower arm quadrangle is defined

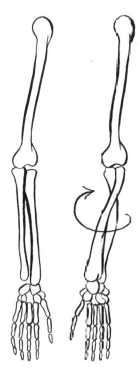

Figure 3-21. *Pronation and supination.*

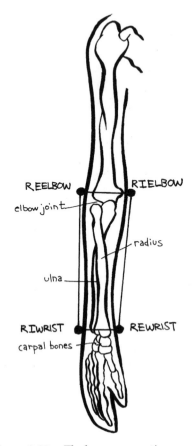

Figure 3-22. *The lower arm motion segment.*

by IELBOW, EELBOW, IWRIST, and EWRIST (see Figure 3-22). The IWRIST marker should be placed at the bottom of the ulna, and the EWRIST marker should be located at the bottom of the radius. It is also possible, if it suits the particular performance, to place these markers between the radius and ulna, at the anterior and posterior side of the lower forearm. The idea is to place them as close to the hand as possible without affecting them by hand movements, so they should be located above the carpal bones.

Hand

The hand is usually captured as a whole segment when using a body capture system, but a bend-sensing glove, such as the Cyberglove, can be used simultaneously. If this is done, a parallel and synchronized stream of information will be

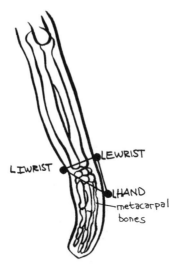

Figure 3-23. *The hand motion segment.*

collected and must be merged after the fact. For optical capture of the rigid hand segment, you can use both wrist markers (IWRIST and EWRIST) plus the HAND marker, located above the metacarpals. The use of both wrist markers will ensure that the elbow rotations stay where they belong. Figure 3-23 shows the hand motion segment.

Upper Leg

The hip joint is capable of flexion, extension, abduction, adduction, and both medial and lateral rotations, but it is not possible to capture its exact pivot point location because it is located internally. Its position can be adjusted in post-processing. Use the HIP, EKNEE, and IKNEE markers to create the segment triangle, as shown in Figure 3-24. Both knee markers should be placed on the lower end of the femur, over the lateral and medial condyles. If the motion does not permit having two markers on each side of the knee joint, one of them can be moved to the mid-femur area, but doing so will require more fine-tuning after the fact.

Lower Leg

The lower leg segment is based on the movements of the knee, which is capable of flexion and extension primarily, but can also rotate a few degrees in lateral and medial directions. Most of the rotational movements, though, are based on the hip rotations and abduction and adduction of the foot. To capture the motion segment

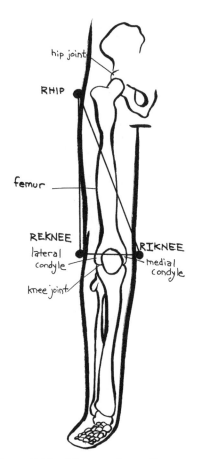

Figure 3-24.   *The upper leg motion segment.*

of the lower leg, use EKNEE, IKNEE, and ANKLE, which should be placed over the lateral malleolus (see Figure 3-25). If one of the knee markers is not present, you can place another marker in the mid-frontal area of the lower leg, where the tibia is closest to the skin.

Foot

The foot has a very large number of joints — 31, to be precise. Most marker setups consider the foot as one single motion segment, but I believe that a minimum of two segments is acceptable for most projects. It is best to wear hard shoes if possible when capturing the foot, since all its complicated mechanism is filtered into two segments that can be captured by an optical system.

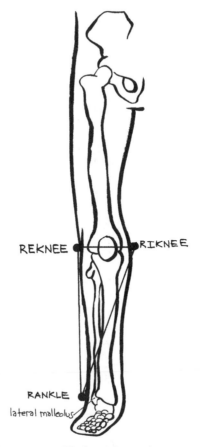

Figure 3-25. *The lower leg motion segment.*

We cannot break the foot in exactly two segments based on its mechanical structure, but I will assume that the first segment starts at the ankle joint and ends somewhere along the metatarsals. The reason for this division line is that the rotation of the second segment is a combination of many joints, including the tarsometatarsal, metatarsophalangeal, and interphalangeal. The first segment is defined by ANKLE, HEEL, and FOOT. HEEL should be placed in the back of the shoe, as low as possible, because this marker will be used to define where the floor is for this segment. FOOT should be located where the shoe bends when the foot is in flexion.

The second segment is assumed to be strictly capable of flexion and extension, so only a line is required, formed by FOOT and TOE. TOE should be placed in the front of the shoe, as close to the floor as possible, because it will define the location of the floor for this segment. Figure 3-26 shows the foot segments.

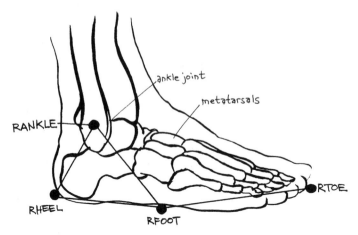

Figure 3-26.   *The foot motion segments.*

Capture Schedule

You have prepared a candidate table, which you have sorted in different ways according to categories. You have hired the talent, built the props, looked at the rigs, and know how many different characters and configurations you have to deal with. Each shot has a detailed blueprint as well. It is time to put together the capture schedule.

You will now use some of those categories you created earlier, since you will build the schedule using the category constants and variables. A *constant* is something you cannot change in the time it has been scheduled, such as the availability of a performer. *Variables* are the categories you can schedule any time you want. The category types that are important for scheduling a session are the ones that have to do with volume, characters, interaction, props and rigs, and character setup. The latter category, character setup, is used indirectly, as each character setup will translate into one or more marker setups. The categories based on blending are used during the session and data application, and the ones based on delivery priority are used during post-processing.

You can use different scheduling methods depending on the size of your project. At TSi, we generally used Microsoft Project. There are analytical methods that can produce a mathematically optimal result, but unless the project is extremely complicated, such a solution would be overkill. Choosing a solution has more to do with the number of categories than with the number of shots, because each category creates either a new marker setup or a new stage configuration, and the idea is to minimize the number of times you reconfigure the stage and the marker setup. You could have a job for which you need to capture 500 shots, but if it involves no props, no interactions, no rigs, and only one character, it becomes a very simple scheduling problem.

The best way to illustrate the scheduling task is by using a low-tech model established by film production, where the shooting calendar is created by using a production board such as the one shown in Figure 3-27. I like this approach because it helps visualize the overall production timetable. The talent, character name, and marker setup are listed horizontally on the right side of the board, whereas the shots with their stage configuration are shown vertically. You can rearrange the shots because they are listed on moveable strips and color coded by stage configuration. Gaps between shot groups indicate days or half-days. This method is better illustrated by a simple example.

Suppose you have scheduled two days of motion capture at an optical studio. The whole project calls for three different camera configurations based on volume, plus there are two different characters, Stan and Ollie, performed by different actors. Stan has two shots in which he's wearing a harness and two in which he's interacting with a surfboard, so you will have different marker configurations for those groups of shots. Also, there are two shots in which two characters appear together, and you have decided to have them perform simultaneously.

You already know that your shots have the following marker setups:

Stan shots with harness:	2
Stan shots without harness:	8
Stan holding surfboard:	2
Ollie shots:	4
Multiple shots:	2
Total shots:	18

Notice that you have five different marker configurations. A marker configuration is defined by every time there is even a minor difference in the marker setup, such as a different character, a character and an interactor or prop, multiple characters, and so forth.

You will fill out a moveable strip with each shot's information. The strips are color coded by stage configuration, so you'll have three colors to work with. An example of a production board with the information already transferred is shown in Figure 3-28; you can see the two capture sessions divided by a black gap. The strips have been placed in a way such that stage configuration takes precedence over other variables, such as talent availability, but if we had restrictions or constants, we could easily reorganize the board to reflect them. All shots with the volume 1 configuration and most with volume 2 will be captured on the first day, finishing with all shots requiring a rig and harness. The second day, the remaining

Shot:		
Client reference:		
Estimated prod. time (minutes):		
Samples per second:		
Title:		
Director:		
Client:		
Character	Setup	Talent

Figure 3-27.   *Production board.*

Shot:	0S02	0S03	0S07	0S08	0S09	0S18	0S01	0S05	0S06	0S10	0S12	0S13	0S15	0S04	0S11	0S14	0S16	0S17
Client reference:	S23	S32	S12	S09	S65	S37	S21	S98	S42	S45	S98	S04	S73	S11	S43	S19	S06	S91
Estimated prod. time (minutes):	30	30	30	30	30	30	30	30	60	60	30	45	45	30	30	45	45	30
Collection samples per second:	120	120	240	120	120	120	120	120	120	120	120	240	120	120	120	120	120	120
Title: Stan & Ollie go surfing	VOLUME 1	VOLUME 1	VOLUME 1	VOLUME 1	VOLUME 1	VOLUME 1	VOLUME 2	VOLUME 2	VOLUME 2	VOLUME 2	VOLUME 2	VOLUME 2	VOLUME 2	VOLUME 3	VOLUME 3	VOLUME 3	VOLUME 3	VOLUME 3

Director: John Director

Client: Peter Client

Character	Setup	Talent	0S02	0S03	0S07	0S08	0S09	0S18	0S01	0S05	0S06	0S10	0S12	0S13	0S15	0S04	0S11	0S14	0S16	0S17
Stan	Normal	Paul Talent	X	X	X	X	X			X								X	X	
Stan	Harness	Paul Talent									X	X								
Stan	Surf-board	Paul Talent																	X	X
Stan, Ollie	Mul-tiple	Paul & Tom												X	X					
Ollie	Normal	Tom Talent				X	X	X												X

Figure 3-28. *Production board with values filled in.*

shots with volume 2 configuration will be shot first. These happen to be the two multiple shots. Then, all volume 3 shots are captured, starting with Stan's shots (including his surfboard ones) and finishing with the last Ollie shot.

The drawback to this schedule is that both actors have to be available for both sessions, but in this case, it is more cost-effective to configure the stage only three times and have the talent come back. If there had been any talent restrictions, we would have had to rearrange the stage a few more times to accommodate.

Rehearsals

The importance of rehearsing can be easily underestimated, because producers sometimes think that the cost of having a performer show up in advance to get familiarized with the motions is higher than the cost of the extra time at the stage. Even if the stage is in-house, this may not be true, as it takes at least two extra people to operate whatever motion capture device is being used, but this is not the only reason.

Provide the talent with the script and all the blueprints in advance and have a preproduction meeting at which you discuss the character and all the motions. Listen to all the performer's concerns and comments about every shot and make sure he or she understands exactly what is expected from the technical and aesthetic standpoints. The talent must know all there is to know about the character.

You want the motions to be rehearsed and learned by the performer in a comfortable environment, that is, without the constricting markers, sensors, or potentiometers that are common to all systems. This practice is consistent with other media, such as theater, where a rehearsal in costume is not done until all the lines and scenes are well learned by everybody. The idea is to get the talent very familiar with the part first; once that is achieved, get him or her familiar with the costume.

Another reason why it is a good idea to rehearse in advance is that the talent may not be capable of performing the motions required. Even though you had casting sessions and the performer you chose looked extremely qualified, it is always possible that some of the motions might be too complex for that particular performer. If you rehearse, you will have time to recast your session.

Finally, make the performer rehearse wearing the motion capture gear, because it will add an extra level of discomfort that you must ensure the performer can handle. Even if the data is to be captured with an optical system, the talent could feel confined by the markers or the black tights.

DURING THE SESSION

If everything was planned as previously described, the actual session should flow very smoothly. You will start with an efficient list of shots, a very clear understanding of each one, well-rehearsed performers, and predefined marker setups. If the preparation was done correctly, there's no need to have everybody involved in the project supervising the session, because they have already given their input as the project evolved. The session is not the right time for changes in the setups, script, or shots.

The people handling the session should consist of a director, a technical supervisor, the motion capture staff, the talent, riggers, choreographers or related motion experts, and additional support personnel. I don't mean to exclude other people associated with the project: They can be present as long as they are not involved, although a big crowd of onlookers is never appropriate. A clear chain of command, headed by the director, is necessary. I've often seen chaos erupt because of lack of planning and excess of opinions, which usually results in unusable data—not because it is unreadable, but because it is either the wrong performance or the wrong setup. It is best to leave changes to the follow-up session, the one that I suggested be scheduled for any corrections and problems that may arise.

Bring at least one camera to the stage in order to shoot each take from a favorable angle. If the project is linear, try to use an angle similar to the final rendering. A monitor should be hooked up to the camera to allow the director to look at the framing and help in the blending and looping of shots.

A clapper like the kind used for motion picture shooting is essential; otherwise, you won't be able to distinguish the data from the video reference. Make sure you write in the clapper all the pertinent information, such as shot name, take number, file name, project name, character name, director name, and date, even if the video is synchronized with the captured data.

When dealing with stationary props that need to match with digital props, make sure to capture at least one file of only the props with enough markers to make out all of their dimensions. After this data is captured, there is no need to place markers on these props again, provided they remain in the same position throughout the session.

Sometimes it is better to collect a motion at a very high sampling rate, especially if the motion is very fast, because it helps if you need to do post-tracking (as you would with an optical system). The markers are closer frame after frame, which aids the software to find the continuity a lot better. Many motion capture operators believe that a higher capture sampling rate increases the post-process work, but that is not the case if the cameras operate at the same resolution at the high and low sampling rates.

Try to use a capture frame rate that is divisible by the final frame rate for the project. For example, if you will ultimately need 24 frames per second, don't collect data at 30 or 60; instead, use 48, 96, or any other multiple of 24 if possible. If your equipment is only capable of multiples of 30, then use a higher sampling rate so there will be more data available for a cleaner down-sampling.

Figure 3-29.   *Character in a neutral pose.*

The Base Position

When you model a character, you choose a neutral pose that is appropriate for the kind of deformations the model will go through. When the character is humanoid, a good neutral pose is standing up with arms about 45° apart from the body, palms facing in, and legs apart about 30°, as shown in Figure 3-29. Only if the character's performance will be in a predetermined position throughout the project would you want to model it in a nonneutral pose. If your character will be sitting in all shots, for example, you might as well model a sitting character, since you can come up with good deformations while modeling.

The base position in motion capture serves a similar purpose. When setting up the character, you need a neutral pose with which to begin—a pose that will match your modeled character's neutral position. It is also a definition of the character's initial set of coordinate systems, which I describe later.

The modeling of the character should ideally happen after the base position has been captured, but this rarely happens. Also, it is preferable to model a character using the performer's proportions, but this is sometimes impossible as well. If you have modeled the character in advance, it is necessary to capture a matching base position by measuring the angle of rotation of limbs and helping the performer adopt that stance.

Since all you need is one frame of matching data, the capture of the base position can include motion. As you set up the character you can pick the closest frame to the model. Pose the performer's legs at the right angle of separation, and make sure the back is straight. Have the performer rotate his or her arms from a position close to the body to a total extension pose, making sure the palms are pointing in the right direction and that the arms are aligned with the body. That will most likely yield a frame that matches the arm rotations. Also, make sure the performer is facing the right axis, whether it is negative Z or anything else, so that the collected data is facing you when looking at the front orthogonal view of your animation software. Finally, make sure the performer is standing at the origin.

When capturing a base position, place an extra marker on the floor. It could be at the front, back, or any side, as long as you remember where it is and you always do it the same way. This marker will tell you where the front and back of the data are.

Depending on the file format you will use for your final product, the base position may or may not be a pose of your character's skeleton in which all the joints have a transformation value of zero. I cover this in the next chapter when I talk about file formats.

Directing the Motion Capture Session

Directing a motion capture session is very similar to directing live action. A film director runs the acted performance and, at the same time, controls the technical aspects of the shoot, such as the camera roll and sound. The motion capture director controls the performance as well as the video shooting and the collection of the data. Directing motion capture includes more technical elements that apply exclusively to this type of performance, such as interactions, blending, loops, and nonlinear action in general, plus all the constraints of the virtual space in which the action takes place. A director must have a very clear vision of the performer's motion as filtered into the final character, and must enforce the character's limitations on the performer.

Capturing motion for crowds in the background of a scene is very different from capturing the lead character, so if the shots to be captured are very important to the project, it is advisable that the director of the project be the one directing the session. In feature film, a second-unit director is responsible for running certain less important shots that the director cannot or will not direct, but he or she needs to know exactly what the director is looking for. As the director of the motion capture session, you need to be totally involved and aware of what the project is about.

The first thing you must do as director is to brief the crew, talent, and visitors about what is about to happen and what is not acceptable for them to do while the session is going on. You don't want anybody leaning on a camera stand if you are using an optical system, since this will disturb the calibration and make all the data unusable. Also, people must know not to bring bright objects to an optical stage, or certain metallic objects to an electromagnetic capture session. Make sure people stay within certain boundaries that will not distract you or the talent from the actual performance.

Time should be spent making the talent comfortable and trying to convey what the shot calls for. A well-trained performer is not necessarily used to acting in black tights with white dots or outfitted with sensors and a mechanical suit, and self-consciousness will hurt the performance. You can avoid this by establishing a rapport with the talent, inducing trust while maintaining authority, especially if the talent is a celebrity.

The pace of the session should be as slow as required. Rushing through the moves often doesn't result in good takes. You should look at the taped reference after every good shot to make sure it is a potential final shot; take notes that will allow you to decide this during or after the session. For safety, always capture more than one potential hero shot, as the data could have technical problems.

The monitor attached to the camera can be used to make sure that the blending and looping start and end poses are met. An experienced film director is already familiar with the concept of continuity, which in the case of motion capture can be taken to the extreme. As in film, you should draw or tape marks on the floor and the monitor's screen that will allow the matching of moves. It is possible to use more than one camera/monitor combination if the blending is very complicated. The higher the frame rate of the final medium, the more exact the blending must be at capture time.

When directing a session as captured by optical equipment, you must use the motion capture blueprint to make sure all the interactions are performed with minimum occlusion of markers, and you must make sure no markers are missing during a shot. If the performer needs to interact with nonmarked people on stage, those persons must be careful not to occlude or disturb any markers; however, ultimate responsibility always lies with the director. The technical supervisor should act as an advisor to the director in these and other technical matters.

On one occasion I was asked to provide motion capture services for the opening of a well-known television sitcom. The performer was to be a famous actor, the star of the show. I asked the client for storyboards, but they declined to provide them, saying that they had to be kept confidential. They did describe very roughly what the project would entail and said that it would consist of five or six shots, most of them very simple, except for one in which the actor would have to sit on a chair. They would bring their own director and I wouldn't meet him or the actor until the day of the shoot. You may be asking why I walked into this situation when I should have known better. Well, it wasn't a difficult decision, because we were dealing with a famous star and a high-profile show. Also, it was a paying job and we were looking for those. The risk seemed calculated. On many occasions I had to walk into projects as blindly as in this case, but that is the risk you take when dealing with clients.

A few things went wrong during that session. First, the motions turned out to be much more complicated than expected. The actor had to sit down in a chair, so we had prepared a special chair with a clear back in order to avoid occluding the markers placed on his back. During the shoot, the client decided that a chair would not do, and asked for a couch. To accommodate this new development, we had to add more markers to the actor's front, resulting in a different configuration than the rest of the already collected data. When motion data is delivered, a base position file is included to be used for character setup, and the rest of the data is supposed to be compatible with that file. This change would force the client to have two different character setups, so I decided instead to recompute all the couch data to match the first base position. This was a difficult process and at that time we didn't have an easy way of testing the results, so it took extra work to make it match.

Second, the director was actually a character animator rather than a director, and he had very little knowledge of motion capture issues but wasn't open to many of our suggestions. The performer was a famous actor and had a big attitude about taking direction from an unknown person. We tried to persuade him to do more takes of some shots, especially the one with the couch, but he declined. We customarily use those extra takes as insurance in case the preferred take is not clean. As expected, the couch shot wasn't very clean because we lost many of the markers for a long period of time. Even though we had placed markers in the front, only two cameras could see them when he was sitting, which wasn't enough with the archaic optical system that was the state of the art at the time. We had to work long hours reconstructing some of the motion.

To make a long story short, we managed to finish the job on time, but ended up losing money because of the extra time it took to clean up and recalculate the data. Changing the special chair for a couch is an inconsequential change in a film or television production, but for a motion capture session it meant the difference between profit and loss.

SUMMARY

When deciding whether to use motion capture, you should answer the following questions:

- Do you want realistic-looking motion?
- Is the character human shaped?
- Is the context right?
- If the character is an animal, can a real animal perform the part?
- If enhancements need to be made to the performance, are they reasonably small?

- Will the character require squashing or stretching?
- Will the character require anticipation beyond physical boundaries?
- Will the character require follow-through action beyond physical boundaries?
- Will the character require exaggeration beyond physical boundaries?
- Is it likely that the director will require substantial changes after the capture session?
- Will the shot fit within the available capture volume?
- Will it be possible to capture enough data to feed to an existing character setup?
- Are the interactions affecting the root of the motion?
- Is the number of interactions low enough to make it feasible to use motion capture?
- Will the necessary props interfere with the capture process?
- Will the necessary rigs interfere with the capture process?
- Is it possible to blend the shots together, if necessary, after the capture?
- Is it possible to capture at the necessary sample rate?
- Is it possible to capture the necessary number of performers simultaneously?
- Is it possible to comply with special instructions?

When deciding whether to use motion capture, do *not* make the following assumptions:

- Motion capture will save you money.
- Motion capture will save you time.
- A human can perform a nonhuman character.
- You can do all the shots for a project with motion capture.
- You can do all interactions with motion capture.
- You can fix a bad performance after the fact.
- You can modify timing after the fact.
- A director will accept the captured performance even if he directed it.
- You can produce performance animation without advance planning.

Remember these facts about motion capture:

- Cartoon characters almost never look good if performed.
- If your data is not good, don't fix it: Recapture it.
- Always videotape all captured shots.
- If a move can't be done physically, it can't be captured.

CHAPTER FOUR

The Motion Data

⟡

MOTION DATA TYPES AND FORMATS

Depending on the system you are using, you will have to deal with several different motion data file formats. Real-time systems usually generate a stream of data that can be used directly in the animation software with the help of special plug-ins. Optical systems' data is not generated in real time, so it cannot be streamed into the animation software; instead, it is imported from a data file. Packages such as Softimage, Maya, and 3D Studio Max include converters that allow you to import data files in several file formats, but when performing character setup, it is important to know what data items these files contain. None of these file formats has any information pertaining to the deformation of the character's surfaces; rather, the information pertains to the mechanical aspects of rigid segments. All deformations are specific to the animation software being used.

Optical systems' data files go through a few stages before becoming final. As the data is collected, a video stream file is created for each of the system's cameras, containing the raw images captured. This is termed *raw data*. These files, in combination with a file containing the calibration of the stage, are used to track the three-dimensional data. The second stage is the file generated after tracking, which contains the Cartesian coordinates of each of the markers. The data in this file is called *global translation data*; it represents the position of each marker in reference to the world origin, without including any hierarchy or skeleton definition. I will refer to this type of file as *translational* because it contains no rotations, only translations of independent points in space.

121

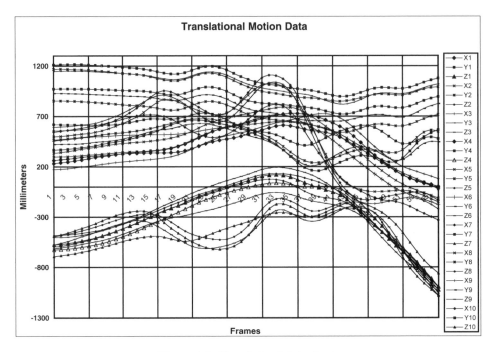

Figure 4-1. *Translational data chart.*

A translational file can be used for performance animation, but there are other levels of simplification, such as files that contain data based on segments or limbs rather than points. Two data types meet this description: the *hierarchical segment translation and rotation* and the *global segment translation and rotation*. Both are based on a definition of a skeleton to be used for driving the motion of the character and are created by combining the points in the translational file. In the hierarchical rotational file, primarily the root point has rotations and translations, and the rest have only initial local translations that define the position and length of each segment, plus a stream of local rotations. The file also contains a set of scale channels that represent the variation in length of each segment. This is necessary because the segments are not exactly rigid, since the markers have to be placed over skin or clothes. The scale channel also helps in the determination of data accuracy. The global rotational file contains translations, rotations, and scale channels for each independent segment; there are no dependencies between the segments.

Rotational files are generally easier to use than translational files because most of the work in setting up a skeleton has already been done for you; however, translational files allow you to create better and more complicated character setups. Experienced users should work mostly with translational data. In addition, because translational files contain no rotations, they are less prone to common problems associated with Euler angle transformations. Figure 4-1 shows a set of curves that represent marker coordinates in a translational file. The data is smooth and does not include any sudden jumps or perturbations.

The primary data file format in use for optical motion capture today is the Acclaim .amc and .asf combination. Other file types available are the Biovision .bva and .bvh files and the Motion Analysis .trc and .htr formats. Many companies have special file formats that fit their particular needs. At TSi, for example, we had the .tsi file, a binary file that was well suited for fast random access, an essential item in video games and data editing tools. Some of the file types mentioned here are rotational and others translational; they're all delimited by tabs. I will later explain each one in detail.

Bringing these files into animation software is not always as easy as it seems. Often the file has to be prepared with certain restrictions, based on the particular program into which it is being imported. The most common restriction has to do with world space. Some animation programs consider *XY* as the front plane, whereas others use *XZ*. Another common difference among off-the-shelf animation software packages is the order of transformations and the order of rotations. Most animation programs have a hard-coded order of transformations. Others have a hard-coded order of rotations, and the data file must be prepared accordingly. It is not enough to change the definitions in the file — the data must be recalculated as well. One more item to consider is the base position: Some programs require their initial skeleton's zero pose to be aligned in a certain way. In addition, the segment scale specified in some files is totally ignored when the data is imported into some animation programs. Other restrictions include naming conventions and units. Translational data is the easiest type to import: Since no hierarchy, rotation, or scale channels are present, most of the restrictions are not applicable. The downside of importing translational data is that the character setup is much more involved; on the other hand, you have better control over what you want to do with the setup.

The Acclaim File Format

The Acclaim file format was developed by Acclaim and Biomechanics for Acclaim's proprietary optical motion capture system. The file format is the most comprehensive of all mainstream formats and is supported by a large majority of commercial animation applications, such as Maya, Alias, Softimage, 3D Studio Max, Nichimen, Prisms, and Houdini. Optical motion capture systems such as the Vicon 8 support the Acclaim format as their primary format.

The format is based on a combination of two files, *Acclaim skeleton format,* or *.asf,* and *Acclaim motion capture,* or *.amc.* The former deals with the definition of a hierarchy of rigid segments, or skeleton, whereas the latter contains the actual data associated with the skeleton. Multiple .amc files can be associated with a single .asf file, which can be beneficial for complicated character setups. Acclaim files can contain translational or rotational data, although rotational is the most commonly used.

The .asf File

The .asf file is much more than just a definition of hierarchy. It contains all the information pertaining to the mechanical function of the skeleton, including units, multipliers, degrees of freedom, limits, and documentation. The only item not included in this file is the data itself, although the file does include the initial pose or base position that is used for character setup. All the data in the associated .amc files is relative to the base position specified.

The .asf file is divided in eight sections identified by the following keywords preceded by a colon: version, name, units, documentation, root, bonedata, hierarchy, and skin, as shown in the following code extract.

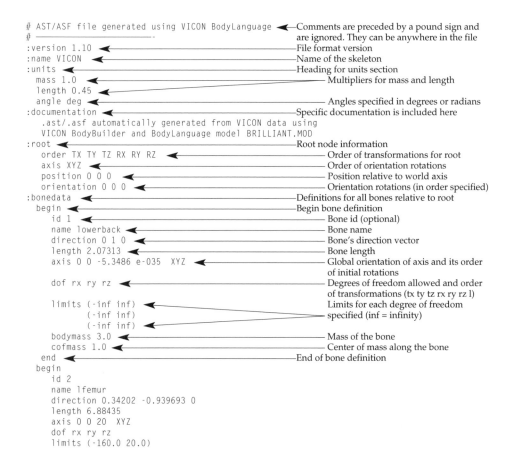

```
            (-70.0 70.0)
            (-60.0 70.0)
    end
    begin
        id 3
        name ltibia
        direction 0.34202 -0.939693 0
        length 7.02085
        axis 0 0 20    XYZ
        dof rx
        limits (-10.0 170.0)
    end
    .
    .
    .
begin
        id 30
        name rthumb
        direction -0.707107 -6.34892e-011 0.707107
        length 1.17742
        axis -90 -45 -2.85299e-015    XYZ
        dof rx rz
        limits (-45.0 45.0)
              (-45.0 45.0)
    end

:hierarchy
    begin
        root lhipjoint rhipjoint lowerback
        lhipjoint lfemur
        lfemur ltibia
        ltibia lfoot
        lfoot ltoes
        rhipjoint rfemur
        rfemur rtibia
        rtibia rfoot
        rfoot rtoes
        lowerback upperback
        upperback thorax
        thorax lowerneck lclavicle rclavicle
        upperneck head
        lclavicle lhumerus
        lhumerus lradius
        lradius lwrist
        lwrist lhand lthumb
        lhand lfingers
        rclavicle rhumerus
        rhumerus rradius
        rradius rwrist
        rwrist rhand rthumb
        rhand rfingers
    end
:skin <filename>
      <filename>
        .
        .
        .
```

Subsequent bone definitions

Parent

Children

Hierarchy definition

List of 3D models that fit this skeleton (optional)

The units section contains three fields: mass, length, and angle. The mass field is a multiplier for segment mass, but it usually is ignored by animation software. length is a multiplier for the bone's length. The angle field specifies whether the orientation data is given in degrees or radians.

The entire hierarchy is relative to the position and orientation of the root, which has an order of transformations as well as a separate axis order that defines its initial orientation. The bone definitions, however, are specified in global space: The direction vector and axis are not relative to the root, but to the world axis.

The dof field is the specification of the allowed degrees of freedom for the particular segment, which can be any or all of tx, ty, tz, rx, ry, rz, and l. The l field is a translation value along the segment's length. A variation in this field's data indicates that the segment is not rigid. These variations can be used in the animation to stretch and compress the character's skin, but they should be reasonably low. The dof tokens are optional and can be specified in any order, which will define the order of transformations for the segment.

In many cases, all translations are omitted from the child segments, except when the file contains only translational data. In such a file, the degrees of freedom for length and rotation would be omitted. I don't recommend omitting any of the rotational degrees of freedom in a rotational file even if a bone, such as the elbow, is supposed to be unable to rotate toward a certain orientation, because the joints are never totally confined.

The limits are used to constrain the motion of a particular degree of freedom and are specified in the same order as the dof tokens, in pairs of minimum and maximum values. The .amc file in most systems is generated within these limits. One should not constrain motion data unless it is absolutely necessary. Most cases where constraining is used include real-time nonlinear video game applications, but there are other cases in which it may be desirable.

Many of the fields in the .asf file are used differently by different software, and some fields are used for special purposes by a particular program. The optional skin section, for example, can be used by animation software to load one or more specific models. bodymass and cofmass are fields used by some systems to calculate certain segment's dynamic characteristics that can be used to implement alternate procedures, such as hair and clothing. The norm is that if a field is not recognized, it is ignored. Preparing an .asf file for importation into some animation software requires special planning. For example, some programs require a different order of rotations or have a differently oriented world axis, which has to be taken into account before creating the .asf and .amc files.

The .amc File

The .amc file contains the actual motion data stream. All the data in this file is relative to the definitions in the .asf file, and the fields are sequenced in the same order as the dof field in the .asf file.

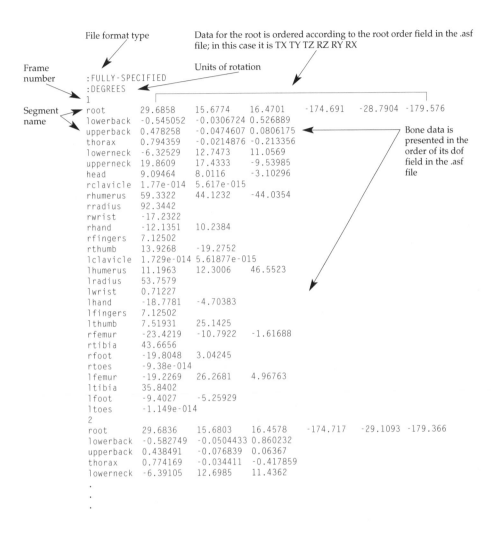

A clear advantage of the Acclaim file over other formats is that each of the bones or segments can have a different order of transformations, whereas other formats specify an order of rotations that applies to all segments and assume that translations occur before rotations. Furthermore, the Acclaim format can contain translational and global rotational data as well as hierarchical rotational data without the need for changing file formats.

The .bva File Format

The .bva file format was created by Biovision, a group of optical motion capture studios specializing in sports analysis and animation. This type of file is very simple because it lists all nine possible transformations without allowing for any changes in order. Each segment's transformations are absolute, or relative only to the world axis, so no hierarchy is necessary. No header is present, only clusters of lines that denote each segment, with the motion data laid out in columns that represent each transformation.

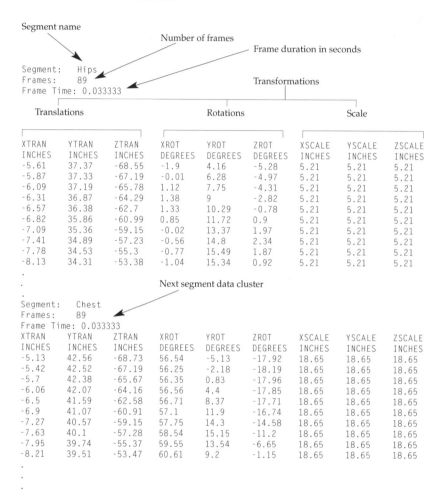

Segment name

Number of frames

Frame duration in seconds

Segment: Hips
Frames: 89
Frame Time: 0.033333   Transformations

Translations   Rotations   Scale

| XTRAN | YTRAN | ZTRAN | XROT | YROT | ZROT | XSCALE | YSCALE | ZSCALE |
INCHES	INCHES	INCHES	DEGREES	DEGREES	DEGREES	INCHES	INCHES	INCHES
-5.61	37.37	-68.55	-1.9	4.16	-5.28	5.21	5.21	5.21
-5.87	37.33	-67.19	-0.01	6.28	-4.97	5.21	5.21	5.21
-6.09	37.19	-65.78	1.12	7.75	-4.31	5.21	5.21	5.21
-6.31	36.87	-64.29	1.38	9	-2.82	5.21	5.21	5.21
-6.57	36.38	-62.7	1.33	10.29	-0.78	5.21	5.21	5.21
-6.82	35.86	-60.99	0.85	11.72	0.9	5.21	5.21	5.21
-7.09	35.36	-59.15	-0.02	13.37	1.97	5.21	5.21	5.21
-7.41	34.89	-57.23	-0.56	14.8	2.34	5.21	5.21	5.21
-7.78	34.53	-55.3	-0.77	15.49	1.87	5.21	5.21	5.21
-8.13	34.31	-53.38	-1.04	15.34	0.92	5.21	5.21	5.21

Next segment data cluster

Segment: Chest
Frames: 89
Frame Time: 0.033333

| XTRAN | YTRAN | ZTRAN | XROT | YROT | ZROT | XSCALE | YSCALE | ZSCALE |
INCHES	INCHES	INCHES	DEGREES	DEGREES	DEGREES	INCHES	INCHES	INCHES
-5.13	42.56	-68.73	56.54	-5.13	-17.92	18.65	18.65	18.65
-5.42	42.52	-67.19	56.25	-2.18	-18.19	18.65	18.65	18.65
-5.7	42.38	-65.67	56.35	0.83	-17.96	18.65	18.65	18.65
-6.06	42.07	-64.16	56.56	4.4	-17.85	18.65	18.65	18.65
-6.5	41.59	-62.58	56.71	8.37	-17.71	18.65	18.65	18.65
-6.9	41.07	-60.91	57.1	11.9	-16.74	18.65	18.65	18.65
-7.27	40.57	-59.15	57.75	14.3	-14.58	18.65	18.65	18.65
-7.63	40.1	-57.28	58.54	15.15	-11.2	18.65	18.65	18.65
-7.95	39.74	-55.37	59.55	13.54	-6.65	18.65	18.65	18.65
-8.21	39.51	-53.47	60.61	9.2	-1.15	18.65	18.65	18.65

In addition to the transformations, each cluster contains a segment name, the number of frames, and the frame duration in seconds. In the given example, each frame has a duration of 0.033333 seconds, which means that the data is supposed to be played back at 30 frames per second.

The scale transformations in the example are all equal for each segment, which means that the segment is rigid throughout the entire data stream.

Having three scale transformations is redundant because only one is required to specify the length of the segment. Note that the example contains equal values for each of the three scale values so that the target animation software can use the one it prefers.

The .bvh File Format

The .bvh file, another Biovision format, is more widely supported than the .bva format. 3D Studio Max and Nichimen, among others, are able to import this file type. The main difference between the .bvh and the .bva files is that the former includes a hierarchy. The file is divided into two major sections: hierarchy and motion. The hierarchy section includes all necessary definitions to create a skeleton in animation software. The motion section contains the data stream.

The hierarchy is defined within blocks of braces. Within each node's braces are defined all of its children, which have their own subblocks.

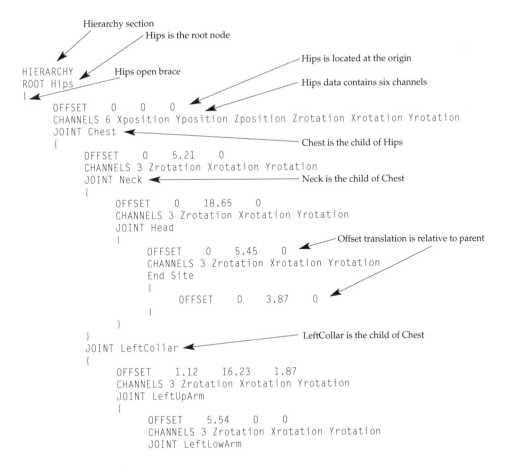

```
                    {
                        OFFSET    0    -11.96    0
                        CHANNELS 3 Zrotation Xrotation Yrotation
                        JOINT LeftHand
                        {
                            OFFSET    0    -9.93    0
                            CHANNELS 3 Zrotation Xrotation Yrotation
                            End Site
                            {
                                OFFSET    0    -7    0
                            }
                        }
                    }
                }
            }
            JOINT RightCollar
            {
                OFFSET   -1.12    16.23    1.87
                CHANNELS 3 Zrotation Xrotation Yrotation
                JOINT RightUpArm
                {
                    OFFSET   -6.07    0    0
                    CHANNELS 3 Zrotation Xrotation Yrotation
                    JOINT RightLowArm
                    {
                        OFFSET    0    -11.82    0
                        CHANNELS 3 Zrotation Xrotation Yrotation
                        JOINT RightHand
                        {
                            OFFSET    0    -10.65    0
                            CHANNELS 3 Zrotation Xrotation Yrotation
                            End Site
                            {
                                OFFSET    0    -7    0
                            }
                        }
                    }
                }
            }
        }
        JOINT LeftUpLeg
        {
            OFFSET    3.91    0    0
            CHANNELS 3 Zrotation Xrotation Yrotation
            JOINT LeftLowLeg
            {
                OFFSET    0    -18.34    0
                CHANNELS 3 Zrotation Xrotation Yrotation
                JOINT LeftFoot
                {
                    OFFSET    0    -17.37    0
                    CHANNELS 3 Zrotation Xrotation Yrotation
                    End Site
                    {
                        OFFSET    0    -3.46    0
                    }
                }
            }
        }
```

```
                }
            }
    JOINT RightUpLeg
    {
            OFFSET     -3.91    0    0
            CHANNELS 3 Zrotation Xrotation Yrotation
            JOINT RightLowLeg
            {
                    OFFSET     0    -17.63    0
                    CHANNELS 3 Zrotation Xrotation Yrotation
                    JOINT RightFoot
                    {
                            OFFSET     0    -17.14    0
                            CHANNELS 3 Zrotation Xrotation Yrotation
                            End Site
                            {
                                    OFFSET     0    -3.75    0
                            }
                    }
            }
    }
}
```

⟵——————————— Hips close brace

Motion section

Number of frames

Frame duration in seconds

```
MOTION
Frames:     89
Frame Time: 0.033333
-5.61   37.37   -68.55   -5.28   -1.9    4.16    -6.55   59.12   -12.24. . . . . . .
-5.87   37.33   -67.19   -4.97   -0.01   6.28    -3.74   57.19   -13.51. . . . . . .
-6.09   37.19   -65.78   -4.31   1.12    7.75    -1.94   56.29   -13.31. . . . . . .
-6.31   36.87   -64.29   -2.82   1.38    9       -1.3    56.47   -12.15. . . . . . .
-6.57   36.38   -62.7    -0.78   1.33    10.29   -1.07   57.02   -10.66. . . . . . .
-6.82   35.86   -60.99   0.9     0.85    11.72   0.84    57.99   -10.03. . . . . . .
-7.09   35.36   -59.15   1.97    -0.02   13.37   5.33    59.11   -11.26. . . . . . .
-7.41   34.89   -57.23   2.34    -0.56   14.8    11.45   59.4    -13.77. . . . . . .
-7.78   34.53   -55.3    1.87    -0.77   15.49   18.07   59      -17.08. . . . . . .
-8.13   34.31   -53.38   0.92    -1.04   15.34   24.45   58.58   -21.20. . . . . . .
-8.42   34.22   -51.46   0.13    -1.36   14.41   29.23   58.31   -24.64. . . . . . .
-8.65   34.26   -49.56   -0.16   -1.66   12.82   31.72   58.38   -25.83. . . . . . .
-8.82   34.44   -47.72   -0.12   -1.74   10.78   32.38   58.63   -24.36. . . . . . .
-8.88   34.77   -45.98   0.12    -1.39   8.65    31.99   58.52   -21.04. . . . . . .
-8.81   35.23   -44.35   0.62    -0.8    6.6     31.13   58.15   -17.16. . . . . . .
-8.62   35.81   -42.81   1.33    -0.17   4.53    29.78   57.78   -13.22. . . . . . .
-8.36   36.47   -41.32   2.13    0.6     2.37    27.75   57.46   -8.980. . . . . . .
-8.07   37.17   -39.89   3.04    1.58    0.03    24.78   57.2    -3.940. . . . . . .
.
.
.
```

Hips Tx, Ty, Tz   Hips Rz, Rx, Ry   Chest Rz, Rx, Ry

Each node has an offset field that defines its translation relative to its immediate parent node, except for the root, where the offset is absolute. In the given example, the node Chest is located 5.21 units in the Y direction from its parent, Hips. The offset order is always XYZ and no orientation is specified. These values also help define the length of the parent segment, but only in the case in which there are no siblings in different locations. There is no assumption in the hierarchy section about the initial orientation of any node, including the root, which leaves it open for interpretation by the animation software. The .bvh file has to be prepared with this in mind.

The brace blocks located at the deepest levels of the chain, called End Site, contain only an Offset field. This offset value defines the length of the last segment in each particular chain.

The Channels field serves two purposes. It defines the allowed transformations for each segment in particular, and it defines the order of occurrence of the transformations. Usually, only the root has any kind of translations, and no scale is used, so all segments are assumed to be rigid. The rest of the segments contain only rotations most of the time. The omission of a scale field makes it difficult to assess each segment's approximation to rigidity, a good measure of margin of error for captured motion data. It is only visually that one can estimate whether the motion is distorted due to marker misplacement or tracking errors.

The Motion section is laid out by column per channel, in the order defined by the hierarchy section. The first fields define the number of frames and the time per frame. In the example, there are 89 frames that last 0.033333 seconds each. Each of the following lines contains a frame of animation for each of the channels defined in the hierarchy section, arranged in the same order. The number of these lines is equal to the number of frames specified.

The .trc File Format

The .trc file is generated by Motion Analysis optical motion capture systems and contains translational data. The first part of the file is a header with global information, such as the sample rates of the data in the file and the data at the time of capture, the number of frames and markers, the measure units, and the file path.

The following file header not only shows the current state of the data, but also that of the original data captured. The data was originally collected at 60 samples per second and the first file generated had 600 frames, or 10 seconds. The final file was sampled down to 30 samples per second and shortened to 55 frames, for a resulting total of 1.83 seconds. This information is useful in case one needs more data for this particular motion; you know that you can always go back to the original file.

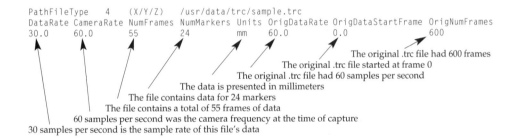

```
PathFileType    4    (X/Y/Z)   /usr/data/trc/sample.trc
DataRate CameraRate NumFrames  NumMarkers Units OrigDataRate OrigDataStartFrame OrigNumFrames
30.0     60.0       55         24         mm    60.0         0.0                600
```

The original .trc file had 600 frames

The original .trc file started at frame 0

The original .trc file had 60 samples per second

The data is presented in millimeters

The file contains data for 24 markers

The file contains a total of 55 frames of data

60 samples per second was the camera frequency at the time of capture

30 samples per second is the sample rate of this file's data

Immediately after the header is the data section. It is organized in columns, the first two being the frame number and the elapsed time, followed by the X, Y, and Z coordinates for each of the markers. The sample file has a total of 74 columns, but only a small portion of it is displayed here due to space limitations.

Frame number

Elapsed time from original data in seconds

Markers

X, Y, and Z coordinates for each marker

Frame#	Time	HeadTop			HeadLeft			. . . . . .
		X1	Y1	Z1	X2	Y2	Z2.	. . . . . .
1	0.817	230.93735	1208.98096	-574.76648	334.8299	1166.96545	-594.16943.	. . . . . .
2	0.85	240.0072	1210.76257	-569.7652	340.59796	1167.55347	-589.94135.	. . . . . .
3	0.883	247.31165	1213.39099	-561.43689	350.31845	1165.92798	-577.86694.	. . . . . .
4	0.917	256.81323	1214.14697	-550.07343	361.84949	1163.37598	-562.20605.	. . . . . .
5	0.95	268.03162	1213.01514	-536.69348	372.88889	1160.41479	-546.67401.	. . . . . .
6	0.983	279.90372	1209.90393	-521.5434	383.58591	1156.65479	-529.50519.	. . . . . .
7	1.017	291.30228	1205.90015	-505.01001	393.53964	1152.14868	-511.16791.	. . . . . .
8	1.05	300.8645	1201.92969	-486.47925	403.14886	1147.81055	-492.53708.	. . . . . .
9	1.083	310.15146	1197.76892	-464.68546	413.05984	1141.46301	-470.33188.	. . . . . .
10	1.117	319.0394	1193.06042	-440.80731	423.74298	1132.39136	-441.99075.	. . . . . .
11	1.15	327.33527	1187.74207	-415.48169	431.36893	1126.23242	-415.71805.	. . . . . .
12	1.183	335.61041	1182.35669	-387.25925	435.79279	1121.53906	-389.98529.	. . . . . .
13	1.217	342.04376	1176.35315	-357.57205	441.3559	1115.30664	-361.85596.	. . . . . .
14	1.25	346.83585	1168.34473	-328.24915	447.29584	1106.78125	-331.64551.	. . . . . .
15	1.283	352.17249	1157.34167	-298.41638	453.83853	1093.90649	-299.004.	. . . . . .
16	1.317	359.34326	1143.95654	-267.88205	462.08264	1076.38452	-264.96805.	. . . . . .
17	1.35	367.59335	1130.49084	-239.15077	471.05423	1061.25952	-235.97731.	. . . . . .
18	1.383	380.05081	1120.76318	-213.7711	483.44202	1052.48083	-212.00629.	. . . . . .
19	1.417	399.8569	1120.18323	-187.46774	501.26627	1053.41492	-190.12701.	. . . . . .
20	1.45	424.87695	1132.76147	-156.1911	523.26544	1068.0321	-167.37	. . . . . .
21	1.483	453.22705	1155.68127	-123.87888	551.185	1091.57129	-138.01402.	. . . . . .
22	1.517	484.33765	1179.08362	-95.45136	583.29871	1114.5094	-109.01964.	. . . . . .
23	1.55	516.72577	1193.46533	-71.39763	614.81665	1127.37964	-84.13749	. . . . . .
24	1.583	546.89313	1195.06714	-47.64498	643.01587	1127.25989	-61.68094	. . . . . .
25	1.617	571.77026	1183.40857	-23.64239	666.65216	1113.55811	-38.76169	. . . . . .
26	1.65	590.37518	1159.01172	-2.46658	685.62512	1087.17603	-14.94808	. . . . . .
27	1.683	604.61987	1126.01575	17.18866	700.51947	1053.99719	4.73558	. . . . . .
28	1.717	618.47876	1092.82764	38.93685	712.78497	1020.67932	21.58421	. . . . . .
29	1.75	635.88593	1064.63171	61.72252	725.93372	990.01843	40.35942	. . . . . .
30	1.783	656.48572	1042.42273	84.18129	741.39056	964.52283	57.84112	. . . . . .
31	1.817	676.87695	1026.60754	103.41233	757.79572	946.63202	69.60565	. . . . . .
32	1.85	694.78033	1015.62036	115.42829	772.42316	935.22876	74.00996	. . . . . .
33	1.883	710.32184	1005.88342	119.15073	784.44037	925.51843	71.607	. . . . . .
34	1.917	721.96924	994.08282	112.42614	790.62396	913.33234	58.56801	. . . . . .

```
35    1.95    729.18774 981.94446  94.91256   787.341    900.19971   32.36996  . . . . . . .
36    1.983   728.96234 972.63641  69.04857   771.02301  890.52222   -4.78092  . . . . . . .
37    2.017   720.39075 965.42316  40.12129   740.43433  885.24048  -44.97452  . . . . . . .
38    2.05    706.97437 956.35742  13.84147   698.77313  881.125    -78.80532  . . . . . . .
39    2.083   689.16138 942.43048  -8.84137   650.47784  874.30579 -100.69447. . . . . . .
40    2.117   664.60425 924.6507   -30.82248  599.46606  864.21606 -110.90468. . . . . . .
41    2.15    633.25525 907.31055  -54.29322  548.83063  854.13361 -119.71699. . . . . . .
42    2.183   597.2608  896.60681  -84.46886  500.12531  848.90173 -136.10138. . . . . . .
43    2.217   554.41614 898.05011 -127.57875  450.83124  852.71204 -164.01965. . . . . . .
44    2.25    500.37473 912.37244 -183.38701  395.72012  865.45477 -204.66075. . . . . . .
45    2.283   437.23184 935.49677 -246.46567  333.65088  883.71863 -257.9906  . . . . . . .
46    2.317   372.21469 959.72858 -313.86023  270.37036  902.46088 -318.92545. . . . . . .
47    2.35    310.91772 977.48767 -382.59006  211.77318  916.40338 -380.58499. . . . . . .
48    2.383   255.18663 984.98004 -451.91742  157.638    921.98083 -444.11844. . . . . . .
49    2.417   204.3597  982.39105 -520.44476  107.93311  917.8783  -509.36462. . . . . . .
50    2.45    158.57669 976.11462 -585.55585  63.39154   910.49255 -573.0976  . . . . . . .
51    2.483   117.98418 975.84723 -650.65942  24.49508   910.52509 -638.02075. . . . . . .
52    2.517   84.24587  987.77338 -720.19849  -8.76104   923.41449 -707.52234. . . . . . .
53    2.55    60.78411 1009.94342 -793.19592  -36.3148   946.66852 -779.4585  . . . . . . .
54    2.583   42.29954 1036.10669 -868.96185  -62.06355  970.36346 -853.00854. . . . . . .
55    2.617   22.16514 1058.95776 -947.20618  -88.7204   984.33331 -926.72235. . . . . . .
```

Notice that the elapsed time in the sample file starts at .817 seconds. That means that the first portion of the original 60-samples-per-second file was cropped after frame 49. If you wanted to go back to the original file, you have all the information necessary to relocate the segment you want.

The .htr File Format

The .htr file is generated by the Motion Analysis optical motion capture system and contains rotational and translational data and scale channels per marker. It is divided into four parts: the header, the segment hierarchy definitions, the base position, and the data stream.

This sample .htr file was converted from the .trc file in the previous section and has 55 frames as well. It has only 24 segments in order to simplify the analysis. Let's first look at the header portion:

```
#Created by TSi Motion Capture Translator on Tue May  7 11:01:18 1996
#Hierarchical Translation and Rotation (.htr) file
[Header]
FileType htr ◄──────────────────── File and data type
DataType HTRS◄──────────────────── For version control use
FileVersion 1◄──────────────────── Number of rigid segments or bones
NumSegments 14 ◄────────────────── Total number of frames
NumFrames 55 ◄──────────────────── Data sample rate
DataFrameRate 30◄───────────────── Rotation order for each segment
EulerRotationOrder ZYX ◄────────── Units at which translations are presented
CalibrationUnits mm ◄───────────── Units at which rotations are presented
RotationUnits Degrees◄──────────── Height axis
GlobalAxisofGravity Y ◄─────────── Axis aligned with segment length
BoneLengthAxis Y ◄──────────────── Factor by which data has been scaled
ScaleFactor 1.000000 ◄
```

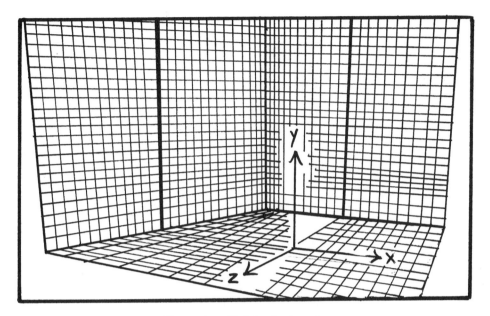

Figure 4-2. *Global axis of gravity.*

The Euler rotation order is important because each segment's orientation is obtained by three successive rotations in a particular sequence. The decision as to what order of rotations will be used must be reached before generating the .htr file. The choice depends largely on the animation software to be used, because some off-the-shelf animation programs have a hard-coded default rotation order that cannot be modified by the user.

Other parameters relevant to this type of file are the axis that points in the direction of gravity and the one that points in the length direction of a segment. These are also subject to the animation software defaults. As shown in Figure 4-2, most packages consider Y as the gravity axis, but some use Z. The axis that corresponds to the bone length is Y in most cases, as seen in Figure 4-3.

The translational data and segment lengths can be scaled to conform to a certain environment size. The `ScaleFactor` field is used to keep track of this modification. This factor pertains to all the data, not to particular segments.

Following the header is the hierarchy and segment definition section, which is where all the segment names and parental links are defined. All segments are listed in the first column; their parents are listed in the second column. If a segment is listed as *global*, it has no parent. It is possible to list all segments as global, resulting in a stream of global segment rotational data. If a hierarchy is defined, the data falls under the hierarchical segment rotational category. In this case there

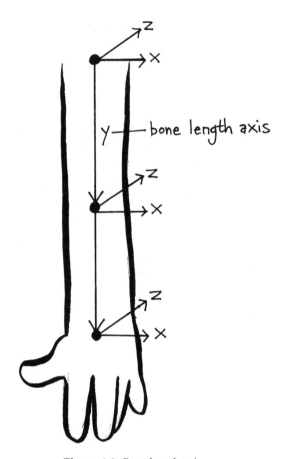

Figure 4-3. *Bone length axis.*

has to be at least one segment marked as global. Figure 4-4 is a graphic representation of the following hierarchy.

```
[SegmentNames&Hierarchy]
#CHILD      PARENT
Head        Torso
Torso       GLOBAL  ◄──────────── The Torso is the root node of this hierarchy
LUpperArm   Torso
RUpperArm   Torso
LLowArm     LUpperArm
RLowArm     RUpperArm
LHand       LlowArm
RHand       RlowArm
LThigh      Torso
RThigh      Torso
LLowLeg     LThigh
RLowLeg     RThigh
LFoot       LLowLeg
RFoot       RlowLeg
```

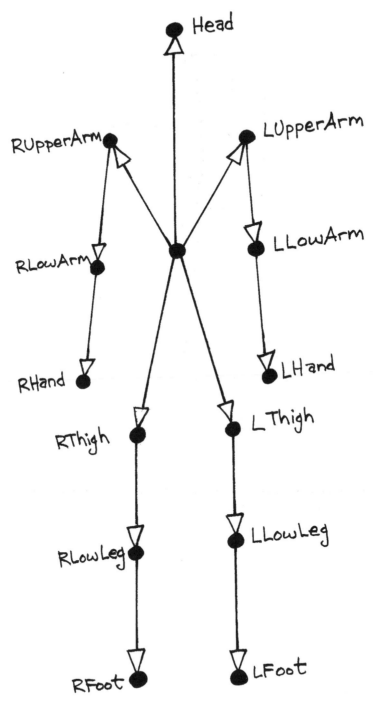

Figure 4-4. *Representation of the hierarchy of the sample file.*

The next section in the .htr file (see the following code) defines the base position, which is the initial pose that was discussed in Chapter 3. During the motion capture session, a file with the neutral pose is captured. A frame in that file is selected to represent the closest pose to the digital character model. This frame will become the common base position and will be embedded in the body of all .htr files as they are generated. The base position is also the initial skeleton of the character in the animation software, so by using a common one for all .htr files, only one character setup is necessary. All motion transformations in the .htr file are relative to this base position. Thus, if all translations and rotations are zeroed out, the skeleton will return to this pose. If the base position is changed, all the data in the file must be recomputed. In Chapter 3 I said that you should not set up your character unless you have already imported a base position file into your animation software. It is possible to avoid this if you can write software to recalculate the data for a predetermined base position based on your character setup.

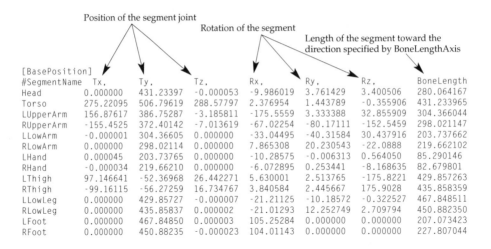

Position of the segment joint

Rotation of the segment

Length of the segment toward the direction specified by BoneLengthAxis

```
[BasePosition]
#SegmentName  Tx.        Ty.        Tz.        Rx.        Ry.        Rz.        BoneLength
Head          0.000000   431.23397  -0.000053  -9.986019  3.761429   3.400506   280.064167
Torso         275.22095  506.79619  288.57797  2.376954   1.443789   -0.355906  431.233965
LUpperArm     156.87617  386.75287  -3.185811  -175.5559  3.333388   32.855909  304.366044
RUpperArm     -155.4525  372.40142  -7.013619  -67.02254  -80.17111  -152.5459  298.021147
LLowArm       -0.000001  304.36605  0.000000   -33.04495  -40.31584  30.437916  203.737662
RLowArm       0.000000   298.02114  0.000000   7.865308   20.230543  -22.0888   219.662102
LHand         0.000045   203.73765  0.000000   -10.28575  -0.006313  0.564050   85.290146
RHand         -0.000034  219.66210  0.000000   -6.072895  0.253441   -8.168635  82.679801
LThigh        97.146641  -52.36968  26.442271  5.630001   2.513765   -175.8221  429.857263
RThigh        -99.16115  -56.27259  16.734767  3.840584   2.445667   175.9028   435.858359
LLowLeg       0.000000   429.85727  -0.000007  -21.21125  -10.18572  -0.322527  467.848511
RLowLeg       0.000000   435.85837  0.000002   -21.01293  12.252749  2.709794   450.882350
LFoot         0.000000   467.84850  0.000003   105.25284  0.000000   0.000000   207.073423
RFoot         0.000000   450.88235  -0.000023  104.01143  0.000000   0.000000   227.807044
```

The translation and rotation values of a segment are relative to its parent. Notice how the value of Ty for the head is almost equal to the torso's bone length. That means that the head is almost exactly at the end of the torso's segment, and we know that the head is the torso's child. Also, notice how the torso's Tx and Tz values are much higher than all the others are. This is because the torso is the only global segment—its transformations are all relative to the world axis, whereas the transformations of all other segments are relative to their direct parents. The only value that is not relative is the bone length.

The fourth section of the .htr file is the data itself. It is divided into subsections per segment, each line representing a frame number.

Frame number

Translations relative to base position

Rotations relative to base position

Scale factor

[Head]

#Fr	Tx	Ty	Tz	Rx	Ry	Rz	SF
1	0.000000	-4.858587	0.000099	10.499692	4.683280	-0.154138	1.013566
2	0.000000	-4.704456	0.000062	10.673701	5.487337	-0.339614	1.014575
3	0.000000	-5.209547	0.000137	11.538472	5.520280	-0.832413	1.014529
4	0.000000	-5.944353	-0.000067	12.095569	5.352387	-1.547831	1.015056
5	0.000000	-5.811870	-0.000099	12.113773	5.297226	-2.093981	1.014358
6	0.000000	-5.177482	-0.000032	12.020602	4.992712	-2.545206	1.014178
7	0.000000	-5.068451	0.000082	12.188824	4.664569	-3.514527	1.014793
8	0.000000	-4.903581	0.000022	12.427092	4.548636	-4.889447	1.017025
9	0.000000	-5.314583	-0.000142	12.031311	4.223691	-5.832687	1.016775
10	0.000000	-6.237838	-0.000062	11.218972	3.141907	-6.143721	1.013859

.
.
.

[Torso]

#Fr	Tx	Ty	Tz	Rx	Ry	Rz	SF
1	0.256104	-4.690031	-901.21180	3.419065	11.191740	1.183391	0.988733
2	6.268514	-4.833825	-899.39510	3.633979	9.386523	1.177484	0.989091
3	12.662476	-4.319671	-898.89568	4.130778	7.166818	1.362676	0.987919
4	20.360730	-3.851736	-898.68094	5.012617	5.342751	1.549584	0.986215
5	28.105710	-4.242471	-897.52817	6.094990	4.100763	1.545525	0.986523
6	33.560872	-5.928574	-892.96085	7.047348	3.505319	1.296721	0.987994
7	38.214739	-7.738103	-887.69563	7.983385	3.506861	1.311696	0.988247
8	43.544279	-9.604294	-882.33720	9.022912	3.708099	1.677518	0.988629
9	48.072781	-10.739373	-875.16154	10.465145	3.904763	1.771565	0.987676
10	50.492413	-11.234768	-864.79241	12.111266	4.148431	1.412131	0.985535

.
.
.

[LUpperArm]

#Fr	Tx	Ty	Tz	Rx	Ry	Rz	SF
1	1.286490	0.963057	0.574860	-7.653392	44.051043	8.626731	1.005609
2	2.559994	1.111917	0.151302	-7.338404	43.176098	9.013981	1.010282
3	4.056162	-0.641842	-0.707999	-7.043097	41.024858	9.262136	1.014424
4	4.616618	-2.865766	-1.335355	-7.426399	38.204100	9.111665	1.015329
5	4.444702	-3.268960	-1.380717	-8.580342	36.165418	8.315740	1.015126
6	4.286494	-2.383443	-1.185014	-9.953407	35.276832	6.634077	1.016061
7	2.765563	-2.713288	-1.117306	-12.110188	34.826341	3.701319	1.020946
8	0.416213	-3.832802	-1.007864	-14.591061	33.521631	0.304836	1.027364
9	-0.619820	-4.311412	-0.618119	-16.499243	30.467864	-2.514869	1.028296
10	-1.814847	-3.660805	-0.214309	-17.731646	27.028367	-5.659754	1.027257

.
.
.

[RUpperArm]

#Fr	Tx	Ty	Tz	Rx	Ry	Rz	SF
1	-0.628667	-10.007628	-0.789967	22.216529	-20.359719	-8.588245	1.024184
2	-2.122022	-9.640057	-0.377274	22.541990	-20.343501	-9.684186	1.020901
3	-4.127241	-8.594386	0.464602	22.742894	-20.373516	-11.309095	1.016075
4	-5.090433	-7.676922	1.081377	22.469946	-19.966937	-12.619528	1.013768
5	-4.973729	-7.047965	1.126349	22.183319	-19.175667	-13.327397	1.011921
6	-4.703499	-6.747547	0.936658	21.930873	-19.265821	-12.519854	1.012378
7	-3.171071	-6.455877	0.873939	21.246082	-19.429001	-10.699060	1.015006
8	-0.836609	-5.405571	0.770152	20.195218	-18.945001	-9.169760	1.016727
9	0.397692	-5.898392	0.380475	19.195593	-18.120445	-8.334362	1.018571
10	1.899746	-8.523217	-0.021126	18.050606	-17.667981	-7.758186	1.024040

.
.
.

```
.
[LLowArm]
#Fr   Tx          Ty          Tz          Rx           Ry           Rz           SF
1     0.000003    1.707023    0.000000    -17.836864   -2.427292    8.876852     0.994353
2     -0.000002   3.129388    0.000000    -19.191384   -1.679347    10.090833    0.980333
3     0.000004    4.390150    0.000000    -21.031146   -0.105618    11.730428    0.975999
4     0.000003    4.665619    0.000000    -22.703322   1.634425     13.370107    0.978072
5     -0.000007   4.603944    0.000000    -24.137978   2.738765     14.980390    0.972584
6     0.000010    4.888471    0.000000    -26.076666   3.162832     17.149450    0.961580
7     0.000000    6.375176    0.000000    -27.982561   3.193934     19.458814    0.954579
8     -0.000004   8.328783    0.000000    -29.160452   2.733712     21.585777    0.961696
9     0.000009    8.612477    0.000000    -29.531369   2.209042     23.412567    0.975206
10    -0.000006   8.296200    0.000000    -29.638691   2.200138     24.648625    0.979509
.
.

[RLowArm]
#Fr   Tx          Ty          Tz          Rx           Ry           Rz           SF
1     0.000000    7.207338    0.000000    4.077527     4.779736     -9.261399    0.997339
2     0.000000    6.228889    0.000000    3.718802     4.740024     -8.438207    1.001040
3     0.000000    4.790671    0.000000    3.249446     4.777283     -7.330081    1.002267
4     0.000000    4.103032    0.000000    2.757547     5.175765     -6.211417    0.998304
5     0.000000    3.552562    0.000000    2.311264     4.783585     -5.304502    0.995057
6     0.000000    3.688861    0.000000    2.874347     3.508883     -6.663122    1.002753
7     0.000000    4.472061    0.000000    3.777142     2.759954     -8.812203    1.008979
8     0.000000    4.985092    0.000000    4.036366     4.543184     -9.327195    0.999816
9     0.000000    5.534443    0.000000    4.044032     7.539941     -9.130649    0.981114
10    0.000000    7.164408    0.000000    4.499946     8.880659     -10.043492   0.962622
.
.

[LHand]
#Fr   Tx          Ty          Tz          Rx           Ry           Rz           SF
1     -0.000015   -1.150439   0.000000    8.243739     1.486729     -8.919611    1.043678
2     -0.000061   -4.006916   0.000000    8.754663     1.456218     -8.584533    1.055827
3     -0.000006   -4.889940   0.000000    9.829340     1.418586     -7.960398    1.055248
4     -0.000081   -4.467616   0.000000    10.936380    1.245752     -6.496042    1.035544
5     -0.000014   -5.585692   0.000000    11.011182    1.099799     -5.658061    1.030126
6     -0.000035   -7.827684   0.000000    11.076282    1.267397     -6.592873    1.040425
7     -0.000027   -9.253875   0.000000    10.745705    1.561329     -8.369294    1.049638
8     -0.000061   -7.804008   0.000000    7.959112     1.591583     -9.831184    1.046414
9     -0.000031   -5.051480   0.000000    5.722562     1.411336     -10.370656   1.032841
10    -0.000107   -4.174827   0.000000    4.688785     1.273762     -10.227041   1.029007
.
.

[RHand]
#Fr   Tx          Ty          Tz          Rx           Ry           Rz           SF
1     -0.000008   -0.584451   0.000000    -2.948995    -0.370179    2.644674     1.019734
2     0.000077    0.228431    0.000000    -4.240219    -0.165327    0.509767     1.019569
3     0.000107    0.498062    0.000000    -4.668479    -0.048645    -0.048041    1.011510
4     0.000072    -0.372647   0.000000    -4.733414    -0.023255    1.129299     0.992169
5     0.000021    -1.085705   0.000000    -5.367082    0.051834     2.634300     0.981505
6     0.000023    0.604676    0.000000    -7.631311    0.208044     3.920976     0.984171
7     0.000043    1.972392    0.000000    -9.173343    0.277757     4.768445     0.994198
8     0.000017    -0.040381   0.000000    -7.029188    0.082563     4.287978     1.007134
9     0.000066    -4.148576   0.000000    -2.578875    -0.163798    4.247556     1.016898
10    0.000056    -8.210634   0.000000    2.125026     -0.614249    5.558822     1.025910
.
.

[LThigh]
#Fr   Tx          Ty          Tz          Rx           Ry           Rz           SF
1     -1.948971   -5.743679   1.216170    4.584717     -1.803198    -2.301923    1.028563
2     -0.819284   -5.643427   -1.622541   4.615649     -3.503848    -2.869945    1.030591
3     0.158322    -5.891428   -5.515270   5.094698     -5.986699    -3.830506    1.033867
4     -0.692296   -6.019829   -7.226451   5.927294     -7.332279    -4.776852    1.038741
```

5	-2.293193	-5.962193	-6.119729	6.874762	-7.096426	-5.249797	1.042618
6	-2.342179	-5.886886	-4.811534	7.378632	-6.509944	-5.284106	1.041001
7	-2.065793	-5.799062	-3.707482	7.864546	-5.981563	-5.689823	1.038133
8	-3.800748	-5.834549	-1.233139	8.284303	-4.674531	-6.110074	1.036010
9	-5.134686	-5.948454	2.060023	8.993702	-3.019969	-6.024278	1.036358
10	-4.070278	-5.600185	3.463773	9.976612	-2.572359	-5.753804	1.037939

.
.
.

[RThigh]

#Fr	Tx	Ty	Tz	Rx	Ry	Rz	SF
1	1.917365	3.396889	4.574878	3.263076	-1.041816	0.892310	1.022364
2	1.460515	3.232908	7.627397	3.558135	-2.758124	0.611140	1.021666
3	1.254415	3.206850	12.467492	4.524791	-5.219322	-0.051084	1.023668
4	1.992551	2.845752	15.895479	6.201461	-6.483182	-0.951123	1.025984
5	2.868044	2.121395	16.976760	8.234925	-6.081634	-1.490023	1.026711
6	2.570853	1.448601	17.569256	10.236563	-5.317917	-1.403521	1.025387
7	1.385562	0.769813	18.910872	13.008264	-4.511639	-1.841973	1.022732
8	0.920314	0.211667	19.865216	17.074544	-2.596840	-2.962349	1.019291
9	0.256353	-0.208364	21.005662	22.052302	-0.184869	-3.433113	1.018606
10	-1.015619	-0.821060	23.861019	26.525253	0.857900	-3.166014	1.015690

.
.
.

[LLowLeg]

#Fr	Tx	Ty	Tz	Rx	Ry	Rz	SF
1	0.000000	12.277876	-0.000005	-9.310979	3.958743	2.994572	0.987525
2	0.000000	13.149770	0.000005	-9.350337	3.621027	3.505744	0.986619
3	0.000000	14.557776	0.000005	-9.343923	3.591080	4.326684	0.985922
4	0.000000	16.652874	0.000008	-9.397132	3.228173	4.814963	0.983453
5	0.000000	18.319480	0.000012	-9.767744	2.445292	4.794431	0.980062
6	0.000000	17.624747	0.000016	-9.847268	2.552874	4.845590	0.977428
7	0.000000	16.391952	0.000001	-9.706737	2.869017	5.127302	0.976938
8	0.000000	15.479248	0.000014	-9.485002	2.161337	4.660242	0.976370
9	0.000000	15.628608	0.000009	-9.413728	1.386960	3.896389	0.975466
10	0.000000	16.308507	0.000013	-9.479881	2.118380	4.032616	0.978753

.
.
.

[RLowLeg]

#Fr	Tx	Ty	Tz	Rx	Ry	Rz	SF
1	0.000000	9.747725	-0.000003	-1.969391	2.713994	-0.256803	0.964314
2	0.000000	9.443244	-0.000004	-2.309806	2.925325	-0.349927	0.965662
3	0.000000	10.315879	-0.000002	-3.293559	3.200043	-0.279514	0.966694
4	0.000000	11.325171	0.000000	-4.596793	2.633765	-0.463029	0.967041
5	0.000000	11.642023	-0.000002	-6.360722	1.133664	-1.235632	0.968146
6	0.000000	11.065212	-0.000002	-8.939798	0.143144	-2.253221	0.970705
7	0.000000	9.908082	-0.000001	-13.063365	0.262553	-2.668486	0.972029
8	0.000000	8.408095	-0.000001	-19.404992	0.503464	-2.941691	0.970976
9	0.000000	8.109777	-0.000001	-26.918280	-0.086212	-3.564932	0.969294
10	0.000000	6.838414	-0.000001	-33.084023	-0.002488	-4.141806	0.969350

.
.
.

[LFoot]

#Fr	Tx	Ty	Tz	Rx	Ry	Rz	SF
1	0.000000	-5.836589	-0.000075	6.849172	0.000000	0.000000	1.014277
2	0.000000	-6.260494	-0.000031	7.131442	0.000000	0.000000	1.007809
3	0.000000	-6.586196	-0.000045	7.382423	0.000000	0.000000	1.008357
4	0.000000	-7.741686	0.000070	7.669603	0.000000	0.000000	1.013625
5	0.000000	-9.328047	-0.000074	8.037170	0.000000	0.000000	1.017301
6	0.000000	-10.560292	-0.000021	8.281682	0.000000	0.000000	1.020076
7	0.000000	-10.789751	0.000048	8.494574	0.000000	0.000000	1.022273
8	0.000000	-11.055420	-0.000067	8.699128	0.000000	0.000000	1.020523
9	0.000000	-11.478071	0.000051	9.061934	0.000000	0.000000	1.016536
10	0.000000	-9.940176	-0.000067	9.780009	0.000000	0.000000	1.017310

```
.
.
.
[RFoot]
#Fr    Tx          Ty          Tz          Rx          Ry          Rz          SF
1      0.000000    -16.090285  -0.000007   0.854710    0.000000    0.000000    0.991550
2      0.000000    -15.482314  0.000083    1.151425    0.000000    0.000000    0.990986
3      0.000000    -15.017190  0.000111    1.753048    0.000000    0.000000    0.996231
4      0.000000    -14.860747  -0.000018   2.355142    0.000000    0.000000    0.997485
5      0.000000    -14.362526  -0.000003   2.974844    0.000000    0.000000    0.996350
6      0.000000    -13.208670  0.000027    3.658937    0.000000    0.000000    0.993913
7      0.000000    -12.611719  0.000000    3.844048    0.000000    0.000000    0.986665
8      0.000000    -13.086514  0.000060    2.895532    0.000000    0.000000    0.976994
9      0.000000    -13.844775  -0.000034   1.293673    0.000000    0.000000    0.975546
10     0.000000    -13.819476  -0.000009   0.294280    0.000000    0.000000    0.983843
.
.
.
[EndOfFile]
```

The SF column in the .htr file is a scale of the particular segment along the axis indicated by BoneLengthAxis. This number represents deviations in the length of the bone caused by the sliding of the skin over the bone. This number must always be very close to 1; otherwise, it indicates a faulty marker location or perhaps a marker placed over loose clothing. If the number is very close to 1 throughout the whole data stream, you may ignore it or approximate it to 1.0, thus assuming that the segment is rigid.

Figure 4-5 is a chart of the segment length scale for the sample file. In this particular case, the scale factor cannot be ignored completely because some values exceed the acceptable rigidity deviation. The LHand segment, for example, has a peak deviation of almost 30%. In a situation like this, it may be necessary to recalculate the .htr file using a different combination of markers. If that doesn't work, the motion may have to be recaptured. The acceptable deviation depends on each particular motion, but it should not exceed 10% in any case.

WRITING A MOTION CAPTURE TRANSLATOR

Most animation programs support at least one motion capture format, but if your application is proprietary, you may have to write your own. The language and platform are not relevant to this discussion, but I will use the C language to illustrate the programming steps. I also present the code in a sequential as opposed to modular way, since I believe the continuity aids in understanding the logic. If you decide to write your own translator, you may want to use more functions and subroutines, a much recommended programming practice.

As a case study, I use the .htr format as the input file and the Acclaim format as the output file. I chose Acclaim as the output format because it is the most complicated one, I have already explained it in detail, and it is the closest to what an animation file format would look like.

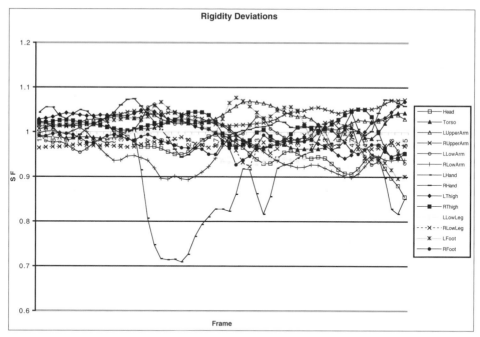

Figure 4-5. *Segment length scale.*

The first step in creating a translator is to define a buffer that will hold all the data of both the input and output files. The .htr file buffer looks like this:

```
/* Hierarchy pairs */
struct htrSegmentHierarchy {
    char *child;                /* child segment  */
    char *parent;              /* parent segment */
};
/* Base position structure */
struct htrBasePosition {
    char *name;                /* segment name   */
    double tx;                 /* initial values */
    double ty;
    double tz;
    double rx;
    double ry;
    double rz;
    double boneLength;
};
/* Frame data */
struct htrFrame {
    int frameNo;               /* frame number         */
    double tx;                     /* transformations      */
    double ty;
    double tz;
    double rx;
    double ry;
```

```
    double rz;
    double SF;                      /* segment scale factor */
};
/* Segment data */
struct htrSegmentData {
    char *segmentName;              /* segment name */
    struct htrFrame *frame;         /* frame data    */
};
/* .htr format wrapper struct */
struct htrFormat {
    char *fileType;             /* file type                  */
    char *dataType;             /* data type                  */
    int fileVersion;            /* file version               */
    int numSegments;            /* number of segments         */
    int numFrames;              /* total number of frames     */
    int dataFrameRate;          /* frame rate                 */
    char *eulerRotationOrder;   /* global order of rotations  */
    char *calibrationUnits;     /* units of translation       */
    char *rotationUnits;        /* units of rotation          */
    char *globalAxisofGravity;  /* global up axis             */
    char *boneLengthAxis;       /* axis along bone            */
    float scaleFactor;          /* global scale factor        */
    struct htrSegmentHierarchy *childParent;   /* hierarchy       */
    struct htrBasePosition *basePosition;      /* base position */
    struct htrSegmentData *segmentData;        /* segment data   */
};
/* .htr data buffer */
struct htrFormat htrFile;
```

htrFile, a variable of type struct hrtFormat, will end up containing the entire data in the .htr file. The first 12 variables in struct hrtFormat correspond to the .htr file's header section. childParent is a buffer that will hold all the child-parent pairs as defined in the SegmentNames&Hierarchy section. This buffer is of the previously defined type struct htrSegmentNamesandHierarchy, which will hold both child and parent strings. basePosition will contain all the data in the BasePosition section. It is of type struct htrBasePosition, where the segment and initial transformations are defined. Finally, segmentData, of type struct htrFrame, will hold the motion data.

The output file is actually a combination of both .asf and .amc files; its structure can be defined as follows:

```
/* This structure will hold each dof's limit pairs */
struct acclaimBoneLimits {
    double minMax[2];               /* min/max values (0 if infinity) */
    int infinity[2];                /* infinity flag (1 if infinity)   */
};
/* Segment's bone data section */
struct acclaimBoneData {
    int id;                                 /* segment id           */
    char *name;                             /* segment name         */
    float direction[3];                     /* direction vector     */
    double length;                          /* segment length       */
```

```
        double axis[3];                          /* global orientation   */
        char axisOrder[5];                       /* order of r for above */
        char dof[20];                            /* dof tokens           */
        int dofNumber;                           /* number of dof tokens */
        struct acclaimBoneLimits *limits;        /* limits defined above */
        float bodyMass;                          /* body mass            */
        float cofMass;                           /* center of mass       */
};
/* Hierarchy section */
struct acclaimHierarchy {
        char *parent;                            /* parent segment */
        char children[MAXLINE];                  /* child segments */
};
/* Skin section */
struct acclaimSkin {
        char *skinFile;                          /* skin file name */
};
/* Motion data section in the .amc file */
struct acclaimMotionData {
        char *segment;                           /* segment name    */
        double tx;                               /* transformations */
        double ty;
        double tz;
        double rx;
        double ry;
        double rz;
        double l;
};
/* Frame data */
struct acclaimFrameData {
        int frame;                               /* frame number */
        struct acclaimMotionData *motionData;    /* segment data */
};
/* Acclaim format wrapper struct */
struct acclaimFormat {
        char* version;                           /* file version      */
        char *name;                              /* skeleton name     */
        float unitsMass;                         /* mass multiplier   */
        float unitsLength;                       /* length multiplier */
        char unitsAngle[5];                      /* angles (deg/rad)  */
        char *documentation;                     /* notes             */
        char rootOrder[20];                      /* root's xform order */
        char rootAxis[5];                        /* initial rot. order */
        double rootPosition[3];                  /* initial position   */
        double rootOrientation[3];               /* initial rotation   */
        struct acclaimBoneData *boneData;        /* segments' data     */
        struct acclaimHierarchy *hierarchy;      /* hierarchy pairs    */
        struct acclaimSkin *skin;                /* skin files         */
        struct acclaimFrameData *frameData;      /* frame data         */
};
/* Acclaim data buffer */
struct acclaimFormat acclaimFile;
```

acclaimFile will hold all the data in the .asf and .amc files. It is of type struct acclaimFormat. The bone information will be located in boneData, and hierarchy will hold all the parent-child relationships. frameData will contain all the data from the .amc file. Notice in the definition of `struct acclaimBoneData` that the integer variable `dofNumber` doesn't actually come from the .asf file. It will contain the number of degrees of freedom available for each particular segment, so that the `dof` line will be parsed only once per segment. Another special-purpose variable is the `infinity` integer inside the definition of `struct acclaimBoneLimits`, which, as its name says, will hold a flag to indicate infinity. `struct acclaimHierarchy` will hold the hierarchy data in pairs of parent and child, as opposed to the way in which the .asf file holds it (i.e., with a parent and all of its children in the same line). If the parent has several children, more than one pair will be generated.

If you compare the definitions above with the actual file structures as explained in the previous section, you will find that most of the variable and type names are very close to those in the files themselves. You will also find that the structures above contain more information than will be used in the conversion from .htr to Acclaim, but including this information in the data structure is good practice in case you need it in the future.

The next step is to start reading the information from the .htr file into the data buffer. Assuming a file is available and its name has already been processed by the program and placed in the string `htrFileName`, we proceed to open the file and then process the header section:

```
#define MAXLINE 500        /* Max length of a line of text  */
#define MAXTOKENS 50       /* Max number of tokens per line */
#define DELIMIT " \t\n"    /* Characters separating tokens  */
#define XYZ 1              /* Order of rotations            */
#define XZY 2              /* Order of rotations            */
#define ZXY 3              /* Order of rotations            */
#define ZYX 4              /* Order of rotations            */
#define YXZ 5              /* Order of rotations            */
#define YZX 6              /* Order of rotations            */
int found;                 /* Boolean variable             */
int value;                 /* Return value                 */
int htrRotOrder;           /* htr order of rotations       */
int numTokens;             /* Number of tokens per line    */
int numParents;            /* Number of parent nodes       */
int numBones;              /* Number of segments           */
int numFrames;             /* Number of frames             */
int i, j, k;               /* Counters                     */
FILE *htrFileHandle;       /* Handle to .htr file          */
char *htrFileName;         /* The .htr file name           */
FILE *asfFileHandle;       /* Handle to .asf file          */
char *asfFileName;         /* The .asf file name           */
FILE *amcFileHandle;       /* Handle to .amc file          */
char *amcFileName;         /* The .amc file name           */
char textLine[MAXLINE];    /* Buffer will hold a line of text */
char *genStr;              /* Generic string               */
char *token[MAXTOKENS];    /* Token buffer                 */


/* Process arguments and other initializations */
```

```
/* Open .htr file */
htrFileHandle = fopen(htrFileName, "r");
if (!htrFileHandle) {
    fprintf(stderr, "\nError: Unable to open %s \n", htrFileName);
    exit();
    }

/* Find the header section */
found = 0;
while (!found && fgets(textLine, MAXLINE, htrFileHandle)) {
    if (strncmp("[Header]", textLine, strlen("[Header]")) == 0)
    found = 1;
    }
if (!found) {
    fprintf(stderr, "\nError: Unable to find 'Header'\n");
    exit();
    }


/* Start reading header data */

/* fileType */
/* Get a line of text */
found = 0;
value = 1;
while (!found && value) {
    value = fgets(textLine, MAXLINE, htrFileHandle);

    /* Skip if comment or newline */
    if (textLine[0] == '\n' !! textLine[0] == '#')
        found = 0;
    else
        if (value)
            found = 1;
    }
if (!found) {
    fprintf(stderr, "\nError: Premature end of file\n");
    exit();
    }

/* Parse line */
numTokens = 0;
token[numTokens++] = strtok(textLine, DELIMIT);
while (token[numTokens-1])
    token[numTokens++] = strtok(NULL, DELIMIT);
numTokens -= 1;

/* Make sure we got two tokens */
if (numTokens != 2) {
    fprintf(stderr, "\nError: Invalid 'fileType'\n");
    exit();
    }

/* Allocate memory and save fileType into buffer */
htrFile->fileType =
    (char *)malloc((strlen(token[1])+1)*sizeof(char));
strcpy(htrFile->fileType, token[1]);

/* dataType */
```

```
/* Get a line of text */
found = 0;
value = 1;
while (!found && value) {
     value = fgets(textLine, MAXLINE, htrFileHandle);

     /* Skip if comment or newline */
     if (textLine[0] == '\n' !! textLine[0] == '#')
          found = 0;
     else
          if (value)
               found = 1;
     }
if (!found) {
     fprintf(stderr, "\nError: Premature end of file\n");
     exit();
     }

/* Parse line */
numTokens = 0;
token[numTokens++] = strtok(textLine, DELIMIT);
while (token[numTokens-1])
     token[numTokens++] = strtok(NULL, DELIMIT);
numTokens -= 1;

/* Make sure we got two tokens */
if (numTokens != 2) {
     fprintf(stderr, "\nError: Invalid 'dataType'\n");
     exit();
     }

/* Allocate memory and save dataType into buffer */
htrFile->dataType =
     (char *)malloc((strlen(token[1])+1)*sizeof(char));
strcpy(htrFile->dataType, token[1]);

/* fileVersion */
/* Get a line of text */
found = 0;
value = 1;
while (!found && value) {
     value = fgets(textLine, MAXLINE, htrFileHandle);

     /* Skip if comment or newline */
     if (textLine[0] == '\n' !! textLine[0] == '#')
          found = 0;
     else
          if (value)
               found = 1;
     }
if (!found) {
     fprintf(stderr, "\nError: Premature end of file\n");
     exit();
     }

/* Parse line */
numTokens = 0;
token[numTokens++] = strtok(textLine, DELIMIT);
while (token[numTokens-1])
```

```
            token[numTokens++] = strtok(NULL, DELIMIT);
numTokens -= 1;

/* Make sure we got two tokens */
if (numTokens != 2) {
    fprintf(stderr, "\nError: Invalid 'fileVersion'\n");
    exit();
    }

/* Save fileVersion into buffer */
htrFile->fileVersion = atoi(token[1]);

/* numSegments */
/* Get a line of text */
found = 0;
value = 1;
while (!found && value) {
    value = fgets(textLine, MAXLINE, htrFileHandle);

    /* Skip if comment or newline */
    if (textLine[0] == '\n' !! textLine[0] == '#')
        found = 0;
    else
        if (value)
            found = 1;
    }
if (!found) {
    fprintf(stderr, "\nError: Premature end of file\n");
    exit();
    }

/* Parse line */
numTokens = 0;
token[numTokens++] = strtok(textLine, DELIMIT);
while (token[numTokens-1])
    token[numTokens++] = strtok(NULL, DELIMIT);
numTokens -= 1;

/* Make sure we got two tokens */
if (numTokens != 2) {
    fprintf(stderr, "\nError: Invalid 'numSegments'\n");
    exit();
    }

/* Save numSegments into buffer */
htrFile->numSegments = atoi(token[1]);

/* numFrames */
/* Get a line of text */
found = 0;
value = 1;
while (!found && value) {
    value = fgets(textLine, MAXLINE, htrFileHandle);

    /* Skip if comment or newline */
    if (textLine[0] == '\n' !! textLine[0] == '#')
        found = 0;
    else
        if (value)
```

```
                        found = 1;
        }
if (!found) {
     fprintf(stderr, "\nError: Premature end of file\n");
     exit();
     }

/* Parse line */
numTokens = 0;
token[numTokens++] = strtok(textLine, DELIMIT);
while (token[numTokens-1])
     token[numTokens++] = strtok(NULL, DELIMIT);
numTokens -= 1;

/* Make sure we got two tokens */
if (numTokens != 2) {
     fprintf(stderr, "\nError: Invalid 'numFrames'\n");
     exit();
     }

/* Save numFrames into buffer */
htrFile->numFrames = atoi(token[1]);

/* dataFrameRate */
/* Get a line of text */
found = 0;
value = 1;
while (!found && value) {
     value = fgets(textLine, MAXLINE, htrFileHandle);

     /* Skip if comment or newline */
     if (textLine[0] == '\n' !! textLine[0] == '#')
          found = 0;
     else
          if (value)
               found = 1;
     }
if (!found) {
     fprintf(stderr, "\nError: Premature end of file\n");
     exit();
     }

/* Parse line */
numTokens = 0;
token[numTokens++] = strtok(textLine, DELIMIT);
while (token[numTokens-1])
     token[numTokens++] = strtok(NULL, DELIMIT);
numTokens -= 1;

/* Make sure we got two tokens */
if (numTokens != 2) {
     fprintf(stderr, "\nError: Invalid 'dataFrameRate'\n");
     exit();
     }

/* Save dataFrameRate into buffer */
htrFile->dataFrameRate = atoi(token[1]);

/* eulerRotationOrder */
```

```
/* Get a line of text */
found = 0;
value = 1;
while (!found && value) {
     value = fgets(textLine, MAXLINE, htrFileHandle);

     /* Skip if comment or newline */
     if (textLine[0] == '\n' !! textLine[0] == '#')
          found = 0;
     else
          if (value)
               found = 1;
     }
if (!found) {
     fprintf(stderr, "\nError: Premature end of file\n");
     exit();
     }

/* Parse line */
numTokens = 0;
token[numTokens++] = strtok(textLine, DELIMIT);
while (token[numTokens-1])
     token[numTokens++] = strtok(NULL, DELIMIT);
numTokens -= 1;

/* Make sure we got two tokens */
if (numTokens != 2) {
     fprintf(stderr, "\nError: Invalid 'eulerRotationOrder'\n");
     exit();
     }

/* Allocate memory and save eulerRotationOrder into buffer */
htrFile->eulerRotationOrder =
     (char *)malloc((strlen(token[1])+1)*sizeof(char));
strcpy(htrFile->eulerRotationOrder, token[1]);

/* calibrationUnits */
/* Get a line of text */
found = 0;
value = 1;
while (!found && value) {
     value = fgets(textLine, MAXLINE, htrFileHandle);

     /* Skip if comment or newline */
     if (textLine[0] == '\n' !! textLine[0] == '#')
          found = 0;
     else
          if (value)
               found = 1;
     }
if (!found) {
     fprintf(stderr, "\nError: Premature end of file\n");
     exit();
     }

/* Parse line */
numTokens = 0;
token[numTokens++] = strtok(textLine, DELIMIT);
while (token[numTokens-1])
```

```
        token[numTokens++] = strtok(NULL, DELIMIT);
numTokens -= 1;

/* Make sure we got two tokens */
if (numTokens != 2) {
    fprintf(stderr, "\nError: Invalid 'calibrationUnits'\n");
    exit();
    }

/* Allocate memory and save calibrationUnits into buffer */
htrFile->calibrationUnits =
    (char *)malloc((strlen(token[1])+1)*sizeof(char));
strcpy(htrFile->calibrationUnits, token[1]);

/* rotationUnits */
/* Get a line of text */
found = 0;
value = 1;
while (!found && value) {
    value = fgets(textLine, MAXLINE, htrFileHandle);

    /* Skip if comment or newline */
    if (textLine[0] == '\n' !! textLine[0] == '#')
        found = 0;
    else
        if (value)
            found = 1;
    }
if (!found) {
    fprintf(stderr, "\nError: Premature end of file\n");
    exit();
    }

/* Parse line */
numTokens = 0;
token[numTokens++] = strtok(textLine, DELIMIT);
while (token[numTokens-1])
    token[numTokens++] = strtok(NULL, DELIMIT);
numTokens -= 1;

/* Make sure we got two tokens */
if (numTokens != 2) {
    fprintf(stderr, "\nError: Invalid 'rotationUnits'\n");
    exit();
    }

/* Allocate memory and save rotationUnits into buffer */
htrFile->rotationUnits =
    (char *)malloc((strlen(token[1])+1)*sizeof(char));
strcpy(htrFile->rotationUnits, token[1]);

/* globalAxisofGravity */
/* Get a line of text */
found = 0;
value = 1;
while (!found && value) {
    value = fgets(textLine, MAXLINE, htrFileHandle);

    /* Skip if comment or newline */
```

```
            if (textLine[0] == '\n' !! textLine[0] == '#')
                    found = 0;
            else
                    if (value)
                            found = 1;
            }
    if (!found) {
        fprintf(stderr, "\nError: Premature end of file\n");
        exit();
        }

/* Parse line */
numTokens = 0;
token[numTokens++] = strtok(textLine, DELIMIT);
while (token[numTokens-1])
    token[numTokens++] = strtok(NULL, DELIMIT);
numTokens -= 1;

/* Make sure we got two tokens */
if (numTokens != 2) {
    fprintf(stderr, "\nError: Invalid 'globalAxisofGravity'\n");
    exit();
    }

/* Allocate memory and save globalAxisofGravity into buffer */
htrFile->globalAxisofGravity =
    (char *)malloc((strlen(token[1])+1)*sizeof(char));
strcpy(htrFile->globalAxisofGravity, token[1]);

/* boneLengthAxis */
/* Get a line of text */
found = 0;
value = 1;
while (!found && value) {
    value = fgets(textLine, MAXLINE, htrFileHandle);

    /* Skip if comment or newline */
    if (textLine[0] == '\n' !! textLine[0] == '#')
            found = 0;
    else
            if (value)
                    found = 1;
    }
if (!found) {
    fprintf(stderr, "\nError: Premature end of file\n");
    exit();
    }

/* Parse line */
numTokens = 0;
token[numTokens++] = strtok(textLine, DELIMIT);
while (token[numTokens-1])
    token[numTokens++] = strtok(NULL, DELIMIT);
numTokens -= 1;

/* Make sure we got two tokens */
if (numTokens != 2) {
    fprintf(stderr, "\nError: Invalid 'boneLengthAxis'\n");
    exit();
```

```
        }

/* Allocate memory and save boneLengthAxis into buffer */
htrFile->boneLengthAxis =
     (char *)malloc((strlen(token[1])+1)*sizeof(char));
strcpy(htrFile->boneLengthAxis, token[1]);

/* scaleFactor */
/* Get a line of text */
found = 0;
value = 1;
while (!found && value) {
     value = fgets(textLine, MAXLINE, htrFileHandle);

     /* Skip if comment or newline */
     if (textLine[0] == '\n' !! textLine[0] == '#')
          found = 0;
     else
          if (value)
               found = 1;
     }
if (!found) {
     fprintf(stderr, "\nError: Premature end of file\n");
     exit();
     }

/* Parse line */
numTokens = 0;
token[numTokens++] = strtok(textLine, DELIMIT);
while (token[numTokens-1])
     token[numTokens++] = strtok(NULL, DELIMIT);
numTokens -= 1;

/* Make sure we got two tokens */
if (numTokens != 2) {
     fprintf(stderr, "\nError: Invalid 'scaleFactor'\n");
     exit();
     }

/* Save scaleFactor into buffer */
htrFile->scaleFactor = atof(token[1]);
```

Now we proceed to load the SegmentNames&Hierarchy section into the buffer. The next step after finding the section is to allocate memory for the branch that will hold this data. We can do this now because we already have loaded the number of segments that we need to process.

```
/* Find the SegmentNames&Hierarchy section */
found = 0;
while (!found && fgets(textLine, MAXLINE, htrFileHandle)) {
     if (strncmp("[SegmentNames&Hierarchy]", textLine,
          strlen("[SegmentNames&Hierarchy]")) == 0)
     found = 1;
     }
if (!found) {
```

```
    fprintf(stderr,
        "\nError: Unable to find 'SegmentNames&Hierarchy' \n");
    exit();
    }

/* Allocate memory based on number of segments */
htrFile->childParent = (struct htrSegmentHierarchy *)
    malloc(htrFile->numSegments *
    sizeof(struct htrSegmentHierarchy));

/* Start reading SegmentNames&Hierarchy data */
for (i=0; i < htrFile->numSegments; i++) {

    /* Get a line of text */
    found = 0;
    value = 1;
    while (!found && value) {
        value = fgets(textLine, MAXLINE, htrFileHandle);

        /* Skip if comment or newline */
        if (textLine[0] == '\n' !! textLine[0] == '#')
            found = 0;
        else
            if (value)
                found = 1;
    }
    if (!found) {
        fprintf(stderr, "\nError: Premature end of file\n");
        exit();
        }

    /* Parse line */
    numTokens = 0;
    token[numTokens++] = strtok(textLine, DELIMIT);
    while (token[numTokens-1])
        token[numTokens++] = strtok(NULL, DELIMIT);
    numTokens -= 1;

    /* Make sure we got two tokens */
    if (numTokens != 2) {
        fprintf(stderr, "\nError: Invalid hierarchy\n");
        exit();
        }

    /* Allocate memory and save hierarchy pair into buffer */
    htrFile->childParent[i].child =
        (char *)malloc((strlen(token[0])+1)*sizeof(char));
    strcpy(htrFile->childParent[i].child, token[0]);
    htrFile->childParent[i].parent =
        (char *)malloc((strlen(token[1])+1)*sizeof(char));
    strcpy(htrFile->childParent[i].parent, token[1]);
    }
```

We continue with the BasePosition section. We are now looking for eight tokens per line that represent the segment name, all six transformations, and the bone length.

```
/* Find the BasePosition section */
found = 0;
while (!found && fgets(textLine, MAXLINE, htrFileHandle)) {
     if (strncmp("[BasePosition]", textLine,
          strlen("[BasePosition]")) == 0)
     found = 1;
     }
if (!found) {
     fprintf(stderr,
          "\nError: Unable to find 'BasePosition' \n");
     exit();
     }

/* Allocate memory based on number of segments */
htrFile->basePosition = (struct htrBasePosition *)
     malloc(htrFile->numSegments *
     sizeof(struct htrBasePosition));

/* Start reading BasePosition data */
for (i=0; i < htrFile->numSegments; i++) {

     /* Get a line of text */
     found = 0;
     value = 1;
     while (!found && value) {
          value = fgets(textLine, MAXLINE, htrFileHandle);

          /* Skip if comment or newline */
          if (textLine[0] == '\n' !! textLine[0] == '#')
               found = 0;
               else
                    if (value)
                         found = 1;
          }
     if (!found) {
          fprintf(stderr, "\nError: Premature end of file\n");
          exit();
          }

     /* Parse line */
     numTokens = 0;
     token[numTokens++] = strtok(textLine, DELIMIT);
     while (token[numTokens-1])
          token[numTokens++] = strtok(NULL, DELIMIT);
     numTokens -= 1;

     /* Make sure we got eight tokens */
     if (numTokens != 8) {
          fprintf(stderr, "\nError: Invalid base position\n");
          exit();
          }

     /* Allocate space and save Baseposition line into buffer */
     htrFile->basePosition[i].name =
          (char *)malloc((strlen(token[0])+1)*sizeof(char));
     strcpy(htrFile->basePosition[i].name, token[0]);
     htrFile->basePosition[i].tx = atof(token[1]);
     htrFile->basePosition[i].ty = atof(token[2]);
     htrFile->basePosition[i].tz = atof(token[3]);
```

```
htrFile->basePosition[i].rx = atof(token[4]);
htrFile->basePosition[i].ry = atof(token[5]);
htrFile->basePosition[i].rz = atof(token[6]);
htrFile->basePosition[i].boneLength = atof(token[7]);
}
```

The last step in loading the .htr file is the processing of the actual segment data. It also consists of eight tokens, but there is one set of data per frame for each segment. We must allocate space for htrFile->segmentData based on the number of segments, and for htrFile->segmentData->frame based on the number of frames.

```
/* Process SegmentData section */
/* Allocate memory based on number of segments */
htrFile->segmentData = (struct htrSegmentData *)
    malloc(htrFile->numSegments *
    sizeof(struct htrSegmentData));

/* Start reading SegmentData data */
for (i=0; i < htrFile->numSegments; i++) {

    /* Get a line of text */
    found = 0;
    value = 1;
    while (!found && value) {
        value = fgets(textLine, MAXLINE, htrFileHandle);

        /* Skip if comment or newline */
        if (textLine[0] == '\n' !! textLine[0] == '#')
            found = 0;
        else
            if (value)
                found = 1;
    }
    if (!found) {
        fprintf(stderr, "\nError: Premature end of file\n");
        exit();
    }

    /* Look for segment name */
    if (genStr = strrchr(textLine, ']'))
        genStr[0] = '\0';

    /* Allocate space for segment name and save w/o brackets */
    htrFile->segmentData[i].segmentName = (char *)
        malloc((strlen(textLine)-1) * sizeof(char));
    strcpy(htrFile->segmentData[i].segmentName, textLine+1);

    /* Allocate space for frame data based on number of frames */
    htrFile->segmentData[i].frame = (struct htrFrame *)
        malloc(htrFile->numFrames * sizeof(struct htrFrame));

    /* Start gathering the segment's data */
    for (j=0; j < htrFile->numFrames; j++) {

        /* Get a line of text */
```

```
      found = 0;
      value = 1;
      while (!found && value) {
            value = fgets(textLine, MAXLINE, htrFileHandle);

            /* Skip if comment or newline */
            if (textLine[0] == '\n' !! textLine[0] == '#')
                  found = 0;
            else
                  if (value)
                        found = 1;
      }
if (!found) {
      fprintf(stderr, "\nError: Premature end of file\n");
      exit();
      }

/* Parse line */
numTokens = 0;
token[numTokens++] = strtok(textLine, DELIMIT);
while (token[numTokens-1])
      token[numTokens++] = strtok(NULL, DELIMIT);
numTokens -= 1;

/* Make sure we got eight tokens */
if (numTokens != 8) {
      fprintf(stderr, "\nError: Invalid frame data\n");
      exit();
      }

/* Save data line into buffer */
htrFile->segmentData[i].frame[j].frameNo = atoi(token[0]);
htrFile->segmentData[i].frame[j].tx = atof(token[1]);
htrFile->segmentData[i].frame[j].ty = atof(token[2]);
htrFile->segmentData[i].frame[j].tz = atof(token[3]);
htrFile->segmentData[i].frame[j].rx = atof(token[4]);
htrFile->segmentData[i].frame[j].ry = atof(token[5]);
htrFile->segmentData[i].frame[j].rz = atof(token[6]);
htrFile->segmentData[i].frame[j].SF = atof(token[7]);
      }
   }

/* Close .htr file */
fclose(htrFileHandle);
```

All of the .htr's file data has now been loaded into memory. At this point, we will start porting the data into the Acclaim format buffer. One could write the data straight into the .asf and .amc files, but moving it first into the buffer will help illustrate this operation in case you decide to write a converter from Acclaim to any other format in the future. If you end up writing a more complicated application in which you can port data between several formats, you could perhaps have a different kind of generic buffer that could save data from any of the file formats. This buffer could be designed in a way that would facilitate other operations as well.

```
/* Start writing data into Acclaim buffer */

/* Allocate space and write version number */
acclaimFile->version = (char *)
     malloc((strlen("1.10")) * sizeof(char));
strcpy(acclaimFile->version, "1.10");

/* Get .htr file name without extension to use as skeleton name */
strcpy(textLine, htrFileName);
if (genStr = strrchr(textLine, '.'))
     genStr[0] = '\0';

/* Allocate space and write skeleton name */
/* You can use any user-defined name here */
acclaimFile->name = (char *)
     malloc((strlen(textLine)) * sizeof(char));
strcpy(acclaimFile->name, textLine);

/* Write unitsMass default value since it is not included in .htr */
acclaimFile->unitsMass = 1.0;

/* Write unitsLength from .htr scaleFactor */
acclaimFile->unitsLength = htrFile->scaleFactor;

/* Write unitsAngle based on .htr rotationUnits */
if (htrFile->rotationUnits[0] == 'R' ||
     htrFile->rotationUnits[0] == 'r')
          strcpy(acclaimFile->unitsAngle, "rad");
else
          strcpy(acclaimFile->unitsAngle, "deg");

/* Allocate space and write notes as needed */
strcpy(textLine, "Created from htr data");
acclaimFile->documentation = (char *)
     malloc((strlen(textLine)) * sizeof(char));
strcpy(acclaimFile->documentation, textLine);
```

Now let's write the `:root` section. The order of transformations in the .htr file always includes translations first and then rotations, followed by scale. Because of this, we will assume all translations occur before all other transformations, and thus we will include code only to process different rotation arrangements. We also save a predefined rotation order value in `htrRotOrder` that we will use later, since the .htr file uses a single order of rotations across the board (unlike the Acclaim format, in which each segment can have a different one).

```
/* We now write the root's xform order and axis      */
/* from eulerRotationOrder. We assume translations    */
/* first because .htr always assumes translations first */
if (strcmp(htrFile->eulerRotationOrder, "XYZ")) {
     strcpy(acclaimFile->rootOrder, "tx ty tz rx ry rz");
     strcpy(acclaimFile->rootAxis, "xyz");
     htrRotOrder = XYZ;
     }
else
```

```
        if (strcmp(htrFile->eulerRotationOrder, "XZY")) {
            strcpy(acclaimFile->rootOrder, "tx ty tz rx rz ry");
            strcpy(acclaimFile->rootAxis, "xzy");
            htrRotOrder = XZY;
            }
    else
        if (strcmp(htrFile->eulerRotationOrder, "ZXY")) {
            strcpy(acclaimFile->rootOrder, "tx ty tz rz rx ry");
            strcpy(acclaimFile->rootAxis, "zxy");
            htrRotOrder = ZXY;
            }
        else
            if (strcmp(htrFile->eulerRotationOrder, "ZYX")) {
                strcpy(acclaimFile->rootOrder,
                    "tx ty tz rz ry rx");
                strcpy(acclaimFile->rootAxis, "zyx");
                htrRotOrder = ZYX;
                }
            else
                if (strcmp(htrFile->eulerRotationOrder, "YXZ")) {
                    strcpy(acclaimFile->rootOrder,
                        "tx ty tz ry rx rz");
                    strcpy(acclaimFile->rootAxis, "yxz");
                    htrRotOrder = YXZ;
                    }
                else
                    if (strcmp(htrFile->eulerRotationOrder, "YZX"))
                        {
                        strcpy(acclaimFile->rootOrder,
                            "tx ty tz ry rz rx");
                        strcpy(acclaimFile->rootAxis, "yzx");
                        htrRotOrder = YZX;
                        }
```

The .htr file uses an actual segment as the parent of all the hierarchy. In the Acclaim format we will move the hierarchy one step down, leaving the .htr's parent node as a child of the root node; the root node is left at the origin at all times. This is very useful because you can use the root to add a transformation offset to the whole tree if desired. One could also do this at the animation software level by adding a parent node, but if you are dealing with a great number of motions, it is better to offset all the motion data files.

```
/* Assume by default that the root bone is the        */
/* parent of all hierarchy in the .htr file and that it */
/* is located at the origin                           */
acclaimFile->rootPosition[0] = 0.0;
acclaimFile->rootPosition[1] = 0.0;
acclaimFile->rootPosition[2] = 0.0;
acclaimFile->rootOrientation[0] = 0.0;
acclaimFile->rootOrientation[1] = 0.0;
acclaimFile->rootOrientation[2] = 0.0;
```

Next, we start saving the bonedata section. We assume that all segments are initially located at the origin, and that the length axis is pointing in the globalAxisofGravity direction. Some variation in this section can exist between animation software packages, because not all of them use this assumption for the initial position of bones. A more elaborate translator should include switches to deal with these software peculiarities.

```
/* Allocate memory for boned ata based on number of segments */
acclaimFile->boneData = (struct acclaimBoneData *)
     malloc(htrFile->numSegments * sizeof(struct acclaimBoneData));

/* Start writing bone data based on base position section */
for (i=0; i < htrFile->numSegments; i++) {

          /* Use i for id # */
          acclaimFile->boneData[i].id = i+1;

          /* Bone name */
          acclaimFile->boneData[i].name = (char *)
               malloc((strlen(htrFile->basePosition[i].name)) *
               sizeof(char));
          strcpy(acclaimFile->boneData.name,
               htrFile->basePosition[i].name);

          /* Write direction vector using globalAxisofGravity    */
          /* The .htr assumption is that all bones' initial       */
          /* length vector is pointing toward the up axis         */
          acclaimFile->boneData[i].direction[0] = 0.0;
          acclaimFile->boneData[i].direction[1] = 0.0;
          acclaimFile->boneData[i].direction[2] = 0.0;
          switch (htrFile->globalAxisofGravity[0])
          {
          case 'X':
               acclaimFile->boneData[i].direction[0] = 1.0;
               break;
          case 'Y':
               acclaimFile->boneData[i].direction[1] = 1.0;
               break;
          case 'Z':
               acclaimFile->boneData[i].direction[2] = 1.0;
               break;
          }

          /* Segment length */
          acclaimFile->boneData[i].length =
               htrFile->basePosition[i].boneLength;
```

Even though the Acclaim format has the ability to select which transformations are available per segment, we have to include them all because the .htr file includes all seven transformations for each of the segments. The limits are also left open, because these are not supported by the .htr format.

```
/* process axis and dof order */
/* using htrRotBone         */
switch(htrRotBone)
{
case XYZ:
     acclaimFile->boneData[i].axis[0] =
          htrFile->basePosition[i].rx;
     acclaimFile->boneData[i].axis[1] =
          htrFile->basePosition[i].ry;
     acclaimFile->boneData[i].axis[2] =
          htrFile->basePosition[i].rz;
     strcpy(acclaimFile->boneData[i].axisOrder, "xyz");
     strcpy(acclaimFile->boneData[i].dof,
          "tx ty tz rx ry rz l");
     break;
case XZY:
     acclaimFile->boneData[i].axis[0] =
          htrFile->basePosition[i].rx;
     acclaimFile->boneData[i].axis[1] =
          htrFile->basePosition[i].rz;
     acclaimFile->boneData[i].axis[2] =
          htrFile->basePosition[i].ry;
     strcpy(acclaimFile->boneData[i].axisOrder, "xzy");
     strcpy(acclaimFile->boneData[i].dof,
          "tx ty tz rx rz ry l");
     break;
case YXZ:
     acclaimFile->boneData[i].axis[0] =
          htrFile->basePosition[i].ry;
     acclaimFile->boneData[i].axis[1] =
          htrFile->basePosition[i].rx;
     acclaimFile->boneData[i].axis[2] =
          htrFile->basePosition[i].rz;
     strcpy(acclaimFile->boneData[i].axisOrder, "yxz");
     strcpy(acclaimFile->boneData[i].dof,
          "tx ty tz ry rx rz l");
     break;
case YZX:
     acclaimFile->boneData[i].axis[0] =
          htrFile->basePosition[i].ry;
     acclaimFile->boneData[i].axis[1] =
          htrFile->basePosition[i].rz;
     acclaimFile->boneData[i].axis[2] =
          htrFile->basePosition[i].rx;
     strcpy(acclaimFile->boneData[i].axisOrder, "yzx");
     strcpy(acclaimFile->boneData[i].dof,
          "tx ty tz ry rz rx l");
     break;
case ZXY:
     acclaimFile->boneData[i].axis[0] =
          htrFile->basePosition[i].rz;
     acclaimFile->boneData[i].axis[1] =
          htrFile->basePosition[i].rx;
     acclaimFile->boneData[i].axis[2] =
          htrFile->basePosition[i].ry;
     strcpy(acclaimFile->boneData[i].axisOrder, "zxy");
     strcpy(acclaimFile->boneData[i].dof,
          "tx ty tz rz rx ry l");
     break;
```

```
    case ZYX:
        acclaimFile->boneData[i].axis[0] =
            htrFile->basePosition[i].rz;
        acclaimFile->boneData[i].axis[1] =
            htrFile->basePosition[i].ry;
        acclaimFile->boneData[i].axis[2] =
            htrFile->basePosition[i].rx;
        strcpy(acclaimFile->boneData[i].axisOrder, "zyx");
        strcpy(acclaimFile->boneData[i].dof,
            "tx ty tz rz ry rx l");
        break;
}

/* Because all data is included in .htr file, dof# = 7 */
acclaimFile->bonedata[i].dofNumber = 7;

/* Allocate space for 7 limits */
acclaimFile->boneData[i].limits = (struct acclaimBoneLimits *)
    malloc(acclaimFile->boneData[i].dofNumber *
    sizeof(struct acclaimBoneLimits));

/* All limits in this particular conversion are open */
for (j=0; j < htrFile->numFrames; j++) {
    acclaimFile->boneData[i].limits[j].minMax[0] = 0;
    acclaimFile->boneData[i].limits[j].minMax[1] = 0;
    acclaimFile->boneData[i].limits[j].infinity[0] = 1;
    acclaimFile->boneData[i].limits[j].infinity[1] = 1;
    }

/* bodyMass and cofMass are not used by .htr file */
acclaimFile->boneData[i].bodyMass = 1.0;
acclaimFile->boneData[i].cofMass = 1.0;
}
```

The hierarchy section in the .asf file is quite different from that in the .htr file. The .asf file lists a parent first, followed by all its children in the same line, whereas the .htr file lists each child first, followed by its parent. The number of lines in the hierarchy section of the .htr file is equal to the number of segments, whereas in the .asf file it is equal to the number of nodes that have children (not counting the root node). Thus, before starting to save the hierarchy in the Acclaim buffer, we must find out how many segments have children.

```
/* Start processing hierarchy */
/* Find out how many bones have children */
numParents = 0;
for (i=0; i < htrFile->numSegments; i++) {
    for (j=0; j < htrFile->numSegments; j++) {
        if (strcmp(htrFile->childParent[i].child,
            htrFile->childParent[j].parent)) {
            numParents++;
            j = htrFile->numSegments;
            }
        }
    }
```

```c
/* Allocate space for hierarchy based on number of parents */
acclaimFile->hierarchy = (struct acclaimHierarchy *)
     malloc((numParents + 1) * sizeof(struct acclaimHierarchy));

/* Start reading .htr file's hierarchy section */
/* Allocate space and save root */
acclaimFile->hierarchy[0].parent = (char *)
     malloc((strlen("root")) * sizeof(char));
strcpy(acclaimFile->hierarchy[0].parent, "root");

/* Find nodes with GLOBAL parent */
for (i=0; i < htrFile->numSegments; i++) {

     /* If GLOBAL is found, add child to list */
     if (strcmp(htrFile->childParent[i].parent, "GLOBAL")) {
         strcat(acclaimFile->hierarchy[0].children,
             htrFile->childParent[i].child);

         /* Add a blank space after child string */
         acclaimFile->hierarchy[0].children[strlen(
             acclaimFile->hierarchy[0].children)] = ' ';
     }
}

/* Remove last space */
acclaimFile->hierarchy[0].children[strlen(
     acclaimFile->hierarchy[0].children)-1] = '\0';

/* Process rest of parent and child nodes */
k = 1;
for (i=0; i < htrFile->numSegments; i++) {
     found = 0;
     for (j=0; j < htrFile->numSegments; j++) {

         /* Find all children of node i */
         if (strcmp(htrFile->childParent[i].child,
             htrFile->childParent[j].parent)) {

             /* If first one, allocate space and save parent */
             if (!found) {
                 acclaimFile->hierarchy[k].parent = (char *)
                     malloc((strlen(htrFile->childParent[j].parent))
                     * sizeof(char));
                 strcpy(acclaimFile->hierarchy[k].parent,
                 htrFile->childParent[j].parent);
                 found = 1;
             }

             /* Cat child's name */
             strcat(acclaimFile->hierarchy[k].children,
                 htrFile->childParent[j].child);

             /* Add a blank space after child string */
             acclaimFile->hierarchy[k].children[strlen(
                 acclaimFile->hierarchy[k].children)] = ' ';
         }
     }
}
```

```
    /* Remove last space */
    if (found) {
        acclaimFile->hierarchy[k].children[strlen(
            acclaimFile->hierarchy[k].children)-1] = '\0';

        /* Update parent number counter */
        k++;
        }
    }

/* I skip the skin section as it is not   */
/* supported by .htr or most animation    */
/* packages                               */
```

Now start saving the data stream. We will not worry yet about the order of transformations. These will be dealt with when we write the .amc file. The 1 channel in the .amc data is not the same as the SF channel in the .htr file, and it must be converted before saving. SF is a scaling factor or a multiplier for the initial segment length, whereas 1 is a translation. This means that an SF value of 1 is equivalent to an 1 value of 0. To convert the scaling factor to a translation, we multiply the initial length by the scaling factor and then subtract the segment length, obtaining the difference in length between the initial length and the length for the frame in question.

```
/* Process motion data stream */
/* Allocate space for data stream based on number of frames */
acclaimFile->frameData = (struct acclaimFrameData *)
    malloc(htrFile->numFrames * sizeof(struct acclaimFrameData));

/* Start processing frames */
for (i=0; i < htrFile->numFrames; i++) {

    /* Write frame number (start at 1 by default) */
    acclaimFile->frameData[i].frame = i+1;

    /* Allocate space for segment data, including root */
    acclaimFile->frameData[i].motionData =
        (struct acclaimMotionData *)
        malloc((htrFile->numSegments+1) *
        sizeof(struct acclaimMotionData));

    /* Write root segment (default at origin) */
    acclaimFile->frameData[i].motionData[0].tx = 0;
    acclaimFile->frameData[i].motionData[0].ty = 0;
    acclaimFile->frameData[i].motionData[0].tz = 0;
    acclaimFile->frameData[i].motionData[0].rx = 0;
    acclaimFile->frameData[i].motionData[0].ry = 0;
    acclaimFile->frameData[i].motionData[0].rz = 0;
    acclaimFile->frameData[i].motionData[0].l = 0;

    /* Allocate memory and write segment name */
    acclaimFile->frameData[i].motionData[0].segment = (char *)
        malloc(strlen("root") * sizeof(char));
```

```
        strcpy(acclaimFile->frameData[i].motionData[0].segment,
            "root");

    /* Read other segment data for this frame */
    for (j=1; j <= htrFile->numSegments; j++) {

        /* Write segment data */
        acclaimFile->frameData[i].motionData[j].tx =
            htrFile->segmentData[j-1].frame[i].tx;
        acclaimFile->frameData[i].motionData[j].ty =
            htrFile->segmentData[j-1].frame[i].ty;
        acclaimFile->frameData[i].motionData[j].tz =
            htrFile->segmentData[j-1].frame[i].tz;
        acclaimFile->frameData[i].motionData[j].rx =
            htrFile->segmentData[j-1].frame[i].rx;
        acclaimFile->frameData[i].motionData[j].ry =
            htrFile->segmentData[j-1].frame[i].ry;
        acclaimFile->frameData[i].motionData[j].rz =
            htrFile->segmentData[j-1].frame[i].rz;

        /* Calculate bone translation deviation using  */
        /* .htr's SF and bone length                   */
        acclaimFile->frameData[i].motionData[j].l =
            acclaimFile->boneData[j-1].length -
            (htrFile->segmentData[j-1].frame[i].SF *
            acclaimFile->boneData[j-1].length);

        /* Allocate memory and write segment name */
        acclaimFile->frameData[i].motionData[j].segment = (char *)
            malloc(strlen(htrFile->segmentData[j-1].segmentName) *
            sizeof(char));
        strcpy(acclaimFile->frameData[i].motionData[j].segment,
            htrFile->segmentData[j-1].segmentName);
        }
    }

/* Save number of segments and frames for later use */
numBones = htrFile->numSegments;
numFrames = htrFile->numFrames;
```

We have now saved all the data in the .htr file into the Acclaim buffer. The next step is to write the actual .asf and .amc files. The number of segments was saved in a variable named numBones and the number of frames in a variable named numFrames because the Acclaim format does not include fields for these values.

```
/* Open .asf file */
asfFileHandle = fopen(asfFileName, "w");
if (!asfFileHandle) {
    fprintf(stderr, "\nError: Unable to open %s \n", asfFileName);
    exit();
    }

/* version */
fprintf(asfFileHandle,":version %s\n", acclaimFile->version);
```

```
/* name */
fprintf(asfFileHandle, ":name %s\n", acclaimFile->name);

/* units section */
fprintf(asfFileHandle, " mass %f\n", acclaimFile->unitsMass);
fprintf(asfFileHandle, " length %f\n", acclaimFile->unitsLength);
fprintf(asfFileHandle, " angle %s\n", acclaimFile->unitsAngle);

/* documentation */
fprintf(asfFileHandle, ":documentation\n");
fprintf(asfFileHandle,   "%s\n", acclaimFile->documentation);

/* doot section */
fprintf(asfFileHandle, ":root\n");
fprintf(asfFileHandle, " order %s\n", acclaimFile->rootOrder);
fprintf(asfFileHandle, " axis %s\n", acclaimFile->rootAxis);
fprintf(asfFileHandle, " position %d %d %d\n",
     acclaimFile->rootPosition[0],
     acclaimFile->rootPosition[1],
     acclaimFile->rootPosition[2]);
fprintf(asfFileHandle, " orientation %d %d %d\n",
     acclaimFile->rootOrientation[0],
     acclaimFile->rootOrientation[1],
     acclaimFile->rootOrientation[2]);

/* bonedata section */
fprintf(asfFileHandle, ":bonedata\n");
for (i=0; i < numBones; i++) {
     fprintf(asfFileHandle, " begin\n");
     fprintf(asfFileHandle, "    id %d\n",
        acclaimFile->boneData[i].id);
     fprintf(asfFileHandle, "    name %s\n",
        acclaimFile->boneData[i].name);
     fprintf(asfFileHandle, "    direction %f %f %f\n",
        acclaimFile->boneData[i].direction[0],
        acclaimFile->boneData[i].direction[1],
        acclaimFile->boneData[i].direction[2]);
     fprintf(asfFileHandle, "    length %d\n",
        acclaimFile->boneData[i].length);
     fprintf(asfFileHandle, "    axis %d %d %d %s\n",
        acclaimFile->boneData[i].axis[0],
        acclaimFile->boneData[i].axis[1],
        acclaimFile->boneData[i].axis[2],
        acclaimFile->boneData[i].axisOrder);
     fprintf(asfFileHandle, "    dof %s\n",
        acclaimFile->boneData[i].dof);

     /* Write limits */
     fprintf(asfFileHandle, "    limits ");
     for (j=0; j < acclaimFile->bonedata[i].dofNumber; j++) {
        if (acclaimFile->bonedata[i].limits.infinity[0])
             fprintf(asfFileHandle, "(-inf");
        else
             fprintf(asfFileHandle, "(%d",
                acclaimFile->boneData[i].limits.minMax[0]);
        if (acclaimFile->bonedata[i].limits.infinity[1])
             fprintf(asfFileHandle, " inf)\n");
        else
             fprintf(asfFileHandle, " %d)\n",
```

```
                        acclaimFile->boneData[i].limits.minMax[1]);
            }
    fprintf(asfFileHandle, " end\n");
    }

/* hierarchy */
fprintf(asfFileHandle, ":hierarchy\n");
fprintf(asfFileHandle, " begin\n");
for (i=0; i < numParents; i++)
    fprintf(asfFileHandle, "     %s %s\n",
        acclaimFile->hierarchy[i].parent,
        acclaimFile->hierarchy[i].children);

/* If there were skin file data, you would write it at this point */

/* Close .asf file */
fclose(asfFileHandle);
```

As we write the motion data, we must deal with the order of transformations per segment. We will use the dof field to determine the order per segment.

```
/* Frame data */
/* Open .amc file */
amcFileHandle = fopen(amcFileName, "w");
if (!amcFileHandle) {
    fprintf(stderr, "\nError: Unable to open %s \n", amcFileName);
    exit();
    }

/* File type */
fprintf(amcFileHandle, ":FULLY-SPECIFIED\n");
if (strcmp(acclaimFile->unitsAngle, "deg"))
    fprintf(amcFileHandle, ":DEGREES\n");
else
    fprintf(amcFileHandle, ":RADIANS\n");

/* Start frame loop */
for (i=0; i < numFrames; i++) {

    /* Frame number */
    fprintf(amcFileHandle, %d\n",
        acclaimFile->frameData[i].frame);

    /* Process root (at origin by default) */
    fprintf(amcFileHandle,
        "root 0.0, 0.0, 0.0, 0.0, 0.0, 0.0, 0.0");

    /* Write bone data for this frame */
    for (j=1; j <= numBones; j++) {

        /* Bone name */
        fprintf(amcFileHandle, "%s",
            acclaimFile->frameData[i].motionData[j].segment);

        /* Process dof tokens */
        numTokens = 0;
```

```
        token[numTokens++] =
            strtok(acclaimFile->boneData[j-1].dof, DELIMIT);
        while (token[numTokens-1])
            token[numTokens++] = strtok(NULL, DELIMIT);
        numTokens -= 1;

        /* Write data to file in the order defined by dof */
        for (k=0; k < numTokens; k++) {
            switch(token[k][0]) {
                case 'l':
                    fprintf(amcFileHandle, " %d",
                        acclaimfile->frameData[i].motionData.l);
                    break;
                case 't':
                    switch(token[k][1]) {
                        case 'x':
                            fprintf(amcFileHandle, " %d",
                                acclaimFile->frameData[i].
                                motionData[j].tx);
                            break;
                        case 'y':
                            fprintf(amcFileHandle, " %d",
                                acclaimFile->frameData[i].
                                motionData[j].ty);
                            break;
                        case 'z':
                            fprintf(amcFileHandle, " %d",
                                acclaimFile->frameData[i].
                                motionData[j].tz);
                            break;
                    }
                case 'r':
                    switch(token[k][1]) {
                        case 'x':
                            fprintf(amcFileHandle, " %d",
                                acclaimFile->frameData[i].
                                motionData[j].rx);
                            break;
                        case 'y':
                            fprintf(amcFileHandle, " %d",
                                acclaimFile->frameData[i].
                                motionData[j].ry);
                            break;
                        case 'z':
                            fprintf(amcFileHandle, " %d",
                                acclaimFile->frameData[i].
                                motionData[j].rz);
                            break;
                    }
            }
        }
        fprintf(amcFileHandle, "\n");
        }
    }

/* Close .amc file */
fclose(amcFileHandle);

/* Clean memory here if you need to */
```

Chapter Five

Setting Up
Your Character

❦

Setting up a digital character involves two main steps: mechanical setup and deformation setup. I'm not talking about modeling or lighting, but about motion setup, which is the action of making a character controllable or poseable. *Mechanical setup* involves creating the skeleton that will drive the character, as well as creating all the controls that will be used to animate the character. *Deformation setup* defines the relationship of each vertex of the character to the skeleton.

This chapter deals only with mechanical setup, because deformation setup is very specific to each particular software package and is implemented in the same way for both keyframed and captured motion data. Nevertheless, when using captured motion data, you must keep in mind that deformations are pushed to the limit. Thus, it is very important to take extra care when creating the mechanical setup that will drive them. Usually, the rotational data that a motion capture studio delivers is not enough to drive a typical vertex-weighting deformation scheme. Keyframe animators can distribute transformations across several joints when posing a character; for example, in twisting an arm, rotations can be partially added to the shoulder, elbow, and wrist in such a way that the character's envelope will not be twisted. Captured motion data does not follow this distribution pattern, but rather behaves in an anatomically correct way, assigning most of the twisting to the segment between the elbow and the wrist. This is usually not friendly to most deformation schemes. Setting up the mechanics of a character to follow the properties of the actual raw data is the key to better deformations.

The rotational motion data formats that were discussed in Chapter 4 include a skeleton for the user. In those cases, the mechanical setup has already been done for you. All you need to do is import the file and, voilà, a skeleton is readily available for your character. I question most of these file formats because the creation of a skeleton is not something to take lightly. In some cases the default skeleton in the motion file will do, but the highest-quality jobs will require a very careful mechanical setup that can only be designed by the same person who is responsible for the setup of the deformations.

To maximize your control over captured motion data, it is best to obtain the data in the simplest format possible. All you need is the tracked marker data, so the translational file will do. This file contains only a stream of marker position coordinates over time. By using this file, you can design the skeleton inside your animation environment and not abide by what a motion capture studio delivers. This method is definitely more time-consuming, so make sure you also obtain the rotational data and determine first if it is of adequate quality and if the skeleton is appropriate enough for your project.

Depending on the animation software to be used, you may need to write expressions or plug-in programs, and mathematics are definitely needed.

SETTING UP A CHARACTER WITH ROTATIONAL DATA

When rotational data is used for motion capture, a skeleton is already included or assumed by the data stream. It is possible that all you need to do is import the data into your software and your character will start moving. It is also possible that the data may be incompatible with your software, or that you may have to change your software's settings in order to receive the data.

Depending on the software used, you may have to create a skeleton before importing the data. If you are dealing with data in the Acclaim format, chances are you only need to load the .asf file. When using other formats, you sometimes have to create the skeletal nodes and then load the data to pose them. If you must do that, you need to find out what the initial orientation and position of the bones should be.

If you load a skeleton in its base position and its pose doesn't match that of the character, the ideal solution is to pose the character to match using the modeling software, but in most cases this is impossible. Another solution is to modify the base position to match the pose of the character. Doing so entails recalculating all the motion data to compensate. A third and most frequently used solution is to add an expression that will add an offset to the data equal to the negative of the offset added to the base position. This is almost equivalent to recalculating all the data, but it is done on the fly. This technique has the advantage of being quick and easy, but it is a hack after all, so it isn't the cleanest solution and may even complicate Euler angle problems that had previously been fixed in the data.

When you import rotational data into animation software, you must make sure that the data is prepared to transform your character in the same order as the software does. In some programs, you are able to change this order—sometimes for each segment or for the whole project. Others are not so flexible. Some programs allow you to change the order of rotations only, whereas others allow you to change when translations, rotations, and scaling happen. You need to know what your particular software supports before preparing the rotational data.

Most programs and motion data formats assume translations will happen before rotations, and scaling will happen after rotations. Most problems that arise usually concern the order of rotations specifically. Three-dimensional rotations are noncommutative, which means you cannot interchange their order and obtain the same result.

SETTING UP A CHARACTER WITH TRANSLATIONAL DATA

The files you use to set up a character with translational data contain a set of markers with positional coordinates over time. You use combinations of these markers to create approximations of rigid segments that will define the skeleton of your character.

Creating the Internal Skeleton

The first step in setting up the character is finding the locations of all the local coordinate systems that will represent the new internal skeleton. There is at least one coordinate system associated with each of the rigid segments, and you need to find equations or formulas that will allow you to find these over time. Once you have these formulas, you can use them in your animation software to position and orient joints.

The bones can be calculated using exclusively the markers that define the rigid segments associated with them, or you can use previously found internal points in combination with markers. The latter approach makes the process easier and ensures that the segments are linked between each other, since considerable inaccuracy is common because markers are placed on the skin and do not exactly maintain their position relative to bones.

Center of Gravity

The location of the character's center of gravity must be determined. Assuming the data was captured using the default marker setup defined in Chapter 3, the

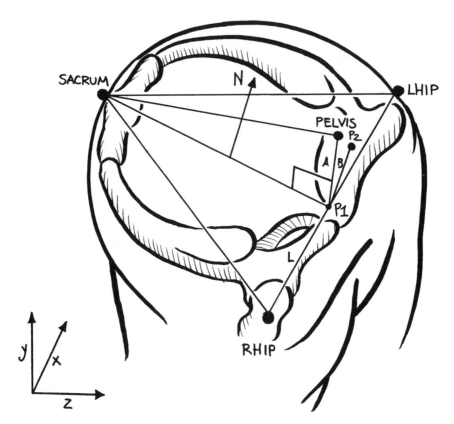

Figure 5-1. *The center of gravity.*

pelvis segment is defined by the SACRUM, LHIP, and RHIP markers. Figure 5-1 is a visualization of the center of gravity, shown in the figure as point PELVIS(x_{PELVIS}, y_{PELVIS}, z_{PELVIS}).

We begin by defining the rigid segment formed by SACRUM, LHIP, and RHIP using the following linear equation of a plane:

$$ax + by + cz + d = 0 \qquad (5\text{-}1)$$

Since we know the coordinates of three points in space, LHIP(x_{LHIP}, y_{LHIP}, z_{LHIP}), RHIP(x_{RHIP}, y_{RHIP}, z_{RHIP}), and SACRUM(x_{SACRUM}, y_{SACRUM}, z_{SACRUM}), the constants (a, b, c, and d) of Equation 5-1 can be calculated by the following determinants:

$$a = \begin{vmatrix} 1 & y_{LHIP} & z_{LHIP} \\ 1 & y_{RHIP} & z_{RHIP} \\ 1 & y_{SACRUM} & z_{SACRUM} \end{vmatrix} \qquad (5\text{-}2)$$

$$b = \begin{vmatrix} x_{LHIP} & 1 & z_{LHIP} \\ x_{RHIP} & 1 & z_{RHIP} \\ x_{SACRUM} & 1 & z_{SACRUM} \end{vmatrix} \tag{5-3}$$

$$c = \begin{vmatrix} x_{LHIP} & y_{LHIP} & 1 \\ x_{RHIP} & y_{RHIP} & 1 \\ x_{SACRUM} & y_{SACRUM} & 1 \end{vmatrix} \tag{5-4}$$

$$d = -\begin{vmatrix} x_{LHIP} & y_{LHIP} & z_{LHIP} \\ x_{RHIP} & y_{RHIP} & z_{RHIP} \\ x_{SACRUM} & y_{SACRUM} & z_{SACRUM} \end{vmatrix} \tag{5-5}$$

We can expand the above equations, obtaining the following:

$$a = y_{LHIP} (z_{RHIP} - z_{SACRUM})$$
$$+ y_{RHIP} (z_{SACRUM} - z_{LHIP})$$
$$+ y_{SACRUM} (z_{LHIP} - z_{RHIP}) \tag{5-6}$$

$$b = z_{LHIP} (x_{RHIP} - x_{SACRUM})$$
$$+ z_{RHIP} (x_{SACRUM} - x_{LHIP})$$
$$+ z_{SACRUM} (x_{LHIP} - x_{RHIP}) \tag{5-7}$$

$$c = x_{LHIP} (y_{RHIP} - y_{SACRUM})$$
$$+ x_{RHIP} (y_{SACRUM} - y_{LHIP})$$
$$+ x_{SACRUM} (y_{LHIP} - y_{RHIP}) \tag{5-8}$$

$$d = - x_{LHIP} (y_{RHIP} z_{SACRUM} - y_{SACRUM} z_{RHIP})$$
$$- x_{RHIP} (y_{SACRUM} z_{LHIP} - y_{LHIP} z_{SACRUM})$$
$$- x_{SACRUM} (y_{LHIP} z_{RHIP} - y_{RHIP} z_{LHIP}) \tag{5-9}$$

We then proceed to find the direction cosines (σ_x, σ_y, σ_z) of the normal N of the plane as follows:

$$\sigma_x = \frac{a}{\sqrt{a^2 + b^2 + c^2}} \tag{5-10}$$

$$\sigma_y = \frac{b}{\sqrt{a^2 + b^2 + c^2}}$$ (5-11)

$$\sigma_z = \frac{c}{\sqrt{a^2 + b^2 + c^2}}$$ (5-12)

We continue by defining a line segment L between points LHIP and RHIP. We will refer to the midpoint between LHIP and RHIP as P_1 and will calculate its coordinates by using the following linear parametric equations:

$$
\begin{aligned}
x &= a_x u + b_x \\
y &= a_y u + b_y \\
z &= a_z u + b_z
\end{aligned}
$$ (5-13)

u is the parametric variable that defines where in the line the point is located. Substituting $u = 0$, we obtain the coordinates of one of the end points; with $u = 1$, we obtain the coordinates of the second end point. $u = 0.5$ will give us the coordinates of P_1, the midpoint in the center of the line segment.

Since we know the coordinates of the end points LHIP and RHIP, to solve the equations we start by substituting the end point coordinates. For the first end point, we assume $u = 0$ and we obtain

$$
\begin{aligned}
bx &= x_{LHIP} \\
by &= y_{LHIP} \\
bz &= z_{LHIP}
\end{aligned}
$$ (5-14)

where x_{LHIP}, y_{LHIP}, and z_{LHIP} are the coordinates of marker LHIP. For the second end point, we substitute $u = 1$ and obtain

$$
\begin{aligned}
x_{RHIP} &= a_x + b_x \\
y_{RHIP} &= a_y + b_y \\
z_{RHIP} &= a_z + b_z
\end{aligned}
$$ (5-15)

Substituting Equation 5-14 into 5-15 gives us

$$
\begin{aligned}
ax &= x_{RHIP} - x_{LHIP} \\
ay &= y_{RHIP} - y_{LHIP} \\
az &= z_{RHIP} - z_{LHIP}
\end{aligned}
$$ (5-16)

Finally, we substitute Equations 5-14 and 5-16 into 5-13 and obtain the coordinates of $P_1(x_1, y_1, z_1)$, where $u = 0.5$:

$$x_1 = 0.5(x_{\text{RHIP}} - x_{\text{LHIP}}) + x_{\text{LHIP}}$$

$$y_1 = 0.5(y_{\text{RHIP}} - y_{\text{LHIP}}) + y_{\text{LHIP}} \tag{5-17}$$

$$z_1 = 0.5(z_{\text{RHIP}} - z_{\text{LHIP}}) + z_{\text{LHIP}}$$

Next, we need to calculate the constant length of line segment A; to do so, we will need to assume that the system is in a base pose where L is aligned with the world x-axis and A is aligned with the world y-axis. In this state, we can further assume the following:

$$x_{\text{PELVIS}} = x1$$

$$y_{\text{PELVIS}} = y_{\text{SACRUM}} \tag{5-18}$$

$$z_{\text{PELVIS}} = z1$$

We make these assumptions because when the system is in its base state, PELVIS is located at the same height as SACRUM and at the same width and depth as P_1. The length of A is then calculated by

$$A = y_{\text{SACRUM}} - y_1 \tag{5-19}$$

We have a line segment B from P_1 to P_2 that is parallel to N and of equal length to A. We know that any two parallel lines in space have the same direction cosines, so the direction cosines of B are the same as the direction cosines of N. The direction cosines for B are computed using the following equations:

$$\sigma_x = \frac{x_2 - x_1}{B} \tag{5-20}$$

$$\sigma_y = \frac{y_2 - y_1}{B} \tag{5-21}$$

$$\sigma_z = \frac{z_2 - z_1}{B} \tag{5-22}$$

Since the only unknown variables are x_2, y_2, and z_2, we can obtain the frame-by-frame location of P_2 as follows:

$$x_2 = x_1 + B\sigma_x \tag{5-23}$$

$$y_2 = y_1 + B\sigma_y \tag{5-24}$$

$$z_2 = z_1 + B\sigma_z \tag{5-25}$$

Next, we need to find the value of θ, the angle between the plane normal and the z-axis. We know that

$$\sigma_z = \cos\theta \qquad\qquad (5\text{-}26)$$

so for a base pose, we can calculate θ by

$$\theta = \arccos(\sigma_z) \qquad\qquad (5\text{-}27)$$

The angle α between A and B is then found by

$$\alpha = -(90-\theta) \qquad\qquad (5\text{-}28)$$

To find the location of PELVIS, we need to rotate P_2 α degrees about the local x-axis at P_1. We perform this operation by first translating P_1 to the origin, then performing the rotation in x, and finally reversing the translation. We achieve this by the following set of matrix transformations:

$$
\begin{bmatrix} x_{\text{PELVIS}} y_{\text{PELVIS}} z_{\text{PELVIS}} 1 \end{bmatrix} =
$$

$$
\begin{bmatrix} x_2 y_2 z_2 1 \end{bmatrix}
\begin{bmatrix}
1 & 0 & 0 & 0 \\
0 & 1 & 0 & 0 \\
0 & 0 & 1 & 0 \\
-x_1 & -y_1 & -z_1 & 1
\end{bmatrix}
\begin{bmatrix}
1 & 0 & 0 & 0 \\
0 & \cos\sigma & \sin\alpha & 0 \\
0 & -\sin\alpha & \cos\alpha & 0 \\
0 & 0 & 0 & 1
\end{bmatrix}
\begin{bmatrix}
1 & 0 & 0 & 0 \\
0 & 1 & 0 & 0 \\
0 & 0 & 1 & 0 \\
x_1 & y_1 & z_1 & 1
\end{bmatrix} \qquad (5\text{-}29)
$$

Vertebral Column

The vertebral column's four segments are used to calculate the position of the four main spinal joints in our setup. The lowest point is LUMBAR, followed by THORAX, LONECK, and UPNECK.

LUMBAR

Point LUMBAR(x_{LUMBAR}, y_{LUMBAR}, z_{LUMBAR}) is located at the same height as marker L1 and at the same width as point PELVIS. Its depth falls somewhere between L1 and PELVIS, so we will assume its location to be right in between them. We will use a very similar method to calculate LUMBAR as we used to calculate PELVIS, using the elements in Figure 5-2.

The location of the midpoint $P_1(x_1, y_1, z_1)$ is found by using Equation 5-17 as follows:

$$x_1 = 0.5(x_{\text{SACRUM}} - x_{\text{PELVIS}}) + x_{\text{PELVIS}}$$

$$y_1 = 0.5(y_{\text{SACRUM}} - y_{\text{PELVIS}}) + y_{\text{PELVIS}} \qquad\qquad (5\text{-}30)$$

$$z_1 = 0.5(z_{\text{SACRUM}} - z_{\text{PELVIS}}) + z_{\text{PELVIS}}$$

We then use Equation 5-19 to find the length of line segment A. This is done by assuming the system is at its base state:

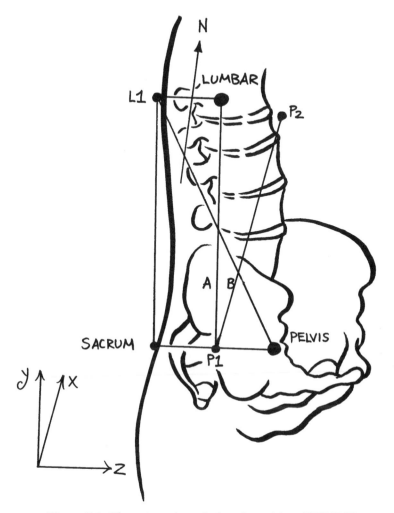

Figure 5-2. *Elements used to calculate the position of LUMBAR.*

$$A = y_{L1} - y_1 \qquad (5\text{-}31)$$

We know the coordinates of three points in space: $L1(x_{L1},\ y_{L1},\ z_{L1})$, $PELVIS(x_{PELVIS},\ y_{PELVIS},\ z_{PELVIS})$, and $SACRUM(x_{SACRUM},\ y_{SACRUM},\ z_{SACRUM})$. The constants ($a$, b, c, and d) of Equation 5-1 can be calculated by the determinants in Equations 5-2 through 5-5, which we can expand as follows:

$$a = y_{L1}\,(z_{PELVIS} - z_{SACRUM})$$

$$+\, y_{PELVIS}\,(z_{SACRUM} - z_{L1}) \qquad (5\text{-}32)$$

$$+\, y_{SACRUM}\,(z_{L1} - z_{PELVIS})$$

$$b = z_{L1} (x_{PELVIS} - x_{SACRUM})$$
$$+ z_{PELVIS} (x_{SACRUM} - x_{L1}) \tag{5-33}$$
$$+ z_{SACRUM} (x_{L1} - x_{PELVIS})$$

$$c = x_{L1} (y_{PELVIS} - y_{SACRUM})$$
$$+ x_{PELVIS} (y_{SACRUM} - y_{L1}) \tag{5-34}$$
$$+ x_{SACRUM} (y_{L1} - y_{PELVIS})$$

$$d = - x_{L1} (y_{PELVIS}\, z_{SACRUM} - y_{SACRUM}\, z_{PELVIS})$$
$$- x_{PELVIS} (y_{SACRUM}\, z_{L1} - y_{L1}\, z_{SACRUM}) \tag{5-35}$$
$$- x_{SACRUM} (y_{L1}\, z_{PELVIS} - y_{PELVIS}\, z_{L1})$$

We proceed to find the plane's normal N direction cosines (σ_x, σ_y, σ_z) using Equations 5-10 through 5-12.

We have a line segment B from P_1 to P_2 that is parallel to N and of equal length to A. We know that any two parallel lines in space have the same direction cosines, so the direction cosines of B are the same as the direction cosines of N. We use Equations 5-20 through 5-22 to obtain the location of P_2:

$$x_2 = x_1 + A\sigma_x \tag{5-36}$$
$$y_2 = y_1 + A\sigma_y \tag{5-37}$$
$$z_2 = z_1 + A\sigma_z \tag{5-38}$$

We know the angle α between A and B is $90°$, so to obtain LUMBAR's position, we need to rotate B $90°$ about the local z-axis at P_1. We use the following set of matrix transformations:

$$\left[x_{LUMBAR}\, y_{LUMBAR}\, z_{LUMBAR}\, 1 \right] =$$
$$\left[x_2 y_2 z_2 1 \right] \begin{bmatrix} 1 & 0 & 0 & 0 \\ 0 & 1 & 0 & 0 \\ 0 & 0 & 1 & 0 \\ -x_1 & -y_1 & -z_1 & 1 \end{bmatrix} \begin{bmatrix} \cos\alpha & \sin\alpha & 0 & 0 \\ -\sin\alpha & \cos\alpha & 0 & 0 \\ 0 & 0 & 1 & 0 \\ 0 & 0 & 0 & 1 \end{bmatrix} \begin{bmatrix} 1 & 0 & 0 & 0 \\ 0 & 1 & 0 & 0 \\ 0 & 0 & 1 & 0 \\ x_1 & y_1 & z_1 & 1 \end{bmatrix} \tag{5-39}$$

THORAX

Point THORAX is calculated by the same method as LUMBAR, using T7, LUMBAR, and L1 instead of L1, PELVIS, and SACRUM. We don't use P_1 at all; instead, we use LUMBAR. The final transformation will yield point P_3, which can then be

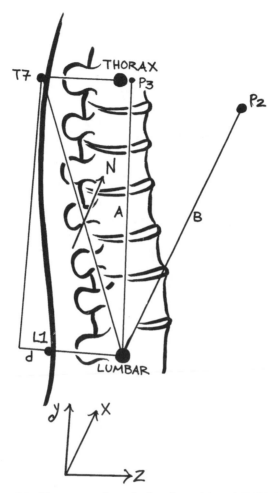

Figure 5-3. *Elements used to calculate the position of THORAX.*

transformed by the depth difference *d*, which can be calculated from the base position. Figure 5-3 shows the elements used to calculate THORAX.

LONECK

Point LONECK is calculated by the same method as THORAX, using T1, THORAX, and T7 instead of T7, LUMBAR, and L1. Figure 5-4 shows the elements used to calculate LONECK.

UPNECK

For point UPNECK, we use the same method as for THORAX, using C1, LONECK, and T1. Figure 5-5 shows the elements used to calculate point UPNECK.

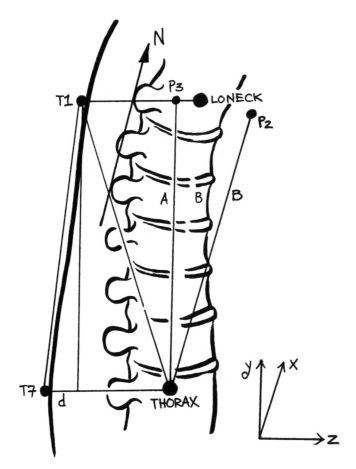

Figure 5-4. *Elements used to calculate the position of LONECK.*

HEAD

Point HEAD is used to help orient the joint that has its root at UPNECK. We assume that it is located between LHEAD and RHEAD. We calculate the location of this point by simply applying Equations 5-13 to 5-17. Figure 5-6 shows the calculation of point HEAD.

Torso

It is a good idea to separate the front part of the rib cage from the spine, since it is not as flexible, especially in the sternum area. We do this by using markers C7 and STERNUM combined with point LONECK, as shown in Figure 5-7.

Point UPTORSO is simply calculated by obtaining a point in between C7 and LONECK, using Equations 5-13 to 5-17 with an appropriate value for parametric variable *u* that is just enough to internalize the point. A value of 0.05 to 0.1 will do

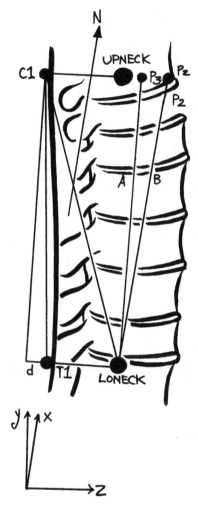

Figure 5-5. *Elements used to calculate the position of UPNECK.*

in most cases, but it really depends on the width of the performer and the diameter of the marker.

Point LOTORSO is used to orient the joint with its root located at UPTORSO. It is calculated in a similar way, using a line between STERNUM and T7 and Equations 5-13 to 5-17. The parametric variable u should also be small enough to just internalize the point.

Shoulder and Arm

Most of the motion capture data files that I have seen do not account for the three joints that form the shoulder complex: the glenohumeral joint between the

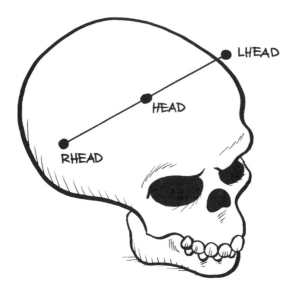

Figure 5-6. *The calculation of point HEAD.*

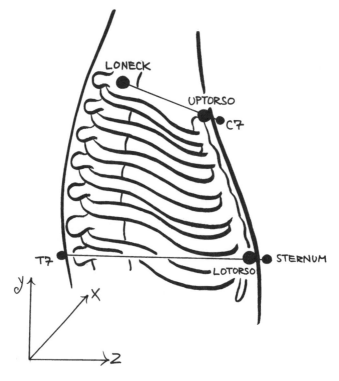

Figure 5-7. *Calculating the position of the torso points UPTORSO and LOTORSO.*

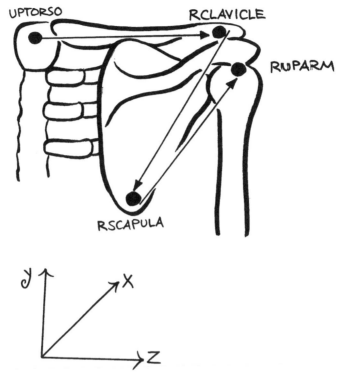

Figure 5-8. *The points that define the shoulder joints.*

humerus and the scapula, the acromioclavicular joint between the distal clavicle and the acromion, and the sternoclavicular joint between the medial clavicle and the manubrium. None of the common deformation schemes works well with shoulders, but it helps to have a somewhat anatomically correct setup. If we use an internal deformation technique, such as a muscle-based system, the correctness is imperative.

The shoulder complex will be formed by joints that go from point UPTORSO to CLAVICLE, down to SCAPULA and back up to UPARM (see Figure 5-8).

We first calculate point CLAVICLE, using markers SHOULDER and SCAPULA and point LONECK. Using Equations 5-13 to 5-17, calculate a point P_1 between the SHOULDER marker and point LONECK. The parametric variable u should be defined so as to place P_1 almost above the acromioclavicular joint. We then calculate point CLAVICLE using the same method for a line between P_1 and SCAPULA. Although it appears that the constructs of the shoulder complex are not well suited for animation, by using SCAPULA and SHOULDER to calculate the position of CLAVICLE we are establishing links between the parts. This setup may not be optimal for keyframe animation, but it is well suited for captured motion data.

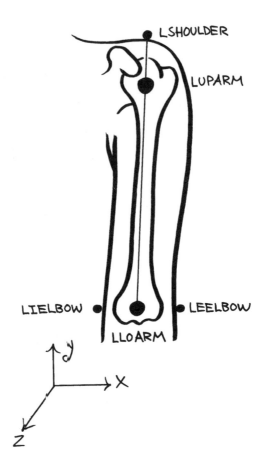

Marker SCAPULA can be used as is, because it only serves as an orientation point for CLAVICLE, but UPARM must be placed at the pivot point of the gleno-humeral or shoulder joint. We do this by calculating a midpoint LOARM between markers IELBOW and EELBOW and using a line between SHOULDER and LOARM to find the location of UPARM (see Figure 5-9).

To replicate as faithfully as possible the rotation of the lower arm, where the radius rotates over the ulna, we will require two bones that we can originate at point LOARM. One will be aligned to point IWRIST and the other to EWRIST. Finally, the hand rotation is obtained by aligning a midpoint P_1, between IWRIST and EWRIST, to the HAND marker (see Figure 5-10).

Leg and Foot

The upper leg pivot point is located at the head of the femur. We trace a line between HIP and PELVIS, and place FEMUR at about 35% of the distance between

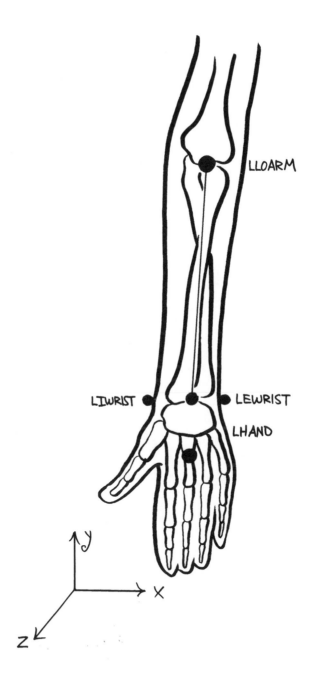

the two. We then use the same line to create UPLEG, just inside the greater trochanter. Point LOLEG, located at the knee, is positioned by calculating the midpoint between markers IKNEE and EKNEE, as shown in Figure 5-11.

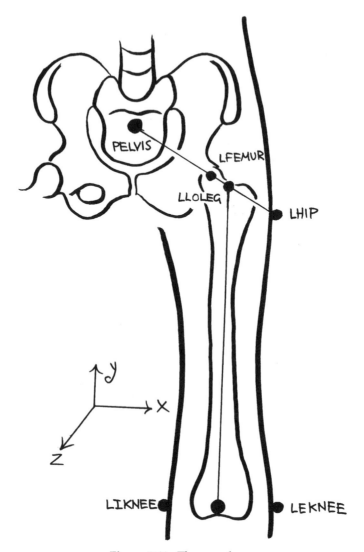

Figure 5-11. *The upper leg.*

Point UPFOOT is obtained via a method similar to that used to calculate LUMBAR, using point LOLEG and markers HEEL and FOOT. We use marker ANKLE later to maintain orientation. LOFOOT is calculated using FOOT, TOE, and UPFOOT.

Orientation of the Bones

You now have a set of points in space where a set of local Cartesian coordinate systems will be located. These represent the roots of joints that will form the mechanical setup. The base position is assumed to be the laboratory frame in time where all these coordinate systems are in their initial state. You can further assume that the longitudinal axis of each segment is the line between the root and target points, but the rotation about the longitudinal axis has to be locked down to a moving rigid segment, such as the ones defined in the marker setup design section in Chapter 3.

Some high-end animation programs, such as Softimage, provide the ability to assign a point in space as a root and another as a target or effector, using other points as orientation constraints. If this is the case, you can now use these points, in combination with the marker sets that were defined as rigid segments in Chapter 3, to place your joints and constrain their primary orientation. If your software does not allow you to do this, you need to perform these calculations yourself, using the direction cosines described previously to calculate the angular changes in the plane and apply them to the bone. In this case, you might want to consider using a nonhierarchical system, as it would require less computations.

TIPS AND TRICKS

Switching the Order of Rotations

There are cases in which your data will be delivered based on a predefined order of rotations with which your software may not be compatible. If this is the case, you will have to recompute your data to reflect an acceptable order. Most of the common captured motion data files contain rotations specified in Euler angles. We will combine all the rotations into one matrix and then decompose it in a way that will yield the desired order of rotations.

The 3×3 rotation matrix of θ about the x-axis is given by

$$\mathbf{R}_x = \begin{bmatrix} 1 & 0 & 0 \\ 0 & \cos\theta & \sin\theta \\ 0 & -\sin\theta & \cos\theta \end{bmatrix} \tag{5-40}$$

The 3×3 rotation matrix of ϕ about the y-axis is given by

$$\mathbf{R}_y = \begin{bmatrix} \cos\phi & 0 & -\sin\phi \\ 0 & 1 & 0 \\ \sin\phi & 0 & \cos\phi \end{bmatrix} \tag{5-41}$$

The 3×3 rotation matrix of ψ about the z-axis is given by

$$\mathbf{R}_z = \begin{bmatrix} \cos\psi & \sin\psi & 0 \\ -\sin\psi & \cos\psi & 0 \\ 0 & 0 & 1 \end{bmatrix} \tag{5-42}$$

We begin by creating the matrix that will contain all the rotations. If the data file contains rotations in the *XYZ* order, we would multiply the matrices in the proper order as follows:

$$\mathbf{R}_{\theta\phi\psi} = \mathbf{R}_x\mathbf{R}_y\mathbf{R}_z \tag{5-43}$$

where θ = rotation about the *x*-axis, ϕ = rotation about the *y*-axis and ψ = rotation about the *z*-axis. We obtain the following matrix:

$$\mathbf{R}_{\theta\phi\psi} = \begin{bmatrix} \cos\phi\cos\psi & \cos\phi\sin\psi & -\sin\phi \\ \sin\theta\sin\phi\cos\psi - \cos\theta\sin\psi & \sin\theta\sin\phi\sin\psi + \cos\theta\cos\psi & \sin\theta\cos\phi \\ \cos\theta\sin\phi\cos\psi + \sin\theta\sin\psi & \cos\theta\sin\phi\sin\psi - \sin\theta\cos\psi & \cos\theta\cos\phi \end{bmatrix} \tag{5-44}$$

Since we know all the values of θ, ϕ, and ψ, we can solve the equations and represent the matrix as follows:

$$\mathbf{R}_{\theta\phi\psi} = \begin{bmatrix} r_{11} & r_{12} & r_{13} \\ r_{21} & r_{22} & r_{23} \\ r_{31} & r_{32} & r_{33} \end{bmatrix} \tag{5-45}$$

We next build the matrix that we will use to extract the new order of rotations. If we had to convert the order of rotations to *ZYX*, for example, we would multiply the matrices in Equations 5-40 to 5-42 as follows:

$$\mathbf{R}_{\theta\phi\psi} = \mathbf{R}_z\mathbf{R}_y\mathbf{R}_x \tag{5-46}$$

where, after decomposing, θ = rotation about the *z*-axis, ϕ = rotation about the *y*-axis, and ψ = rotation about the *x*-axis. We obtain the following equation:

$$\begin{bmatrix} r_{11} & r_{12} & r_{13} \\ r_{21} & r_{22} & r_{23} \\ r_{31} & r_{32} & r_{33} \end{bmatrix} = \begin{bmatrix} \cos\phi\cos\psi & \cos\theta\sin\psi + \sin\theta\sin\phi\cos\psi & \sin\theta\sin\psi - \cos\theta\sin\phi\cos\psi \\ -\cos\phi\sin\psi & \cos\theta\cos\psi - \sin\theta\sin\phi\sin\psi & \sin\theta\cos\psi + \cos\theta\sin\phi\sin\psi \\ \sin\phi & -\sin\theta\cos\phi & \cos\theta\cos\phi \end{bmatrix} \tag{5-47}$$

We simplify the equations by multiplying both sides by $\mathbf{R}_z^{-1}$, which is equal to

$$\mathbf{R}_z = \begin{bmatrix} \cos\psi & -\sin\psi & 0 \\ \sin\psi & \cos\psi & 0 \\ 0 & 0 & 1 \end{bmatrix} \tag{5-48}$$

obtaining

$$\begin{bmatrix} r_{11}\cos\psi - r_{21}\sin\psi & r_{12}\cos\psi - r_{22}\sin\psi & r_{13}\cos\psi - r_{23}\sin\psi \\ r_{11}\sin\psi + r_{21}\cos\psi & r_{12}\sin\psi + r_{22}\cos\psi & r_{13}\sin\psi + r_{23}\cos\psi \\ r_{31} & r_{32} & r_{33} \end{bmatrix}$$

$$= \begin{bmatrix} \cos\phi & \sin\theta\sin\phi & -\cos\theta\sin\phi \\ 0 & \cos\theta & \sin\theta \\ \sin\phi & -\sin\theta\cos\phi & \cos\theta\cos\phi \end{bmatrix} \qquad (5\text{-}49)$$

From Equation 5-49 we can extract

$$r_{11}\sin\psi + r_{21}\cos\psi = 0 \qquad (5\text{-}50)$$

We further simplify Equation 5-50 to obtain

$$r_{11}\sin\psi/\cos\psi + r_{21} = 0 \qquad (5\text{-}51)$$

which can be turned into

$$r_{11}\tan\psi + r_{21} = 0 \qquad (5\text{-}52)$$

We finally obtain the value of ψ by the following:

$$\psi = \tan^{-1} - (r_{11}/r_{21}) \qquad (5\text{-}53)$$

Having ψ, we can calculate the value of θ using Equation 5-49:

$$\sin\theta = r_{13}\sin\psi + r_{23}\cos\psi$$

$$\cos\theta = r_{12}\sin\psi + r_{22}\cos\psi \qquad (5\text{-}54)$$

which can be used to compute θ:

$$\theta = \tan^{-1}[(r_{13}\sin\psi + r_{23}\cos\psi)/(r_{12}\sin\psi + r_{22}\cos\psi)] \qquad (5\text{-}55)$$

We now calculate ϕ using Equation 5-49 in a similar way:

$$\sin\phi = r_{31}$$

$$\cos\phi = r_{11}\cos\psi - r_{21}\sin\psi \qquad (5\text{-}56)$$

so that

$$\phi = \tan^{-1}[r_{31}/(r_{11}\cos\psi - r_{21}\sin\psi)] \qquad (5\text{-}57)$$

Finally, we assign the following values:

Rotation about $x = \psi$

Rotation about $y = \phi$ $\qquad (5\text{-}58)$

Rotation about $z = \theta$

Distribution of Rotations

About the Longitudinal Axis

Some of the most common deformation systems do not yield great results when a joint or bone rotates about its longitudinal axis. The lower arm is almost always a problem area in this respect.

If your character setup does not provide a mechanical solution for pronation and supination as specified in the character setup section, chances are that the longitudinal rotations of the lower arm are attributed to the wrist. An alternative to redesigning the skeletal structure is to distribute the wrist rotations equally between the wrist and elbow. Better yet, distribute the total longitudinal rotations of the arm among the wrist, elbow, and shoulder joints. This is a very easy process, provided that the rotation along the longitudinal axis is the last transformation, which should be standard practice in any character setup.

When using captured motion data from a hierarchical rotational file, assuming that the longitudinal axis is y and that the rotation order is ZXY or XZY, you could simply solve the problem with a set of expressions as follows:

$$\text{TOTAL}_{Ry} = \text{WRIST}_{Ry} + \text{ELBOW}_{Ry} + \text{SHOULDER}_{Ry}$$

$$\text{SHOULDER}_{Ry} = \text{TOTAL}_{Ry} / 3$$

$$\text{ELBOW}_{Ry} = \text{TOTAL}_{Ry} / 3$$

$$\text{WRIST}_{Ry} = \text{TOTAL}_{Ry} / 3 \tag{5-59}$$

You can distribute the rotations in different ways, perhaps applying less to the shoulder.

With Shifting Pivot Point

Another interesting idea is to distribute rotations between joints in a way similar to the actual rotations of the spine, where a single vertebra has a maximum possible range of rotation. The rotation starts with the lowermost vertebra and continues until its maximum range has been reached. At that point, the rotation and pivot point carry over to the next vertebra until it meets its maximum, and so on (see Figure 5-12). For example, if a vertebra has a range of rotation of 10° for a given axis, rotating the whole spine 36° would result in the rotation of the lowermost four vertebrae: the first three by 10° and a fourth by 6°. This method does not yield the same result as rotating the lowest vertebra in the spine by 35° along its single pivot point, but it is close to half, or 18°. Of course, this is dependent on the separation between vertebrae, which needs to be uniform.

The following pseudocode converts a single rotation group into a set of three distributed rotation groups with shifting pivot point. It assumes the rotations are

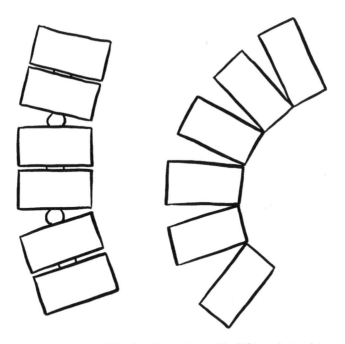

Figure 5-12. *Distributed rotations with shifting pivot point.*

stored in rx, ry, and rz, respectively, that *y* is the longitudinal axis, and that the rotation order is *XYZ*.

```
/* Declare various variables */
int num_joints = 3;                       /* Number of joints      */
float rot_vector[3];                      /* Incoming rotations    */
float rot_residual[3];                    /* Carry over rotations  */
float rot_joint_vector[num_joints][3];    /* Outgoing rotations    */
float rot_joint_limit;                    /* Maximum rot per joint */
int i;                                    /* Loop variable         */

/* Write incoming rotations into array */
/* Double rx and rz to approximate result to single pivot */
rot_vector[0] = rx * 2;
rot_vector[1] = ry;
rot_vector[2] = rz * 2;

/* Set rotation limit per joint */
rot_joint_limit = 15;

/* Initialize residual array */
/* For longitudinal axis divide rotations equally */
rot_residual[0] = rot_vector[0];
rot_residual[1] = rot_vector[1] / num_joints;
rot_residual[2] = rot_vector[2];

/* Start processing rx */
/* If rx is greater than the limit, start distribution */
```

```
if (abs(rot_vector[0]) > rot_joint_limit) {
    i = 0;

    /* Start the distribution loop */
    /* Check if there is carry over and additional joints */
    while (abs(rot_residual[0]) > 0 && i < num_joints) {

        /* If rotations are positive */
        if (rot_vector[0] > 0) {

            /* If the rotation left over is less than limit    */
            /* apply it all to current joint                   */
            if (abs(rot_residual[0]) < rot_joint_limit)
                rot_joint_vector[i][0] += rot_residual[0];

            /* Otherwise, apply limit to current joint     */
            else
                rot_joint_vector[i][0] += rot_joint_limit;

            /* If joint is over limit, save extra in residual */
            if (rot_joint_vector[i][0] > rot_joint_limit) {
                rot_residual[0] +=  rot_joint_vector[i][0] -
                    rot_joint_limit;
                rot_joint_vector[i][0] = rot_joint_limit;
                }

            /* Subtract current rotation from new residual */
            rot_residual[0] -= rot_joint_limit;

            /* Make sure residual isn't negative */
            if (rot_residual[0] < 0)
                rot_residual[0] = 0;
            }

        /* Process negative rotations */
        else {

            /* If the rotation left over is less than limit    */
            /* apply it all to current joint                   */
            if (abs(rot_residual[0]) < rot_joint_limit)
                rot_joint_vector[i][0] += rot_residual[0];

            /* Otherwise, apply limit to current joint     */
            else
                rot_joint_vector[i][0] -= rot_joint_limit;

            /* If joint is over limit, save extra in residual */
            if (abs(rot_joint_vector[i][0]) > rot_joint_limit) {
                rot_residual[0] -=  (rot_joint_vector[i][0] -
                    rot_joint_limit);
                rot_joint_vector[i][0] = -rot_joint_limit;
                }

            /* Subtract current rotation from new residual */
            rot_residual[0] += rot_joint_limit;

            /* Make sure residual isn't positive */
            if (rot_residual[0] > 0)
                rot_residual[0] = 0;
```

```
                }
            i++;

            /* End of loop */
            }
        }

/* If rx is smaller than the limit, apply all to first joint */
else {
        rot_residual[0] = 0;
        rot_joint_vector[0][0] = rot_vector[0];
        }

/* Process ry (longitudinal axis) */
i = 0;
while (i < num_joints) {

        /* Rotate joint */
        rot_joint_vector[i][1] = rot_residual[1];
        i++;
        }

/* Start processing rz */
/* If rz is greater than the limit, start distribution */
if (abs(rot_vector[2]) > rot_joint_limit) {
        i = 0;

        /* Start the distribution loop */
        /* Check if there is carry over and additional joints */
        while (abs(rot_residual[2]) > 0 && i < num_joints) {

                /* If rotations are positive */
                if (rot_vector[2] > 0) {

                        /* If the rotation left over is less than limit    */
                        /* apply it all to current joint                   */
                        if (abs(rot_residual[2]) < rot_joint_limit)
                            rot_joint_vector[i][2] += rot_residual[2];

                        /* Otherwise, apply limit to current joint    */
                        else
                            rot_joint_vector[i][2] += rot_joint_limit;

                        /* If joint is over limit, save extra in residual */
                        if (rot_joint_vector[i][2] > rot_joint_limit) {
                            rot_residual[2] +=  rot_joint_vector[i][2] -
                                    rot_joint_limit;
                            rot_joint_vector[i][2] = rot_joint_limit;
                            }

                        /* Subtract current rotation from new residual */
                        rot_residual[2] -= rot_joint_limit;

                        /* Make sure residual isn't negative */
                        if (rot_residual[2] < 0)
                            rot_residual[2] = 0;
                        }
```

```
                    /* Process negative rotations */
                    else {

                         /* If the rotation left over is less than limit    */
                         /* apply it all to current joint                    */
                         if (abs(rot_residual[2]) < rot_joint_limit)
                              rot_joint_vector[i][2] += rot_residual[2];

                         /* Otherwise, apply limit to current joint    */
                         else
                              rot_joint_vector[i][2] -= rot_joint_limit;

                         /* If joint is over limit, save extra in residual */
                         if (abs(rot_joint_vector[i][2]) > rot_joint_limit) {
                              rot_residual[2] -= (rot_joint_vector[i][2] -
                                   rot_joint_limit);
                              rot_joint_vector[i][2] = -rot_joint_limit;
                              }

                         /* Subtract current rotation from new residual */
                         rot_residual[2] += rot_joint_limit;

                         /* Make sure residual isn't positive */
                         if (rot_residual[2] > 0)
                              rot_residual[2] = 0;
                         }
               i++;

               /* End of loop */
               }
          }

/* If rz is smaller than the limit, apply all to first joint */
else {
     rot_residual[2] = 0;
     rot_joint_vector[0][2] = rot_vector[2];
     }

/* Apply new values to all joints */
```

Using Parametric Cubic Curves

Other methods for creating smoother relationships between joints involve the generation of curves using markers or calculated points as control points. A parametric cubic curve can be generated using two or four points. To produce a parametric cubic curve using two points, use the following three polynomials of the third order:

$$x(u) = a_x u^3 + b_x u^2 + c_x u + d_x$$

$$y(u) = a_y u^3 + b_y u^2 + c_y u + d_y \tag{5-60}$$

$$z(u) = a_z u^3 + b_z u^2 + c_z u + d_z$$

where u is the parametric variable that has an interval from 0 to 1. $u = 0$ represents the first point, and $u = 1$ represents the second point. Any value in between can be used to calculate additional points as needed.

The slope of the curve is given by the two tangent vectors located at the ends of the curve. The components of each tangent vector are given by differentiating Equations 5-60 as follows:

$$x^u = \frac{dx(u)}{du} = 3a_x u^2 + 2b_x u + c_x$$

$$y^u = \frac{dy(u)}{du} = 3a_y u^2 + 2b_y u + c_y \qquad (5\text{-}61)$$

$$z^u = \frac{dz(u)}{du} = 3a_z u^2 + 2b_z u + c_z$$

By solving the equations using $u = 0$ and $u = 1$ where the two points are known, you can obtain the values of the coefficients (a, b, c, and d) and then proceed to calculate intermediate points.

When linking two point segments, such as in the vertebral column, make sure that the tangent vectors at the ends of the curves are matching, thus resulting in a single smooth curvature.

Interpolation

There are many instances when you will need to interpolate rotations between different captured motion data files. Common cases are the blending or stitching of different motions or creating a looping motion for actions like walking or running.

As I've stated in previous chapters, the success of blending or looping depends a great deal on the compatibility of the motion data. The points where the data files are to be blended need to be similar in their pose and have a similar timing of motion. If this is true, half the work is already done.

Quaternions

Rotations in captured motion data files are usually represented by Euler angles combined with a predefined order of rotations. This is not the best format to use when interpolating between two rotations because in order to reach the final orientation, three ordered rotations about separate axes have to occur. There are 12 combinations by which the final orientation can be reached, resulting in different representations of the 3×3 rotation matrix. Furthermore, Euler angles have the problem commonly known as gimbal lock, whereby a degree of freedom is lost due to parametric singularity. This happens when two axes become aligned, resulting in the loss of the ability to rotate about one of them.

Interpolating translations using Cartesian coordinates works mainly because translations are commutative, which means that to arrive at a certain location in space the order of translations is not important; thus, there are no dependencies between the transformations. Rotations represented by Euler angles are noncommutative, which means that their order cannot be changed and still yield the same final orientation. It also means that the transformations depend on each other.

Interpolation between orientations is best done by using *quaternions,* which, as their name implies (from Latin), are sets of four numbers, one of which represents a scalar part and three that represent a vector part. A quaternion q can be represented by the following equation:

$$q = a + bi + cj + dk \qquad (5\text{-}62)$$

where the coefficients a, b, c, and d are real numbers and $\mathbf{i}$, $\mathbf{j}$, and $\mathbf{k}$ are the axes. As in complex numbers of the form

$$z = a + ib \qquad (5\text{-}63)$$

where $\mathbf{i}^2 = -1$, for quaternions, each of $\mathbf{i}^2$, $\mathbf{j}^2$, and $\mathbf{k}^2$ are also equal to -1. Thus, quaternions are extensions of complex numbers that satisfy the following identities:

$$
\begin{aligned}
\mathbf{i}^2 + \mathbf{j}^2 + \mathbf{k}^2 &= -1 \\
\mathbf{ij} &= -\mathbf{ji} = \mathbf{k} \\
\mathbf{jk} &= -\mathbf{kj} = \mathbf{i} \\
\mathbf{ki} &= -\mathbf{ik} = \mathbf{j}
\end{aligned}
\qquad (5\text{-}64)
$$

The condensed notation for a quaternion is

$$q(s, \mathbf{v}) \qquad (5\text{-}65)$$

where s is the scalar part and $\mathbf{v}$ is the vector part, so that

$$
\begin{aligned}
s &= a \\
\mathbf{v} &= b\mathbf{i} + c\mathbf{j} + d\mathbf{k}
\end{aligned}
\qquad (5\text{-}66)
$$

Quaternion multiplication can be expressed as follows:

$$q_1 q_2 = (s_1 s_2 - \mathbf{v}_1 \bullet \mathbf{v}_2,\; s_1 \mathbf{v}_2 + s_2 \mathbf{v}_1 + \mathbf{v}_1 \times \mathbf{v}_2) \qquad (5\text{-}67)$$

Quaternion multiplication is noncommutative, so $q_1 q_2$ is not the same as $q_2 q_1$. The magnitude of a quaternion can be determined by the following equation:

$$|q| = \sqrt{q\bar{q}} = \sqrt{s^2 + \left|\mathbf{v}^2\right|} \qquad (5\text{-}68)$$

where $\bar{q}$ is the conjugate of the quaternion, defined as

$$\bar{q} = q(s, -\mathbf{v})$$ (5-69)

A unit quaternion has a magnitude of 1, so from Equation 5-68 we can determine that

$$\bar{q}q = 1$$ (5-70)

where q is a unit quaternion. Unit quaternions are used to represent rotations, and can be portrayed as a sphere of radius equal to one unit. The vector originates at the sphere's center, and all the rotations occur along its surface. Interpolating using quaternions guarantees that all intermediate orientations will also fall along the surface of the sphere. For a unit quaternion, it is given that

$$a^2 + b^2 + c^2 + d^2 = 1$$ (5-71)

The inverse of a quaternion is defined as

$$q^{-1} = \frac{\bar{q}}{|q|^2}$$ (5-72)

but for a unit quaternion it can be reduced to

$$q^{-1} = \bar{q}$$ (5-73)

A unit vector $\mathbf{p}$ can be represented in quaternion notation as one without a scalar part, also called a *pure* quaternion:

$$P(0, \mathbf{p})$$ (5-74)

The rotation of $\mathbf{p}$ can be computed by the following equation:

$$P' = qPq^{-1}$$ (5-75)

where P' is also a pure quaternion. This rotation can also be achieved by applying the following matrix:

$$\mathbf{R} = \begin{bmatrix} 1 - 2c^2 - 2d^2 & 2bc - 2ad & 2bd + 2ac & 0 \\ 2bc + 2ad & 1 - 2b^2 - 2d^2 & 2cd - 2ab & 0 \\ 2ad - 2ac & 2cd + 2ab & 1 - 2b^2 - 2c^2 & 0 \\ 0 & 0 & 0 & 1 \end{bmatrix}$$ (5-76)

Before we start looking at the interpolation process, we need to establish that a rotation of θ about a unit vector **p** can be performed by using the following unit quaternion:

$$q\,(s, \mathbf{v}) = (\cos\,(\theta/2), \mathbf{p}\,\sin\,(\theta/2)) \qquad (5\text{-}77)$$

which means that separate rotations about the *x*, *y*, and *z* axes can be represented as

$$q_x = (\cos\,(\theta/2), \sin\,(\theta/2), 0, 0)$$

$$q_y = (\cos\,(\phi/2), 0, \sin\,(\phi/2), 0) \qquad (5\text{-}78)$$

$$q_z = (\cos\,(\psi/2), 0, 0, \sin\,(\psi/2))$$

respectively. We can now convert our Euler angles from the captured motion data file into quaternion space by simply multiplying the quaternions in the proper order. For example, a rotation in *XYZ* order would be given by using Equation 5-67 to perform the following multiplication:

$$q_{xyz} = q_x q_y q_z \qquad (5\text{-}79)$$

Converting a rotation matrix to a quaternion is a simple process. Assume we have a 4×4 transformation matrix of the form

$$\mathbf{R} = \begin{bmatrix} r_{11} & r_{12} & r_{13} & 0 \\ r_{21} & r_{22} & r_{23} & 0 \\ r_{31} & r_{32} & r_{33} & 0 \\ 0 & 0 & 0 & 1 \end{bmatrix} \qquad (5\text{-}80)$$

We obtain the *trace*, which is the sum of its diagonal elements r_{11}, r_{22}, and r_{33} so that

$$\text{Tr}(\mathbf{R}) = r_{11} + r_{22} + r_{33} \qquad (5\text{-}81)$$

To find the converted quaternion $q(W, X, Y, Z)$, we start by finding the value of the scalar *W* using Equation 5-81:

$$W = \frac{\sqrt{\text{Tr}(R)}}{2} \qquad (5\text{-}82)$$

The vector elements are calculated as follows:

$$X = (r_{12} - r_{21})/4W \qquad (5\text{-}83)$$

$$Y = (r_{20} - r_{02})/4W \qquad (5\text{-}84)$$

$$Z = (r_{01} - r_{10})/4W \qquad (5\text{-}85)$$

Once we are in quaternion space, we can proceed with the interpolation. The most commonly used interpolation method for quaternions is called *spherical linear interpolation, or slerp*. Because of its spherical nature, this method guarantees that any intermediate quaternions will also be unit quaternions. Slerp computes the angle θ between both quaternions as vectors in two-dimensional space using their scalar product. If we have two quaternions q_1 and q_2, we can find θ as follows:

$$\theta = \cos^{-1}(q_1 \bullet q_2) \tag{5-86}$$

To calculate quaternion q' in between q_1 and q_2 using slerp, we use a parametric variable u with interval from 0 to 1 and the following equation:

$$q' = q_1 \left(\frac{\sin[(1-u)\theta]}{\sin \theta} \right) + q_2 \frac{\sin u\theta}{\sin \theta} \tag{5-87}$$

If θ is equal to 0, the slerp will run into computational problems due to division by zero. If this is the case, instead of using slerp we just use linear interpolation. Other problems with slerp occur when θ is equal to multiples of $\pi/2$. Those problems can be avoided by changing either one of q_1 or q_2 to an approximation. For example, we can use q_2 and q_3, an adjacent keyframe, to generate a third quaternion q_4 that is as close to q_2 as possible without falling in the problem area, then we could proceed with the original interpolation using q_1 and q_4 instead of q_1 and q_2.

We now must convert q' (W, X, Y, Z) back into a rotation matrix $\mathbf{R}$ of the form shown in Equation 5-80. We use the matrix in Equation 5-76, which now becomes

$$\mathbf{R} = \begin{bmatrix} 1-2Y^2-2Z^2 & 2XY-2WZ & 2XZ+2WY & 0 \\ 2XY+2WZ & 1-2X^2-2Z^2 & 2YZ-2WX & 0 \\ 2XZ-2WY & 2YZ+2WX & 1-2X^2-2Y^2 & 0 \\ 0 & 0 & 0 & 1 \end{bmatrix} \tag{5-88}$$

We can finally decompose $\mathbf{R}$ into Euler angles if we need to, using the method explained in the section "Switching the Order of Rotations."

Keyframe Reduction

In some situations you may want to reduce the number of keyframes in your data. This is not the same as down-sampling, as you will keep the same sampling rate or frames per second at which the data is supposed to play back. Depending on what the purpose is, you may be able to reduce the number of keyframes automatically, but for the highest quality you may have to do it manually.

Removing every *n*th keyframe is not a good method, because it doesn't take into account the ratio of change from one keyframe to the next. The preferred method is to find areas in your curve that are smooth and don't fluctuate too much and then delete all keyframes that fall within two predetermined boundary keyframes. This is a long process if you have a character with dozens of joints, but you can accelerate it by using an algorithm that looks for differences in the curves.

There are many commercial software solutions that allow you to perform several types of fitting to your curves. Many load your data into a spreadsheet where you can perform a variety of manual or automatic operations, including smoothing and other noise reduction methods. A good method for curve fitting is the least squares method, which most software packages support.

Readaptation of Captured Data

It is a fact that in most cases your data will not fit your digital character's proportions. A few algorithms exist that allow you to adapt your data to different models. One of the best approaches is the one outlined by Michael Gleicher in his paper "Retargetting Motion to New Characters." Unfortunately, none of the known algorithms is capable of handling the weight and gravity properties of the motion. Consider the application of data captured from a heavy wrestler to the model of a small child. Even if you manage to adapt the data perfectly in order to avoid problems like feet sliding, your performance is most likely not going to be what you'd expect from a small child.

Your performer should fit the proportions of the target character as closely as possible, but even following this recommendation is not enough sometimes. A sample problem case would be a character that is supposed to be only a few inches high that is being performed by a full-sized actor who matches its proportions very closely. It is clear that the closer the data is to the character in both size and proportion, the better. If the differences are small, you will benefit greatly from an algorithm such as the one mentioned above or a trick like the one following.

When adapting data to a character of different proportions, it is always better to use translational data. Rotational data incorporates already computed angular displacements between limbs, which will not change if you translate or scale them. When using translational data, you first adapt the data and then let your software recompute the rotations to fit the new structure.

A good way to remap translational data to a character that is close to a performer's proportions is to scale groups of points by carefully placed pivot points that are generated from the data itself. It isn't desirable to add translation offsets to the points, because their ratio of transformation will not change, just their base location. When you scale, you are ensuring that the range of motion for that point will scale as well.

The first step in bringing the data into a model is to scale the whole data set to fit the most problematic area in the model with regard to the animation. If the character is walking most of the time, the biggest problem area may be the legs, so you will start by scaling all the data to match the length of the legs. By doing this you have eliminated the problem of the hips and feet, but not that of the knees. If you just displace the knee point, you will not get the desired result, but if you scale it using a pivot point located at the hip, it will work much better. You obviously need to continue scaling it throughout the animation. Another solution for the knee is to use a two-joint inverse-kinematics chain without actually using the knee point except for alignment of the hip. The process of scaling different points using different moving pivot points should be used in this fashion until the whole structure has been fitted.

Conclusion

꒱꒰

Motion capture is not a new technology, but is still raw in the field of performance animation. The tools we have today are not enough to make it a user-friendly resource, but that is not easy to find out, as it appears to be a plug-and-play alternative to keyframe animation. There is a lack of learning resources, mainly caused by the fact that not many people have used motion capture on a regular basis. Most motion capture users end up being one-time users who share a bad experience, and, because nobody likes to talk about failure, these experiences don't become lessons to others. The controversy that surrounds motion capture in the computer animation industry is mostly due to overestimation of what the technology is capable of, which in turn is due to lack of communication.

One of the main purposes of this book was to defuse the misconception, so at times it may have sounded as if I were trying to dissuade you from using motion capture at all. This is definitely not the case. I would love to see motion capture used at the peak of its potential, but that has yet to happen, and there is a price to pay. The idea is to make that price a cost that can be determined in advance.

The papers that have been written about motion capture-related topics usually don't cover the production and political problems that are associated with the tool. I tried to write this book in a less academic and more production-oriented language, sometimes dealing with problems in a way that may not be mathematically perfect, but one that is well fitted for an animation production environment. After all, this is not medicine; we are allowed to manipulate the numbers somewhat, as long as we obtain what we are looking for visually, and we must take advantage of that freedom.

I couldn't possibly cover everything that pertains to motion capture. Most notably, I didn't cover facial motion capture in detail. I could write a whole book based on this topic alone, and maybe I will in the future, but the most interesting aspects are still under development and are still protected by company and project secrecy. In addition, I don't believe most of what is commercially available today as far as facial tracking software, dedicated hardware, and character setups, is capable of producing high-quality facial motion. Most real-time facial tracking devices can capture only two-dimensional information and the systems that are able to capture three-dimensional information still generate an undesirable amount of high-frequency noise, especially when the number of markers is high.

The topics I did cover in detail should be used as seed knowledge for bigger undertakings. The captured motion data files that are dissected in Chapter 4 should help you understand any other format that may be out there, and you should be able to write a converter for any combination of formats. The character setup example is definitely not best suited for any case, but the concepts should be useful to anybody setting up a character for motion capture, where external markers need to be converted to an internal skeleton. In addition, most common motion capture problems can be solved with math procedures similar to the ones used in Chapter 5. Nothing is as valuable, however, as the commentary from people who have used the tool. The best perspective of the process is gained by reading and using those experiences in your own projects.

Although this book doesn't provide the answers to all existing problems, I hope it provides enough help in creating your own solutions. Most of all, I hope it provides some help in deciding whether motion capture is a good answer for the project at hand, and if it is, I hope it helps you achieve success.

Motion Capture Equipment and Software Manufacturers

OPTICAL TRACKING SYSTEMS
ACTI System

www.actisystem.fr
41, Quai Gauthey
21000 Dijon
France
Phone: +33-0-380-450-974
Fax: +33-0-380-451-571

Products

Akination: Optical tracking system capable of acquisition with up to 16 cameras. Compatible with 3D Studio Max, Softimage, Lightwave, Maya, Alias and Famous. It supports time-code recording and both active and passive markers.

Adaptive Optics Associates, Inc.

www.adaptiveoptics.com
54 Cambridge Park Drive
Cambridge, MA 02140
USA
Phone: (617) 864-0201
Fax: (617) 864-5855

Products

Multitrax: Windows NT-based optical motion tracking system.

Ariel Dynamics, Inc.

www.arielweb.com
6 Alicante Street
Trabuco Canyon, CA 92679
USA
Phone: (619) 874-2547
Fax: (619) 874-2549

Products

Ariel Performance Analysis System (APAS-99): Camera independent optical tracking system. It supports any number of regular video cameras or high-speed cameras of up to 10,000 Hz. It can use any kind of markers but it doesn't require them.

Bioengineering Technology & Systems (BTS)

www.bts.it
Via Cristoforo Colombo, 1A
20094 Corsico
Milano
Italy
Phone: +39-2-45875-1
Fax: +39-2-4586707-4

Products

ELITE Plus: Optical motion tracking system with up to eight camera configurations.
BTSWIN: General-purpose motion analysis software.

Biomechanics, Inc.

www.biomechanics-inc.com
200 N. Cobb Parkway, Suite 216
Marietta, GA 30062
USA
Phone: (770) 424-8195
Fax: (770) 424-8236

Products

Motion Reality: Optical tracking system with up to 12 cameras. Additional features include multiple-subject capability plus real-time display of human skeletons.
Nuance: Motion-editing tool for motion capture purposes. Supports a variety of file formats including Acclaim .amc/.asf and can load geometry in .obj format.

Digits 'n Art, Inc.

www.dnasoft.com
305 de la Commune West, Suite 100
Montreal, Quebec
Canada H2Y2E1
Phone: (514) 844-8448
Fax: (514) 844-8844

Products

LifeSource: Combination electromagnetic/optical/piezo-resistive system. It includes magnetic sensors for body capture, optical markers for facial capture, and resistive sensors for hand capture.

Human Performance Technologies, Inc.

www.hpt-biolink.com
825 South US Highway One, Suite 200
Jupiter, FL 33477
USA
Phone: (561) 744-5204
Fax: (561) 744-5204

Products

Biolink: Dual camera optical motion tracking system for sports-related applications.

Mikromak GmbH

www.mikromak.com
Am Wolfsmantel 18
D-91058 Erlangen
Germany
Phone: +49-9131-69096-0
Fax: +49-9131-69096-18

Products

WINanalize: Motion evaluation software.
Mikrokam: High-speed motion analysis camera systems.

MIE Medical Research, Ltd.

www.mie-uk.com
6 Wortley Moor Road
Leeds LS12 4JF
United Kingdom
Phone: +44-113-2793-710
Fax: +44-113-2310-820

Products

Kinemetrix: Optical tracking system based on pulsed infrared array. Available in configurations of up to 6 cameras.

Motion Analysis Corporation

www.motionanalysis.com
3617 Westwind Boulevard
Santa Rosa, CA 95403
USA
Phone: (707) 579-6500
Fax: (707) 526-0629

Products

ExpertVision HiRES: PC-based optical motion tracking system.
FaceTracker: Single-camera 2D facial tracking system.

Northern Digital, Inc.

www.ndigital.com
103 Randall Drive
Waterloo, Ontario
N2 V 1C5
Canada
Phone: (519) 884-5142
Fax: (519) 884-5184

Products

OPTOTRAK 3020: Real-time optical motion measuring device that employs active markers as opposed to the typical retro-reflective markers. Markers emit infrared light that is identified by position sensors. The system is capable of sampling rates up to 750 Hz, and the manufacturer claims it can capture face, hands, and full body simultaneously. Entertainment applications include performance animation, motion control, and virtual reality.

Peak Performance Technologies, Inc.

www.peakperform.com
7388 S. Revere Parkway, Suite 603
Englewood, CO 80112
USA
Phone: (303) 799-8686
Fax: (303) 799-8690

Products

Peak Motus: Optical tracking system available in configurations of up to 12 cameras. Besides marker-based tracking, the system is capable of videotape-based tracking, where no markers are required. This is useful when capturing in uncontrolled environments. It exports data to 3D Studio MAX, Lambsoft's Pro-Motion, Alias PowerAnimator, TAV and Maya; Nichimen N-World, Softimage, Lightwave and Kaydara's FiLMBOX.

PhaseSpace, Inc.

www.phasespace.com
1937 Oak Park Blvd, Suite A
Pleasant Hill, CA 94523
USA
Phone: (510) 945-6533
Fax: (510) 945-6718

Products

The OWL (Optical Wave Locator): Affordable real-time optical tracking system available in configurations of up to 16 cameras at up to 300 samples per second. It uses up to 120 LED active markers.

Phoenix Technologies Inc.

www.ptiphoenix.com
Kent Corporate Center
Unit 550-655 West Kent Ave. N
Vancouver, BC V6P 6T7
Canada
Phone: (604) 321-3238
Fax: (604) 321-3286

Products

Visualeyez System: Facial and full-body optical tracking system compatible with Softimage, Maya, 3D Studio Max, and others.

Qualisys Inc.

www.qualisys.com
41 Sequin Drive
Glastonbury, CT 06033
USA
Phone: (860) 657-3585
Fax: (860) 657-3595

Products

ProReflex: Optical tracking system available in configurations of up to 32 cameras. It can collect at a maximum frame rate of 1000 Hz.
MacReflex: Optical tracking system available in configurations of up to 7 cameras. It can capture a maximum of 50 markers at 60 samples per second.

Vicon (Oxford Metrics, Ltd.)

www.vicon.com
15455 Red Hill Avenue, Suite C
Tustin, CA 92780
USA
Phone: (714) 259-1232
Fax: (714) 259-1509

Products

Vicon 8: Optical tracking system for performance animation production. Available configurations of up to 24 cameras at a maximum sampling rate of 240 Hz. Specific performance animation features include SMPTE and genlock support, integrated MPEG movie capture, and support for Acclaim file formats.

X-IST Realtime Technologies GmbH

www.x-ist.de
Hans-Böckler Str. 163
D-50354 Hürth
Germany
Phone: +49-02233-518000
Fax: +49-02233-518089

Products

Facial Expression Tracker: Single camera real-time facial tracker. It tracks the position of up to 36 markers. It supports Softimage, Wavefront, Prisms, 3D Studio Max, Lightwave and Vuppetmaster.

Head-Room: 3D Studio Max plug-in for muscle-based facial animation.

Vuppetmaster: Real-time performance animation software. Compatible with Polhemus, Ascension, and other tracking devices.

ELECTROMAGNETIC TRACKING SYSTEMS

Ascension Technology Corporation

www.ascension-tech.com
P.O. Box 527
Burlington, VT 05402
USA
Phone: (802) 893-6657
Fax: (802) 893-6659

Products

MotionStar: Tethered electromagnetic tracker. Available in configurations of up to 90 sensors at 120 samples per second.

MotionStar Wireless: Wireless electromagnetic tracker. Available in configurations of up to 20 sensors at 100 samples per second.

Flock of Birds: Tethered electromagnetic tracker. It can capture up to 4 sensors simultaneously at 144 samples per second.

pcBird: Pc-based single-sensor device.

Polhemus, Inc.

www.polhemus.com
1 Hercules Drive
P.O. Box 560
Colchester, VT 05446
USA
Phone: (802) 655-3159
Fax: (802) 655-1439

Products

*STAR*TRAK:* Wireless electromagnetic tracker. Available in configurations of up to 32 sensors at 120 samples per second.

ULTRATRAK PRO: Tethered electromagnetic tracker. Available in configurations of up to 32 sensors at 60 samples per second.

FASTRAK: Tethered electromagnetic tracker. Available in configurations of up to 4 sensors at 120 samples per second.

Skill Technologies, Inc.

www.skilltechnologies.com
1202 E. Maryland Avenue, Suite 1G
Phoenix, AZ 85014
USA
Phone: (602) 277-7678
Fax: (602) 277-2326

Products

Phoenix: Tethered electromagnetic tracker. Available in configurations of up to 4 sensors at 120 samples per second.
Imperial: Tethered electromagnetic tracker. Available in configurations of up to 32 sensors at 60 Hz or 16 sensors at 120 Hz.
Genius: Wireless electromagnetic tracker. Available in configurations of up to 16 sensors at 120 Hz.

ELECTROMECHANICAL TRACKING SYSTEMS

Analogus

www.analogus.com
24 Shotwell Street
San Francisco, CA 94103
USA
Tel: (415) 487-0800
Fax: (415) 487-0898
Distributed by
ID8 Media (formerly CADCrafts)
www.id8media.com
731 Market St. #520
San Francisco, CA 94103
Phone: (415) 495-3930
Fax: (415) 495-4970

Products

The Gypsy 2.5: Electromechanical full-body motion capture system. Compatible with 3D Studio Max, Biped, Lightwave, Softimage, Alias, Maya, Kaydara FiLMBOX, and BioVision. Additional options include a wireless kit.
The AnimaTTon 2: Same as the Gypsy 2 except no global translation mechanism.
The Torso 2: Upper-body electromechanic suit.

Digital Image Design Inc.

www.didi.com
72 Spring Street
New York, NY 10012
USA
Tel: (212) 343-2442
Fax: (212) 343-0440

Products

Monkey 2: Desktop poseable electromechanical device for stop-motion and real-time puppeteering. It can be reassembled for different character layouts. Compatible with Softimage, Alias Power Animator, 3D Studio Max, N-World, Lightwave, and JACK.

PuppetWorks

www.puppetworks.com
3425 Harvester Road, Suite 203
Burlington, Ontario
Canada L7N 3N1
Tel: (905) 333-1905
Fax: (905) 333-5547

Products

J2000: Re-configurable digital puppet system. It includes 20 digital encoders and plug-in software for Maya, Alias Power Animator, Softimage, 3D Studio Max, and Houdini.

J1000: Upper body digital puppet system with 10 encoders. For use with 3D Studio Max and Character Studio.

Body Tracker: Digital body tracking device with position tracking. Various configurations are available.

HAND TRACKING DEVICES
Fifth Dimension Technologies

www.5dt.com
Pretoria
South Africa
Phone: +27-12-349-1400
Fax: +27-12-349-1404

Products

5DT Data Glove: Glove with 5 fiber-optic sensors, one per finger.

Infusion Systems, Inc.

www.infusionsystems.com
425 Carrall Street, Suite 316
Vancouver, BC
V6B 6E3
Canada
Phone: (604) 684-3646
Fax: (604) 684-3656

Products

TouchGlove: Glove with 6 force-sensitive sensors, mounted on palm and each fingertip.

Virtual Technologies, Inc.

www.virtex.com
2175 Park Boulevard
Palo Alto, CA 94306
USA
Phone: (650) 321-4900
Fax: (650) 321-4912

Products

CyberGlove: Glove with flexible sensors, which measures the position and movement of the fingers and wrist. It is available in two models and for either hand, with either 18 or 22 sensors.

OTHER TRACKING TECHNOLOGIES

The Character Shop, Inc.

www.character-shop.com
9033 Owensmouth Avenue
Canoga Park, CA 91304
USA
Phone: (818) 718-0094
Fax: (818) 718-0967

Products

Waldo: Telemetric input devices for controlling puppets and animatronics. Custom-built for specific applications.

Charnwood Dynamics, Ltd.

www.charndyn.com
Victoria Mills
Fowke Street
Rothley
Leicestershire LE7 7PJ
United Kingdom
Phone: +44-116-2301-060
Fax: +44-116-2301-857

Products

CODA mpx3O: Uses cross-correlation techniques to locate the positions of active LED markers. The sensors and associated DSP processors are located in a host PC. The system is capable of capturing up to 6 markers at 800 samples per second and up to 28 markers at 200 samples per second. Acquisition and display are both real-time processes. Many scanners can be used simultaneously.

Motion Capture Service Bureaus and Virtual Content Providers

❧❧

3D Creations, Inc.

www.3dcreations.com
545 5th Avenue
New York, NY 10017
USA
Phone: (212) 907-1213
Fax: (212) 687-8023

Equipment: Ascension Technologies Flock of Birds electromagnetic tracker, X-IST facial tracking system, and 5th Dimension Data Glove.
Output compatibility: Alias|Wavefront Advanced Visualizer and others.
Types of projects: Video games and broadcast projects.
Services: Body, face, and hand capture.

Acclaim Motion Studios

www.acclaim.net
Phone: (516) 656-2510

Equipment: Proprietary optical system.
Output compatibility: Acclaim.
Types of projects: Film and video games.
Services: Body capture.

AudioMotion Studios

www.audiomotion.com
Beaumont Road
Banbury, Oxon
OX17 7RH
United Kingdom
Phone: +44-0-1295-266622
Fax: +44-0-1295-266685

Equipment: Vicon 370E optical systems, Ascension Technologies Flock of
   Birds electromagnetic tracker and 5th Dimension Data Gloves.
Output compatibility: Biovision, Acclaim, 3D Studio Max, and others.
Types of projects: Various multimedia-related projects.
Services: Body, face, and hand capture. Data cycling and customized skeletons.

Biovision Sport Centers

www.biovision.com
Indian Wells Studio
44-460 Indian Wells Lane
Indian Wells, CA 92210
USA
Phone: (760) 341-5007
Fax: (760) 773-4004

St. Louis Studio
812 Mid Point Drive
O'Fallon, MO 63366
USA
Phone: (877) 379-0880
Fax: (314) 281-0880

Equipment: Vicon 370E optical system.
Output compatibility: Biovision, Acclaim, 3D Studio Max, and others.
Types of projects: Sports related.
Services: Body capture, proprietary software for sports analysis.

Electrashock

www.electrashock.com
1320 Main Street
Venice, CA 90291
USA
Phone: (310) 399-4985

Equipment: Adaptive Optics optical motion capture system.
Output compatibility: Various formats.
Types of projects: Film, television, and video games.
Services: Body capture. Graphic concept creation.

Film East

www.filmeast.com
9 East Stow Road
Marlton, NJ 08053
USA
Phone: (609) 810-1090
Fax: (609) 810-1077

Equipment: MotionStar DC wireless magnetic tracker.
Output compatibility: Most formats.
Types of projects: Film and television.
Services: Body capture, 3D scanning, 3D animation, motion control.

FutureLight

www.smstudios.com/fl/fl_index.html
3025 W. Olympic Blvd.
Santa Monica, CA 90404
USA
Phone: (310) 264-5566
Fax: (310) 264-5572

Equipment: Northern Digital Optotrak system with 8 cameras. SGI Reality-Engine2. Proprietary real-time performance animation software.
Output compatibility: Biovision, Acclaim, .htr, 3D Studio Max, Maya, Softimage, Prisms, Houdini, Alias.
Types of projects: Film and television.
Services: Real-time body capture. Full production facility.

House of Moves

www.moves.com
5318 McConnell Ave.
Los Angeles, CA 90066
USA
Phone: (310) 306-6131
Fax: (310) 306-1351

Equipment: Vicon 8 optical system with 24 cameras.
Output compatibility: Most formats.
Types of projects: Film, television, and video games.
Services: Facial and body capture, motion data application, resizing, and
    blending. Off-site services available. Custom programming.

Lamb & Company

www.lamb.com
2429 Nicollet Avenue
Minneapolis, MN 55404
USA
Phone: (612) 872-1000
Fax: (612) 879-5776

Equipment: Ascension Flock of Birds magnetic system with 16 sensors.
Output compatibility: Most formats.
Types of projects: Film and television.
Services: Facial, body, and hand capture; full production studio with propri-
    etary software.

Medialab

www.medialab3d.com

USA
310 N. Canon Drive #228
Beverly Hills, CA 90210
Phone: (310) 247-0994
Fax: (310) 247-0998

France
34-36 Rue de la Belle Feuille
92100 Boulogne Billancourt
Phone: +331-55-19-55-19
Fax: +331-55-19-55-60

Equipment: A variety of puppeteering devices, including electromagnetic tracking.
Types of projects: Broadcast and film-based projects using Clovis PA, Medialab's proprietary real-time puppeteering software.

Metropolis Digital

www.metro3d.com/motion.htm
12 S. First Street, 11th Floor
San Jose, CA 95113
USA
Phone: (408) 286-2900
Fax: (408) 286-2970

Equipment: Ascension Flock of Birds electromagnetic tracker.
Output compatibility: Alias | Wavefront, Softimage, and 3D Studio.
Types of projects: Film, television, and video games.
Services: Body capture. Full digital production.

Motek

www.motek.org

The Netherlands
Oostelike Handelskade 11
1019BL Amsterdam
Phone: +310-204-19-11-11
Fax: +310-204-19-22-22

USA
131 Daniel Webster Hwy
Nashua, NH 03060
Phone: (603) 891-8321
Fax: (603) 888-5085

Equipment: Optical and electromagnetic systems.
Output compatibility: Most major software packages.
Types of projects: Film, television, video games, sports analysis, and teleco-
munications.
Services: Facial and body capture.

Motion Capture Magic

www.beam.com.au/mcm
14 Queens Road
Melbourne, Victoria
Australia 3004
Phone: +61-3-9866-8300
Fax: +61-3-9866-8674

Equipment: Vicon 370E Optical motion capture system.
Output compatibility: Acclaim, Softimage, Alias, 3D Studio, and others.
Types of projects: Video games, film, and video.
Services: Facial and body capture, custom effects, and custom skeleton mapping.

Pacific Title Mirage

www.pactitle.com
1149 North Gower Street
Hollywood, CA 90038
USA
Phone: (323) 769-3700
Fax: (323) 769-3701

Equipment: Life F/x proprietary facial performance system. Electromagnetic
tracking system. Orad virtual studio.
Output compatibility: Several formats.
Types of projects: Film and broadcast.
Services: Facial performance skin reconstruction and body capture.

Pyros Pictures

www.pyros.com
3197 Airport Loop Drive
Costa Mesa, CA 92626
USA
Phone: (714) 708-3400
Fax: (714) 708-3500

Equipment: Motion Analysis optical motion capture system.
Output compatibility: .htr, .trc and other formats.
Types of projects: Video games, film, and video.
Services: Facial and body capture. Full animation production capabilities.

Protozoa, Inc.

www.protozoa.com
2727 Mariposa, Studio 100
San Francisco, CA 94110
USA
Phone: (415) 522-6500
Fax: (415) 522-6522

Equipment: A variety of puppeteering devices, including an electromagnetic
tracker.
Types of projects: Broadcast and web-based projects using Alive, Protozoa's
proprietary real-time puppeteering software.

QuantumWorks

www.quantumworks.com
Phone: (818) 906-3322
Fax: (818) 906-3331

Equipment: Electromagnetic tracker and 2D optical face capture system.
Types of projects: Broadcast, location-based and web-based projects using
Gepetto, Quantumwork's proprietary standalone performance animation
software.

Rainbow Studios

www.rainbo.com
3830 N. 7th Street
Phoenix, AZ 85014
USA
Phone: (602) 230-1300
Fax: (602) 230-2553

Equipment: Polhemus 32-sensor electromagnetic system.
Output compatibility: Lightwave, 3D Studio Max, and others.
Types of projects: Broadcast, film, and video game projects.

SimGraphics

www.simg.com
1137 Huntington Drive
South Pasadena, CA 91030
USA
Phone: (323) 255-0900
Fax: (323) 255-0987

Equipment: Proprietary combination optical/magnetic system called VActor Performer.
Types of projects: Broadcast, trade-show, and location-based entertainment projects using SimGraphics' proprietary software and hardware solution.

Televirtual

www.televirtual.com
Park House
31 Cattle Market Street
Norwich, NR1 3DY
United Kingdom
Phone: +44-0-1603-767493
Fax: +44-0-1603-764946

Equipment: Magnetic and optical motioncapture tracking devices.
Output compatibility: A variety of formats.
Types of projects: Film and video.
Services: Facial, hand, and body capture. Full animation production capabilities.

Virtual Celebrity Productions

www.virtualceleb.com
3679 Motor Ave., Suite 200
Los Angeles, CA 90034
USA
Phone: (310) 253-5131
Fax: (310) 253-5139

Equipment: Combination of different tracking technologies along with VCP's proprietary software solutions.
Types of projects: VCP's technology is geared toward the creation of virtual celebrity performers for film, broadcast, and location-based entertainment projects.

Waxworks

www.waxworks.com
100 Baffin Place
Waterloo, Ontario
Canada N2V 1Z7
Phone: (800) 281-9333
Fax: (519) 886-6990

Equipment: Combination of different tracking technologies.
Types of projects: Broadcast, web, corporate, and multimedia applications.

Other Sources

❦

SOFTWARE

Beam International

www.famoustech.com
14 Queens Road
Melbourne, Victoria
Australia 3004
Phone: +61-3-9866-8300
Fax: +61-3-9866-8674

Products

Famous: A facial animation system for use with facial motion capture. It allows the clustering of polygonal models using a 3D paint approach, assigning regions to captured marker data. It allows for customized expressions and keyframe adjustments. Famous can be used as a plug-in for Softimage, 3D Studio Max, and Maya, and runs under Windows NT. It can import captured data in a variety of formats, including Vicon and X-ist.

Dreamteam Ltd.

www.dreamteam-ltd.com
3 Maskit Street
Herzliya Pituach
Israel 46733
Phone: +972-9-9559855
Fax: +972-9-9559615

Products

Typhoon: Performance animation software for real-time productions. Compatible with Ascension, Polhemus, PuppetWorks, Northern Digital, and Expert-Vision 3D systems, plus other types of input devices, such as midi, joysticks, and data gloves. It has animation software support for Softimage and Alias Power Animator.

Kaydara

www.kaydara.com
4428 St. Laurent, Suite 300
Montreal, Quebec
Canada H2W 1Z5
Phone: (514) 842-8446
Fax: (514) 842-4239

Products

Filmbox: Performance animation software for real-time productions. Compatible with Softimage, Alias, Lightwave, and 3D Studio Max.

Lambsoft

www.lambsoft.com
2429 Nicollet Avenue
Minneapolis, MN 55404
USA
Phone: (612) 813-3737
Fax: (612) 879-5776

Products

Smirk: A facial animation plug-in for 3D Studio Max. Its idea is based on facial sub-expressions that can be combined and associated to keyframe animation or captured motion data.

Pro Motion: A plug-in for Kinetix 3D Studio MAX for filtering, editing, blending, and applying motion data to characters. It supports most motion capture formats.

MoveTools: A software package that moves cameras, lights, motion data, motion hierarchies, and geometry between several packages, including 3D Studio Max, Alias Power Animator, Maya, Softimage, Lightwave, and Wavefront Advanced Visualizer.

TestaRossa

www.toolsinmotion.com
1250 Long Beach Ave.
Los Angeles, CA 90021
USA
Phone: (213) 488-1191
Fax: (213) 488-1464

Products

Mirai Tools: Human performance animation tools integrated into Nichimen's Mirai animation software.

MISCELLANEOUS RESOURCES

Simulation Special Effects

www.simulationfx.com
112 Privada Luisita
Los Gatos, CA 95030
USA
Phone: (408) 261-0851
Fax: (408) 261-0851

Products

Performance Animation Wear: Mounts and harnesses for electromagnetic sensors.

Viewpoint Datalabs

www.viewpoint.com
625 S. State
Orem, UT 84058
USA
Phone: (800) 328-2738
Fax: (801) 229-3000

Products

Motion Data: Stock motion data from House of Moves and BioVision.

Index

Related Titles from Morgan Kaufmann

Morgan Kaufmann

http://www.mkp.com

- **THE ART AND SCIENCE OF DIGITAL COMPOSITING**
  Ron Brinkmann
  1999   ISBN: 0-12-133960-2

- **TEXTURING & MODELING:**
  A PROCEDURAL APPROACH, SECOND EDITION
  David S. Ebert, F. Kenton Musgrave,
  Darwyn Peachey, Ken Perlin, Steven Worley
  1998   ISBN: 0-12-228730-4

- **3D MODELING AND SURFACING**
  Bill Fleming
  1999   ISBN: 0-12-260490-3

- **RENDERING WITH RADIANCE**
  Gregory Ward Larson, Robert Shakespeare
  1998   ISBN: 1-55860-499-5

- **PRINCIPLES OF DIGITAL IMAGE SYNTHESIS**
  Andrew S. Glassner
  1995   ISBN: 1-55860-276-3

- **ADVANCED RENDERMAN:**
  CREATING CGI FOR MOTION PICTURES
  Anthony A. Apodaca, Larry Gritz
  2000   ISBN: 1-55860-618-1